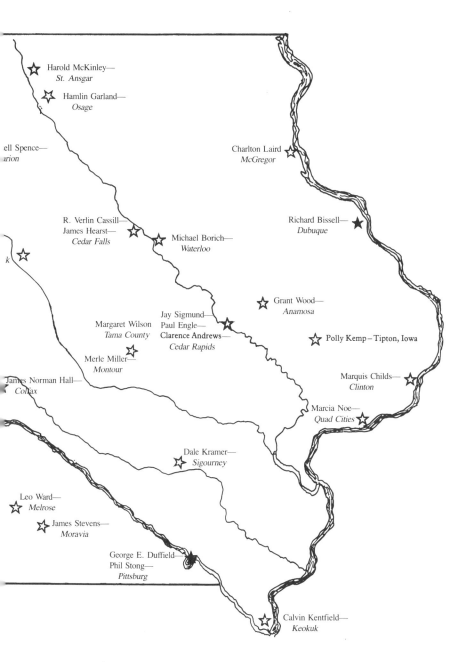

Harold McKinley—
St. Ansgar

Hamlin Garland—
Osage

ell Spence—
arion

Charlton Laird—
McGregor

R. Verlin Cassill—
James Hearst—
Cedar Falls

Michael Borich—
Waterloo

Richard Bissell—
Dubuque

k

Grant Wood—
Anamosa

Jay Sigmund—
Paul Engle—
Clarence Andrews—
Cedar Rapids

Margaret Wilson
Tama County

Polly Kemp – Tipton, Iowa

Merle Miller—
Montour

Marquis Childs—
Clinton

James Norman Hall—
Colfax

Marcia Noe—
Quad Cities

Dale Kramer—
Sigourney

Leo Ward—
Melrose

James Stevens—
Moravia

George E. Duffield—
Phil Stong—
Pittsburg

Calvin Kentfield—
Keokuk

810.9
And

DATE DUE

810. 9
And

This Is
IOWA

A Cavalcade of the Tall Corn State

This Is
IOWA

A Cavalcade of the Tall Corn State

Clarence A. Andrews

Midwest Heritage Publishing Company

108 Pearl Street
Iowa City, Iowa
52240

Library of Congress Cataloging in Publication Data

Main entry under title:

This Is Iowa / A Cavalcade of the Tall Corn State

   1. American literature – Iowa   2. Iowa – Literary
collections   3. Children – Iowa – Literary collections.   4. Authors – Iowa
– Biography – Addresses, essays, lectures, poems.   I. Andrews,
Clarence A.   81 – Library of Congress Catalog Card Number 061137.

ISBN 0-934582-04-1

For Ollie,
my favorite Iowan . . .

Acknowledgments

Grant Wood. *Dinner for Threshers.* 1933. Two studies for left and right sections of the painting. Pencil. Each 17¾ x 26¾ inches. Collection of Whitney Museum of American Art.

Hartzell Spence. "Heresy at Cherokee" from *One Foot in Heaven,* 1942. Drawing by Donald McKay. Both used by permission of Hartzell Spence.

Marquis Childs. "River Town," from *Mighty Mississippi: Biography of a River,* by Marquis Childs. Copyright 1982 by Marquis Childs. Reprinted by permission of Ticknor and Fields, a Houghton Mifflin Company.

Grant Wood. "Fall Plowing." Collection of Deere Company. Used by permission of Deere and Company and Mrs. Nan Wood Graham.

Gary Gildner. "Touring the Hawkeye State." Reprinted from *Nails,* by Gary Gildner, by permission of the University of Pittsburgh Press. Copyright 1975 by Gary Gildner.

Phil Stong. Selection from *Stranger's Return.* Copyright 1933 by Phil Stong, renewed 1961. Reprinted by permisison of the Harold Matson Co., Inc.

Paul Engle. "That Old Time Fourth of July." Copyright Meredith Corporation, 1958. Used by permission of Paul Engle.

Paul Engle. "Remember Memorial Day." Copyright Meredith Corporation, 1959. Used by permission of Paul Engle.

Paul Engle. "State Fair." Copyright by Paul Engle. Used by permission of Paul Engle.

Paul Engle. "Iowa." Copyright by Paul Engle. Used by permisison of Paul Engle.

"Last Song," from *The Black Hawk Songs,* by Michael Borich. Copyright 1975 by the Board of Trustees of the University of Illinois. Used by permission of Michael Borich and the copyright owner.

"Rebellion in the Potato Fields," by Stanley High. Used by permisison of *The Nation.*

Richard Bissell, "Good Old Dubuque," reprinted from *Holiday* magazine, now published by Travel/Holiday, Floral Park, New York 11001.

Drawings by William J. Wagner, FAIA, used by permission of Mr. Wagner.

Josephine Herbst, "Feet in the Grass Roots," in "Life in the United States" series, *Scribner's Magazine,* Vol. XCIII, January, 1933. Copyright 1933, Charles Scribner's Sons; copyright renewed. Reprinted with the permission of Charles Scribner's Sons.

Michael Walker, "AGRI: Getting Iowa's 'Gold' to Market," *The IOWAN,* Summer, 1982. Used with permission of *The IOWAN* and Michael Walker.

Merle Miller, "Land That They Love," from *Collier's Weekly.* Used by permission of Merle Miller.

Photograph of 1932 Farm Strike. Used by permission of the Iowa State Historical Department.

"Memories of Pioneer Iowa," from *Annals of Iowa.* Used by permission of the Iowa State Historical Department.

MacKinlay Kantor, "Miller Adam" and "The Snow of the Okoboji" from *Turkey in the Straw,* 1935. Copyright by MacKinlay Kantor. Reprinted by permisison of Paul R. Reynolds, Inc., 12 East 41st Street, New York, New York.

Wallace E. Stegner, "The Trail of the Hawkeye," from *The Saturday Review of Literature,* used by permission of Wallace E. Stegner. Copyright by Wallace E. Stegner.

Raymond Kresensky. "The Old Families." Copyright 1965 by Westburg and Associates, Fenimore, WI. From *The Special Raymond Kresensky* Edition of the North American Anthology of Poets. Used by permission.

B. Paul Chicoine. "Sioux City's Steamboat Days." *The Iowan,* Winter, 1981. Used by permission.

"Iowa Stubborn" by Meredith Willson. Copyright 1957, 1958 FRANK MUSIC Corp. and RINIMER CORPORTATION. International Copyright Secured. All Rights Reserved. Used by Permission.

"Iowa Corn Song." Lyric by R. W. Lockard & George Hamilton, Music by Edward Riley & George Botsford. Copyright EDWIN H. MORRIS & COMPANY, A Division of MPL Communications, Inc. Renewed by EDWIN H. MORRIS & COMPANY, A Division of MPL Communications, Inc., 1949. International Copyright Secured. All Rights Reserved. Used by Permission.

Photograph of Susan Glaspell from the Berg Collection, The Research Libraries, The New York Public Library, Astor, Lenox, and Tilden Foundations. Used by permission.

Dust jacket by Ted Kooser.

Contents

Illustrations

Introduction

HERE IS A BOOK about Iowa and its history, written not by historians, dusty and dry from their endless toil in dim library stacks, but by and large by the people who made it. Michael Borich, who has links to the Mesquakie settlement at Tama, translates the last words of Black Hawk into verse, and MacKinlay Kantor, who grew up listening to tales of "the snow of the Okoboji" from people who had been there at the time of the Spirit Lake massacre, versifies his recollection of those winter tales. George C. Duffield, Phil Stong's maternal grandfather, narrates his pioneer journey from Ohio to Iowa; Herbert Quick, Charles Aldrich and Hamlin Garland all describe experiences they had on the virgin Iowa prairie as it was converted into farmland.

Here you will find words telling how an Iowa village was built on the banks of the Red Cedar River, and how a pioneer church came to be built. In succeeding pages, you will experience life on turn of the century farms and in a turn of the century Iowa village. Then, moving right along, you will come upon a new generation, both in village and town, and on the farm as well.

Like many areas of the Great Valley of the Mississippi, Iowa was settled by immigrants from several European nations. So here you will read about the immigration and settlement of a "German grandfather," of an Irish couple, of immigrants from Holland, and, all too briefly, of the Scotch who came to Iowa.

You will see Iowans as they remember their ancestors on a day set aside for that purpose and you will see them as they celebrated the anniversary of their independence from a Europe their ancestors left behind. You will hear about "stubborn Iowans," and how one Iowa family, in a minor rebellion of sorts, turned against their own government. You will visit the Iowa State Fair, that most typical of Iowa celebrations, and you will visit the Iowa Great Lakes, one of Iowa's major recreational areas.

You will tour an internationally-famous Iowa industry and one of Iowa's great educational institutions; you will take a tongue-in-cheek tour through Dubuque, a more serious tour through a major Iowa city (here called "Winslow") and a "guided" tour through an Iowa county seat town.

And you will meet a number of Iowa people: farmers, housewives, writers, a cartoonist, an artist, a song writer, poets, students, a minister who had one foot on earth and "one foot in Heaven." All of these fascinating, mind-boggling tales about the state "where the tall corn grows" come to you through the words and art of almost three dozen Iowans, most of whom became nationally famous for their work in telling and showing a nation and the world something about the great state they were natives of—IOWA.

Iowa

"IOWA," said Paul Engle, "is the land of pigs and poets." Engle could make that statement with authority.   He grew up on an Iowa farm outside of Cedar Rapids, and he spent most of his life within hog-calling range of Iowa's porcine herds.   As Iowa's best-known poet, he has known every major American poet of the last half-century and quite a few minor poets as well.

In 1940, a book of verses labeled Oh, Millersville! *came into Engle's view, and he reviewed it for the* Des Moines Register. *"There is so warm a feeling of validity about these [fifty-eight] verses, and so accurate a sense of individual character, their final impact is far stronger than a simple amusement at girlish simplicity," he said.*

You will learn more about Oh, Millersville! *a few pages further.   But here, to get this collection of good things about Iowa off to a great start, I have placed Fern Gravel's paean to her native state (and to herself as well).*

Iowa

by Fern Gravel

Of all the different states in our country so grand
Iowa is the best, and that is my land.
It raises more corn than any other state
And we ship thousands of hogs and cattle to Chicago by freight.
We have only one poet so far as I know,
Mr. Beyers, who wrote some songs a long time ago.
He was very famous in the Civil War.
"Marching Through Georgia" was one. He wrote many more.
I am writing another kind of poetry,
And some of my poems are beautiful to me.
I hope, some day, people will travel
To see the home of the poetess, Fern Gravel,
Like they go to Longfellow's home, and Whittier's;
And then I'll remember the day I wrote this verse.

Home of Iowa Author Katherine Buxbaum

Indians in Iowa

ALTHOUGH THE FREQUENCY OF INDIAN NAMES encountered in driving around Iowa may suggest otherwise, the white settlers in Iowa had very few contacts with Iowa's first inhabitants. True, as Richard Bissell tells us later on, Julien DuBuque, Iowa's first prominent business man, married an Indian girl, Potosa, and, as we do not learn any other place in this collection, General Joseph Street and Wapello were good friends at Agency City near Ottumwa. Black Hawk, whom we will meet in Michael Borich's "Last Song," came over frequently from his home on the Rock River, but he, Keokuk, and any others left alive after Bad Axe, were expelled from Iowa before whites were allowed to enter.

The one serious encounter between whites and Indians in Iowa produced what is called the "Spirit Lake Massacre"—treated here briefly in Kantor's "The Snow of the Okoboji," and, later, even more briefly in Verlin Cassill's essay on the Iowa Great Lakes. Some years after writing this poem, Kantor produced Spirit Lake *(1961), a work guaranteed to provide anyone with more than they ever wanted to know about that massacre.*

"Last Song" is a poetic rendering of Black Hawk's own words in his autobiography.

Black Hawk, a member of the Sauk tribe (also Sac or Saukie) was one of the three great Heartland Indian war chiefs whose misfortune it was to be caught up in the struggles between English and Americans for possession of the American Heartland and, later, to be overwhelmed by the political and military maneuverings accompanying the beginnings of immigration into the Iowa prairie and woodlands. In what Leland Sage calls the "tragi-comedy of the so-called Black Hawk War," he was imprisoned and forced to yield his beloved Saukenuk village (on the plain where Rock Island, Illinois, presently is situated) to the sovereignty of the Federal government.

Michael Borich, whose maternal grandmother was a full-blooded Sac and Fox Indian, was born in Waterloo, educated in Waterloo's parochial schools and at the University of Northern Iowa. Michael has taught in the Waterloo public school system, on the Irvine campus of the University of California, on the Green Bay campus of the University of Wisconsin, and presently teaches at Kirkwood Community College in Cedar Rapids.

MacKinlay ("Mack") Kantor was born in Webster City, in 1904, the descendant on his mother's side of pioneer settlers in Iowa; his father was a Chicago cantor. As a boy, Kantor listened to tales of the Spirit Lake massacre and of the Civil War. He was the author of some thirty books, including the Pulitzer-prize-winning Andersonville *(1955).*

Black Hawk

Last Song

In my sixty-seventh year I am prisoner
of the whites. Between the spaces
of barred metal, my people, my dead
people, appear sullen as judges.

Sun Fish is gone. Thunder is gone.
Nea-a-pope is gone. White Beaver is gone.
Wa-Pel-lo is gone. Quash-qua-me is gone.
Ma-ta-tah is gone. Gomo is gone.
Wash-e-own is gone. Singing Bird is gone.
Wa-co-me is gone. Ra-she-pa-ho is gone.
Mu-ka-ta-quet is gone. Ma-she-na is gone.

The arrow of execution, the waiting
arrow of death, the goose-quilled
scratching shaft of black blood
is taking the lands east of the

Kishwaukee, is taking the lands
between the Rock and the Great
River, is taking all Indian lands,
is taking all wild game. Our

brother buffalo is gone.
Bear and deer refuse to shake
newborn from their bellypouch.
No thing escapes the white man's

guns. And the coming arrow
is opening its raven teeth and bending the weight my dying
skin wrinkles before it.

Otawa are dying. Chippewa are dying. Potawatomi are dying.
Fox and Winnebago are dying.
Sioux are dying. Menominee are dying.
Cree and Kickapoos are dying.
Osage and Cherokee are dying.

Delaware and Muscow are dying.
Omaha and Quapaw are dying.
Ponca are dying. Kansa are dying.
Sauk are dying.

The white blade is stroking
flesh of all Indian peoples.
In the blue marsh our bones
twitch and thrash their invisible

flesh. Molds of arm and leg
become rock and press into
limestone paths on journeys
deeper along the way our

leading, rigid tracks bring us.
We are the color of earth clay.
Our spirits have shown us how to
shape soil in holy image.

Clear streams run in our veins.
Pure air wings our bodies home.
Our sorrow for lost lands
and lost people is the sorrow

of spirits, the sorrow of our fathers,
earth sorrow. Our lives are rising
in wings of smoke from bone
fires on mountainsides into
the shuddering black torch of sky,
into flaming night,
into dreams and song.

. . . Michael Borich, *Black Hawk Songs* (1972)

Shau-hau-napo-tinia
An Ioway Chief

The Snow of the Okoboji

Now all brave Iowayans listen to me,
I'll tell of a dreadful massacree;
I know that it was long before
I went away to the Civil War. . . .
    Inkpaduty is wild and brown:
    Up the hills and over and down
    He's rode away with a maiden fair
    From the snow of the Okoboji!
Oh, it was a cold and mournful night
When the settlers saw a hideous sight —
Those Indian fires against a sky
Coppery-red as the tongues leaped high —

Indian fingers picking at the door,
Indian drums down under the floor,
Indian teeth a-waiting outside —
And Indian feet like a catamount's glide. . . .
I've heard tell how Herriott died:
Seven Sioux corpses lying at his side,
And his brave face set at a frozen grin
With his brains half out and his brains half in;

Doctor Herriott clung like the itch
To his rifle, busted across the breech.
No part of that gun was fit to save. . . .
But his hands still grasped it in his grave!
    Inkpaduty is brown and wild;
    He's rode away with a red-lipped child.
    His teepees smoke on the plains so far
    From the snow of the Okoboji!
Gardners, Marbles, Mattocks and more —
Butchered and dragged from their humble door.
Oh, sad those winds on the northern hills
As Inkpaduty's war cry chills.

Inkpaduty's uncle was
The chief Sidominadoty. . . .
He's carried Abbie Gardner away
To the buffalo grass of Dakoty!
All praise for the Pioneer Company
For one of those rescuers was me!
And all this happened long before
I went away to the Civil War.

. . . MacKinlay Kantor, *Turkey in the Straw* (1935)

Abbie Gardner

Coming Into Iowa in 1837

GEORGE C. DUFFIELD was one of Philip ("Phil") Duffield Stong's grandfathers. In this selection from Volume VI, number 14, of the Annals of Iowa, *we see one of the stages of the Duffields' migration from Ohio to Iowa, a journey which was to form the basis for two of Phil Stong's later novels,* Buckskin Breeches *(1937) and* Ivanhoe Keeler *(1939).*

As Duffield reports, James Duffield's claim was staked out on land from which Keokuk and his people had been expelled in 1832, and from which they were soon to be driven again. There were, therefore, some contacts between the settlers and the Indians, but they were brief and friendly, although in Buckskin Breeches, *Stong shows a dispute between Old Eli and some old Indians, and a brief skirmish between one of the boys and an Indian lad.*

Eventually the area which James Duffield settled was to become the site of "Pittsville," the imaginary town which was the setting for many of Phil Stong's novels.

Coming Into Iowa in 1837

ON THE 9TH DAY OF MARCH, 1837, James and Margaretta Duffield, with their eight children, arrived at Appanoose, on the left bank of the Mississippi river. On the right bank was Fort Madison. Samuel Swearingen and wife, with their seven children, were the only persons there who were acquainted with the Duffields before they reached this point, but an hour's meeting between men in those days was enough to make them fast friends. A number of families were there that morning, all having waited over night to be ferried across.

We camped at a tavern the evening we reached the river; and camped is the name for it, because our mother and Mrs. Swearingen, with the girls, were the only ones who slept in the house. The men and boys cuddled into the hay ricks and under the wagons. The next morning we drove to the edge of the water. Our wagon was driven on to a flat-boat. This boat was about 30 feet long and 12 feet wide. There were two sets of row-locks on each side, one man to each oar. A man stood at the stern with a long steering oar and guided the boat. Getting on the boat was quite a job, for there were a great many families waiting to be taken over, and each took its turn. Each family would be numbered, and when that number was called would be put aboard as quickly as possible, those remaining being only too glad to lend a hand in order to hurry their turn along. Each man who crossed helped to row. There was but one boat, and it took a greater part of a day to get our party over. The rapid current carried us down stream, and with the best management it was nearly always necessary for the men to jump ashore when the bank was reached, either in coming over or going back, and tow the boat back up stream to the landing.

At last we were over. "Gwine to the Ioway settlement?" we would be asked. "Yes; whar mought the trail be?" in response. "Leadin' out 'twixt them big bluffs, thar," pointing the way a mile from the river. The Iowa "settlement" was then but a small part of our present State, and still a part of Wisconsin Territory.

As the boat came to the shore on its different trips, men and boys would be busy reloading the wagons. Axeltrees were tarred, linchpins carefully adjusted; feather beds, blankets, pots and skillets, the axes and rifles loaded in. These were indispensable, and there were few other things so considered, and really few other things to care for. "Dick" and "Buck," the patient, faithful oxen, were yoked and hitched to the four-wheeled wagon, and "Jule," an old blind mare, was hitched to the "pint" of the tongue. This wagon had a bed with "over-jets" above the wheels, and hand-shaved bows, with cover, making a roomy and comfortable conveyance. The women were in supreme possession of this wagon, with a man or boy to drive. "Bright" and "Berry," the second yoke, drew the two-wheeled cart, and in it were the few rude farming tools, and what riding was done by any boy large enough to keep pace afoot with an ox, was on this cart. None of the time were all riding, and some of the time all walked.

After reaching the hills or bluffs, we were amazed at their steepness and size. The trail led in and out to the head of a ravine that ran in from the prairie. It was a hard climb. Yet when we reached the more level ground we found a mere trail. Every foot of the way was on wild prairie sod which was hardly killed even where the hoofs of the oxen and wheels of the wagons trampled it, and between the tracks was a row of tall dead grass never broken, and as high as that on either side of the trail. One might think that this would make a good road. So it might at almost any other season. But most roads are poor in March of any year. These roads in March, 1837 – when nearly every day was rainy, and the soft, rich soil let the hoofs and wheels down to the stalling point – were the very worst. How many times did every one of the party have to get out, and nearly every article be unloaded! At such a time it was lucky there were large families. It took father and eldest sons to goad the oxen and encourage "Jule"; mother and each of the younger ones to carry a load apiece of the things taken from the wagon, and if father or larger sons could be spared from their tasks, it was to pry and push over or through quagmire after quagmire, until night overtook the tired company, sometimes not more than a mile from the place of their early morning start. It might be thought that the trail could be left and new ways taken. But when this was tried it was found that it took not more than one wagon to ruin the track, and not a rod of the way over which we came had not thus been cut up by others in our situation.

In those days I think every traveler coming west from Fort Madison stopped at Pittman's. We had worried, and worked, and tugged, until man and beast were tired out. Patience and strength were well nigh exhausted, and in the rain our party drew up at Pittman's door at dark. Mother and Mrs. Swearingen were crying out of discouragement, and what mother did was none too bad for every child she had to do, and hardly so for father. Lewis Pittman had settled on the trail before there was any travel west. In 1837 he had a very well improved farm. He had a good sized family, and yet Swearingen's nine and ours of ten were taken in that night. And when our bedraggled troop marched into the large room where the big fire-place blazed, it was with the feeling that it was housed in the palace of a lord. A meal was prepared before the fireplace, and without other lights than the flaring chunks, though candles were used in the other room. We were fed as became a generous host and hungry guests. And when the table was cleared away, and the party gathered around the fire to exchange the experiences and reminiscences common to their lives, it was a scene that I shall not forget. Swearingens and Pittmans and Duffields; three couples with their broods; no more than six chairs in the whole house; the little ones at their mothers' feet, scorching their faces and nodding their tired heads; the larger ones at play in the shadows at the rear, and the girls and boys in their teens, shy and bashful, sat apart from the group, yet not near each other, neither interested in the talk of their elders nor offering to visit among themselves. Then came the retiring time. If that household required no more than six chairs in its waking hours, where had it room for twenty-five or thirty persons to sleep?

We stayed at the Pittmans' several days resting and waiting for better weather. West Point, four miles beyond, was reached in a day. There was a stop, after leaving West Point, at Mr. Long's. His was the only family between West Point and Utica, where William Goodall lived. Now we began to think we were nearing our journey's end. Utica prairie was known far and wide. Here the trail leading on up the divide was left by those going in other directions, and all trails became faint. We took a southwesterly course, passed one or two cabins and came to the edge of civilization which was bounded on the west by the Des Moines river.

Father had visited this section in 1836, and had selected a claim west of the river some two miles, at the time beyond any land yet surveyed, and entirely out of the usual path of claim hunters. It was on the left bank of a creek which the Indians called Chequest, that empties into the Des Moines river some four miles below the sharp turn southward on the first curve of the great bend or "Ox Bow." Our camp was made on the left bank of the river and exactly opposite the mouth of Chequest creek. On the right bank and above the creek's mouth was the only cabin within the present limits of the State of Iowa west of the Des Moines river. It was built by Samuel Clayton in 1836; beyond it there was not one single human habitation, except those of the Indians.

On that side of the river, above and below Chequest creek, and in the valley of the creek back from the river for miles was the Indian camp of Keokuk, numbering, I should think, seven hundred. Here they were making sugar from the hard maples that thickly covered the banks of creek and river. For years afterward we could see the marks they made on the trees. They had no augers nor "spiles" such as the settlers used, so they would take their tomahawks, cut the bark from the tree in the shape of the letter "V," the point being perhaps a foot below the upper parts which reached two-thirds of the way around the tree. A flat peg or chip was driven into the tree below the point of the "V," the flat side up and the outer end lower than that next the tree. The sap would come out from the bark, follow around to the chip, run out to its point and drop into the troughs. These troughs were ingeniously made. They would cut a pole six or eight inches in diameter and about every two or three feet they would cut the bark in a zigzag way around the pole, so that when it was unrolled from the pole it would be a solid seamless strip say two feet long, with long, slender, pointed projections at the ends. These projections would be about a foot long, and about two inches wide at the body of the trough. These ends were drawn together by tough bark as tightly as possible, and this would curl up the bark to the size of the pole before it was stripped off, and would hold sometimes a couple of gallons of water. Of course the ends of the trough where they were puckered up, and occasionally a crack or hole through the body, would leak. To mend this, the Indians would take the inner bark of the slippery elm, beat it into a pulpy mass, and daub it into the cracks and openings, and this would make the whole thing water tight. They would gather the sap into storage troughs made, as their canoes were made, from the largest walnut trees. These they would make by cutting down the trees, taking off the bark and chipping off the upper side until it was flat and the size they wished the upper part of their trough to be. Then they would take coals and brands from their fires, lay them along the flat surface, burn the log a little then knock off the fire, put it out and with their tomahawks cut out the charred part. This they repeated until they would work out as fine a trough as could be made with the most improved modern tools. Their canoes were often made in fantastic shape, with walls so thin that they were as light as if made from bark. From 1836 to '40 there were many sugar troughs and hundreds of canoes in the woods and along the streams.

It would interest the curious to see our party crossing the Des Moines river on the 4th of April, 1836. No flatboats had been made, nor were there any other arrangements provided for crossing with anything more bulky or heavy than a man. Our camp on the left bank had attracted a large party of Indians, and their canoes were drawn up along the bank by dozens. I do not suppose they had ever seen a wagon, certainly never two at once, while the cover, the yoking of the cattle and the hitching of old "Jule" were all interesting to them. The river was too high and swift to ford; it would even have been dangerous to try to swim the cattle and "Jule" over. Father hit upon the plan of hiring a couple of the largest of the canoes, placing them side by side and lashing them together with puncheons placed crosswise over them; then taking everything out of the wagons and taking them apart the pieces were loaded on this craft and with the help of the Indians it was poled and paddled across. The last trip would have made a good picture. Indians and settlers; men, women and children; household goods, dogs, and finally "Jule," towed along, swimming in the water behind. But all were finally and safely landed.

The families were quartered in the Clayton cabin. The Claytons had seven in their family; our party nineteen; twenty-six souls were housed in great comfort in the one-roomed cabin.

During this week the men erected a cabin on our claim. Then for the last time that ox team was hitched to our moving wagon. It was a happy procession, drawing up and away from the river on the gentle slope of the ridge formed by the breaks of Chequest creek and the Des Moines river, then along its crest where a path was traced by the hoof of deer and buffalo and the moccasin of Indian brave. No shod hoof, much less a wagon-tire had ever marked this road. How "Dick" and "Buck" crowded and hooked to get the advantage of the trail, while "Jule" switched along its easy, crooked line with a swing and a stride that showed that she knew its meaning. For a few short miles, then off down to the left, through the sloping open woods, then out into an opening to a fresh, new, one-roomed cabin – HOME!

. . . George C. Duffield (1823-1908)

The Land and the People

IN THESE BRIEF EXCERPTS from three book-length works and one journal article we see the land of Iowa as the settlers saw it, and a catalog of some of the people who came on the land. Herbert Quick's brilliant description of the Iowa Prairie (Vandemark's Folly, 1922) was singled out for praise by Iowa's greatest student of the prairie, Bohumil Shimek, a University of Iowa professor who frequently came into his classroom dripping wet with marsh mud and water but holding triumphantly in his outstretched hand some new specimen of plant life he had found. Quick was born on the Iowa Prairie in 1861.

Charles Aldrich's description of a prairie slough is taken from "The Old Prairie Slough," Annals of Iowa, 1901. Aldrich had encountered the sloughs in central Iowa when he came into the state in 1857, and he knew from that personal experience the "terrors" the sloughs presented to "wagons westward."

Quick's tally of the people who came to Iowa with his young hero and his hymeneal to the marriage of John Deere's steel plow (seen in Grant Wood's painting) and the virgin prairie sod are from Vandemark's Folly. Garland's "Ploughing" is from his Boy Life on the Prairie (1899), a book which has a chapter on the breaking of the prairie sod.

Margaret Wilson's Scotch hymn to the fertile Iowa soil is from her 1923 The Able McLaughlins; her narrative of the coming of the Scotch to north Tama County won her both the Harper Prize Novel Award and the Pulitzer Prize for fiction. She was born in Traer in 1882, "a descendant of the same Scottish Covenanter clan that produced Iowa's 'Tama Jim' Wilson, long-time U.S. Secretary of Agriculture. She was the author of nine other novels, one of which (The Law and the McLaughlins, 1936) is a sequel to The Able McLaughlins.

(John) Herbert Quick was born in Steamboat Rock, on the Grundy-Hardin county line, in 1861, the son of pioneer immigrants. His only education was in a Grundy County rural school—"not to have had a college education might be considered a virtue," he later said. Nevertheless, he became a lawyer, a politician (he was Mayor of Sioux City from 1898 to 1900) and the author of twenty books, several of which explicate his political and educational theories. He died in 1925 while on a trip to lecture at the University of Missouri.

Charles Aldrich (1828-1980) was a historian; for the last fifteen years of his life he edited Annals of Iowa, *a publication of the State Historical Society.*

Hamlin Garland *was born in 1860 on a coulee farm near LaCrosse, Wisconsin, but spent his formative years on a prairie farm northeast of Osage, Iowa—the farm buildings are still preserved and used by a farm family not related to Garland. After graduation from the Cedar Valley Seminary in Osage, Garland lived for a time in Boston, where he continued his education on his own. In Chicago, he was encouraged to write about his farm experiences by Joseph Kirkland, who—emulating his mother, Caroline—was an early American writer in the realistic tradition. Ultimately, as the author of a score of books, including one play, numerous verses, short stories, novels and reminiscences of his experiences as an author, Garland won a Pulitzer Prize and a reputation as "Dean of American Letters."*

Grant Wood *(1891-1942) was born on a farm near Anamosa, took his public school education in Cedar Rapids, got some formal art education in Minneapolis and Chicago, but was largely self-educated as an artist (like many of the older contributors to this book, he was reared in the Emersonian principle of "self-reliance"). He soon discarded European concepts of the techniques of art and began developing his own "regional" theories of painting and drawing. His* Fall Plowing *was commissioned by the John Deere Company in 1931, the centenary of John Deere's invention of the iron-shared plow, the "Plow that Broke the Plains," and made settlement on the prairies feasible.*

• HOME OF HERBERT QUICK ⇀ NEAR GRUNDY CENTER, IOWA •

The Land and the People

I COULD SEE THE IOWA PRAIRIE sweeping away as far as the eye could see. I shall never forget the sight. It was like a great green sea. The old growth had been burned the fall before, and the spring grass scarcely concealed the brown sod on the uplands; but all the swales were coated thick with an emerald growth full-bite high, and in the deeper, wetter hollows grew cowslips, already showing their glossy, golden flowers. The hillsides were thick with the woolly possblummies in their furry spring coats protecting them against the frost and chill, showing purple-violet on the outside of a cup filled with golden stamens, the first fruits of the prairie flowers; on the warmer southern slopes a few of the splendid bird's-foot violets of the prairie were showing the azure color which would soon make some of the hillsides as blue as the sky; and standing higher than the peering grass rose the rough-leafed stalks of green which would soon show us the yellow puccoons and sweet-williams and scarlet lilies and shooting stars, and later the yellow rosin-weeds, Indian dye-flower and goldenrod. The keen northwest wind swept before it a flock of white clouds; and under the clouds went their shadows, walking over the lovely hills like dark ships over an emerald sea.

The wild-fowl were clamoring north for the summer's campaign of nesting. Everywhere the sky was harrowed by the wedged wild geese, their voices as sweet as organ tones; and ducks quacked, whistled and whirred overhead, a true rain of birds beating up against the wind. Over every slew, on all sides, thousands of ducks of many kinds and several sorts of geese hovered, settled or burst up in eruptions of birds, their back-feathers shining like bronze as they turned so as to reflect the sunlight to my eyes; while so far up that they looked like specks, away above the wind it seemed, so quietly did they circle and sail, floated hugh flocks of cranes—the sand-hill cranes in their slaty-gray, and the whooping cranes, white as snow with black heads and feet, each bird with a ten-foot spread of wing, piping their wild cries which fell down to me as if from another world.

It was sublime! Bird, flower, grass, cloud, wind, and the immense expanse of sunny prairie, swelling up into undulations like a woman's breasts, turgid with milk for a human race. I forgot myself; my heart swelled and my throat filled. I sat looking at it, with the tears trickling from my eyes, the uplift of my soul more than I could bear. It was my happiness in finding the newest, strangest, most delightful, sternest, most wonderful thing in the world—the Iowa prairie—that brought the tears to my eyes. . . .

. . . Herbert Quick (1860-1925)

THE PRAIRIE SLOUGH was always an interesting object and a wonder to me. In the winter it would be frozen solid—as cold and dead as an iceberg. Some of the larger ones, however, would be studded with muskrat houses, huge piles of coarse weeds and mosses, which the animals tore up from the bottoms of the sloughs. These creatures wintered in their houses safe from everything except the spears of the Musquakie Indians. But in the summers the prairie sloughs were fairly alive—and with a variety of life. Several species of small mollusks— coiled shells—had lived and died in our prairie sloughs for countless ages. The winds drifted the bleached and empty shells ashore, where they often looked like piles of small white gravel. Several species of birds nested in the weeds and coarse grasses which grew out in the water. Yellow-headed blackbirds were the most conspicuous. They were about the size of the purple grackle (crow blackbird). The head and neck almost to the shoulders were a bright yellow and glistened like polished gold. They were very beautiful birds, but their notes were terribly harsh—as distressing as the filing of a saw. The beautiful red-wings also made their homes in the sloughs, as did the marsh wrens. They ingeniously wove together several stalks of coarse grass and made themselves strong nests—safe from predatory wolves and foxes. In point of numbers the red-wings far surpassed the others, breeding by millions in our prairie sloughs. When minks were plenty, they also had their abodes in and about the sloughs. Ducks, geese and cranes summered in these damp regions, often appropriating the muskrat houses for their nests. And there were mosquitoes beyond any computation. They simply swarmed in clouds.

No two prairie sloughs were alike. We had ponds or lakelets, where the water was open, in rare instances abounding with fish—and others, where the surface was covered with dense growths of bulrushes and coarse grasses, which looked black from a little distance. One could go around such places dry shod. Little valleys with but gradual descent, down which the water slowly crept through the grass roots and the black ooze, were also called sloughs, as were wide reaches of swamp lands. These last were the teamsters' and travelers' terror, for it was impossible to go around them. In the spring and in rainy seasons they became almost impassable, and when a wagon stuck fast, the horse or oxen had a wonderful penchant for lying down, no doubt in great discouragement—and there you were!   ...Charles Aldrich

I DROVE OUT TO THE HIGHWAY, and turning my prow to the west, I joined again in the stream of people swarming westward. The tide had swollen during the week. The road was rutted, poached deep where wet and beaten hard where dry, or pulverized into dust by the stream of emigration. Here we went, oxen, cows, mules, horses; coaches carriages, blue jeans, corduroys, rags, tatters, silks, satins, caps, tall hats, poverty, riches; speculators, missionaries, land-hunters, merchants; criminals escaping from justice; couples fleeing from the law; families seeking homes; the wrecks of homes seeking secrecy; gold-seekers bearing southwest to the Overland Trail; politicians looking for places in which to win fame and fortune; editors hunting opportunities for founding newspapers; adventurers on their way to everywhere; lawyers with a few books; Abolitionists going to the Border War; innocent-looking outfits carrying fugitive slaves; officers hunting escaped negroes; and most numerous of all, homeseekers "hunting country"—a nation on wheels, an empire in the commotion and pangs of birth. Down I went with the rest, across ferries, past a thousand vacant sites for farms toward my own farm so far from civilization, shot out of civilization by civilization itself.   ...Herbert Quick

First school teacher arrives in Council Bluffs

THE NEXT DAY WAS A WEDDING DAY—the marriage morning of the plow and the sod. It marked the beginning of the subdual of that wonderful wild prairie of township and farm. No more fruitful espousal ever took place than that—when the polished steel of my new breaking plow was embraced by the black soil with its lovely fell of greenery. Up to that fateful moment, the prairie of the farm and of the township had been virgin sod; but now it bowed its neck to the yoke of wedlock. Nothing like it takes place any more; for the sod of the meadows and pastures is quite a different thing from the untouched skin of the original earth. Breaking prairie was the most beautiful, the most epochal, and most hopeful, and as I look back at it, in one way the most pathetic thing man ever did, for in it, one of the loveliest things ever created began to come to its predestined end.

The plow itself was long, low, and yacht-like in form; a curved blade of polished steel. The plowman walked behind it in a clean new path, sheared as smooth as a concrete pavement, with not a lump of crumbled earth under his feet—a cool, moist, black path of richness. The furrow-slice was a long, almost unbroken ribbon of turf, each one laid smoothly against the former strand, and under it lay crumpled and crushed the layer of grass and flowers. The plow-point was long and tapering, like the prow of a clipper, and ran far out under the beam, and above it was the rolling colter, a circular blade of steel, which cut the edge of the furrow as cleanly as cheese. The lay of the plow, filed sharp at every round, lay flat, and clove the slice neatly from the bosom of earth where it had lain from the beginning of time. As the team steadily pulled the machine along, I heard a curious thrilling sound as the knife went through the roots, a sort of murmuring as of protest at this viola-tion—and once in a while, the whole engine, and the arms of the plow-man also, felt like a jar, like that of a ship striking a hidden rock, as the share cut through a red-root—a stout root of wood, like red cedar or mahogany, sometimes as large as one's arm, topped with a clump of tough twigs with clusters of pretty whitish blossom.   . . . Herbert Quick

Grant Wood mural—Library—Iowa State University

Fall Plowing—Grant Wood

Ploughing

A lonely task it is to plow!
   All day the black and clinging soil
Rolls like a ribbon from the mould-board's
   Glistening curve. All day the horses toil
Battling with the flies—and strain
   Their creaking collars. All day
The crickets jeer from wind-blown shocks of grain.

          . . . Hamlin Garland

THE ELDER McLAUGHLIN SIGHED WITH SATISFACTION AS HE TALKED. Even yet he had scarcely recovered from that shock of incredulous delight at his first glimpse of the incredible prairies; acres from which no frontiersman need ever cut a tree; acres in which a man might plow a furrow of rich black earth a mile long without striking a stump or a stone; a state much larger than all of Scotland in which there was no record of a battle ever having been fought—what a home for a man who in his childhood had walked to school down a path between the graves of his martyred ancestors—whose fathers had farmed a rented sandpile enriched by the blood of battle among the rock of the Bay of Luce. Even yet he could scarcely believe that there existed such an expanse of eager virgin soil waiting for whoever would husband it. Ten years of storm-bound winters, and fever-shaken, marketless summers before the war, had not chilled his passion for it—nor poverty so great that sometimes it took the combined efforts of the clan to buy a twenty-five cent stamp to write to Scotland of the measureless wealth upon which they had fallen. From the time he was ten years old he had dreamed of America. He had had to wait to realize his dream till his landlord had sold him out for rent overdue. What Wully remembered gallingly about that sale was that his grandmother had been present at it, and her neighbors, thinking she bought the poor household stuff to give back to her son, refused to bid for it against her. Then having got it all cheap she sold it at a considerable profit, and pocketed the money. That was why, taught by his father, he despised everything that suggested Scotch stinginess. Nor had he wept a tear when the old woman died, soon after, and his father, taking his share of her hoardings, had departed for his Utopia. Some of the immigrants had long since lost their illusions. But not John McLaughlin. He loved his land like a blind and passionate lover. Really there was nothing glorious that one was not justified in imagining about a nation to be born to such an inheritance. And he told Wully that he might at least console himself with the thought that those months in [a Civil War] prison had made him the possessor of such land, that with the possible exception of the fabled Nile valley, there was probably in the world no richer. And the McLaughlins prided themselves on the fact that they were no American "soil-scratchers," exhausting debauchers of virgin possibilities. Their rich soil, they promised themselves, was to be richer by far for every crop it yielded.

. . . Margaret Wilson

Pioneer Village and Town

AND SO THE PEOPLE CAME to these rolling grassy prairies. Some settling near the streams, as the Duffields, built their first homes of logs. Others, settling in areas where grass and only grass grew as far as the eye could see, built "soddies," homes laid up from the foot-thick strips of sod they ripped from the land before they plowed. Or else they dug into hillsides, returning, until something better could be contrived, to the kind of shelters their caveman ancestors had moved out of aeons before.

Wheat was a major crop for many of these first Iowa farmers, and wheat required mills and millers. So mills sprang up wherever a head of water could be dammed on a stream; Mitchell County in north-central Iowa had perhaps three dozen mills at one time.

"Miller Adam" is a poetic tribute to Kantor's maternal grandfather, Adam McKinlay, a "small man . . . round-shouldered, and with chronic asthma from years in the dust-laden mills" of Webster City; Kantor's great-grandfather, Lt. Joseph Bone, was also a miller.

Raymond Kresensky's (1897-1955) poem is a tribute to the "Old Families" of Algona, his birthplace. Several of the families named in the poem became prominent in Iowa history. Kresensky was a Des Moines resident at the time of his death.

Towns began to grow around the settlements and mills. Pittsburg developed at the point where the Chequest Creek in Van Buren County flows into the Des Moines River, just south of George C. Duffield's farm. Webster City grew around mills such as Lt. Bone's on the Boone River. Algona grew around homes built by Asa and Ambrose Call.

The two 1921 Palimpsest *articles by H. Clark Brown and Charlton Laird recall the development of another Iowa town, Bradford, and the building of Iowa's most famous church, "The Little Brown Church in the Vale," nearby. Laird, whose father was a McGregor lumberman, later wrote two historical novels,* Thunder on the River *(1949) and* West of the River *(1953) about the relationships between whites and Indians which led up to the "Bad Axe Massacre" in southeast Minnesota, an incident which ended Black Hawk's dreams of retaining his Illinois and Iowa bases.*

Paul Engle's "Ancestral Iowa" looks back at his ancestors in the Cedar Rapids area. Later, in "Remember Memorial Day?" you will travel with young Paul Engle to visit the graves of these ancestors.

Miller Adam

Miller Adam is gray and thin;
He walks like a lame deer limping.
(But there was a time when his ruddy grin
Studied his courtship primping).

Behind his years the wheat fields stare,
And rivers with black floods flowing—
His is the thought of the meal bags there,
And the thought of the meal piles' growing.

He rode from the east when fields were damp,
When cries of the geese were shriller;
He built his dam by Mesquakies' camp,
And prided himself as a miller.

And times when he treads the roaring street
I can see the brown-red riding
Of an ancient Sioux on a mustang fleet,
His face from the wild sun hiding;

And times when he stares by the window-pane
I can hear the spring storm rushing—
Dammed in the swirl of a battered rain
As the stones go grating, crushing. . . .

Oh, Adam, some have a panelled room
With their velvet and bright lace sunning—
You faced the howl of a midnight flume
While a vicious sea was running!

Wherever you limp with your sad old cane,
And the snow on your bent back falling,
Your pride is one with forgotten grain,
And the early, keen brant calling.

. . . MacKinlay Kantor, *Turkey in the Straw* (1935)

The Old Families

We are members of the old families,
Our blood runs purple
Through four generations.
We preempted the land
On which your town now stands.

We built log cabins
Among the ravines
And drove ox teams to Fort Dodge
For supplies.
We sent for a parson and a teacher.

We fought the railroad when it came through
And we prompted our own real estate schemes.
The railroad built its own town—
And we built ours.

We had money to lend
And we organized banks
The interest built our home
And sent our daughters to Paris,
And our sons to Rome.
It paid for these stores.

We are members of the old families
And our bones lie in Riverview Cemetery.
Drop down honeysuckle, fern and wild sweet william.

Here is the first white child
Born in Algona.
Here is the stage coach driver.
The first mayor, the first parson,
And the first homesteaders.

We are the Calls, the Blackfords, the Inghams,
The Daltons, the Smiths,
The Hendersons, the Lessings, Heckerts, Hudsons,
McGetchies and the Kings.
Our blood runs purple through generations
And now . . .

There is the gray-haired old maid
And a few others, bearing new names —
A street loafer and a bankrupt;
The others have gone.

Count the stones in a long row,
And read the gray names.
Kick your toe in the gravel path
And roll a stone
While you look north to the river and the hills
In search of us.

There are two black lines
Up the north valley.
The stage coach went there.

We are members of the old families
And our bones lie
In Riverview Cemetery.

. . . Raymond Kresensky

-ST. CHARLES CEMETERY-
ST. CHARLES. IOWA.

A Prairie Village — Civil War Times

IN TIMES PAST, the rising sun each morning spread its rays over the great expanse of undulating prairie grassland, and quickened to life the pulse of a little prairie village in its heart. Bradford, in Chickasaw County, was a bit of old new England set down on the rolling land of northeastern Iowa. The site was far from new when the first white settler discovered it. It was an early habitation of the Indians; the little stream which had cut its way through this region, the silvery fish in it, the little glades of its tributaries with their shade, their wild life and their wild fruits, all combined to make this a favored spot with the Indian, a delectable place for a camping ground. Here too, beside the stream, was the Land of the Passing Ones where the Indians placed the bark-encased bodies of their dead on log structures above the ground.

Then came the first white man, and a trading post was established at the Indian village. Little did the Indians realize what this outpost of the white man's power would mean to them. But the time came when it seemed as though their gods had entirely forsaken them; discouraged and saddened with the thoughts of leaving the camping-grounds of their ancestors they turned one last, long glance toward the land of their memories, then set forth to a new home beyond the wide Missouri. The heritage of their forefathers was no longer theirs. Is it any wonder that they looked upon these white intruders with such bitterness?

With the departure of the Indians, log cabins sprang up on every side, for the white man also found this a pleasant vale for the location of a home. The great red cedars, which gave the stream its name, and the great walnuts were felled, and within a fortnight, it almost seemed— so rapidly was the prairie silence broken—a little village appeared on the Iowa prairies. In the course of time it became a thrifty place, a metropolis of the prairies. All the stage lines of that region included it in their daily routes. When the stagecoaches reached the main street, the horses were driven at a terrific speed, for the entrance of the stages was a matter of great importance. They were the only communication with the outside world and many of the town worthies made it a point to be on hand when they arrived. The occasions were of especial importance to the small boys of the village; their fancies pictured a wild rush from one bandit holdup to another.

Down the long main street of the village the coaches came wildly dashing—past the brown church, the school house, the red brick Academy which was the pride of the day, past the old log courthouse, the wagon shop, the brewery, the saw-mills, the blacksmith's, and the public square. It stopped only when it arrived at the big Bronson House. Here at the hotel the mail had to be left, new mail bags taken on, and a change of horses made. Passengers got off and on, occasions of wondering stares or friendly salutations as the situation demanded. Then the coaches were free to continue on their ways over the prairie, traversing a distance of nearly twenty miles before the next villages were reached. Occasionally they ran parallel to the Indian trails which were worn deep in the prairie soil, but for the most part the voyages were monotonous excursions except for those passengers who happened to be awake to the wonders of bird and plant life about them.

. . . H. Clark Brown

FAP mural, Council Bluffs, Iowa

The Little Brown Church in the Vale

AT THE EDGE of the now-deserted village of Bradford stands a little, weather-beaten, old church, painted a quiet brown and half hidden among the trees. The bit of forest that civilization has left clustering about the building half hides and half discloses it; the short square belfry is only partly screened by the boughs of several oaks and a towering pine. This is the church immortalized in Dr. William Pitts's lyric song, "The Little Brown Church in the Vale."

The church itself is very plain—plain in a simple, homely way that gives to it a rare charm and beauty. In the simplicity and dignity of the structure are reflected the New England ancestry and training of the architect, the Reverend J. K. Nutting. The main gabled building, low and rather broad, is fronted with a dignified little tower. Everything is neat and unadorned; even the old doors of the Gothic portal are without ornament.

Little and plain as the church is, it represented courageous undertaking on the part of the inhabitants of the village. It was built just after a panic and during a period of inflated war prices. Money was practically unknown; Mr. Nutting indicated this when he wrote that his cash salary for 1859—four dollars—had been brought into the community by an Easterner. In the year 1862 poverty because of war conditions compelled the parish to reduce the minister's salary from five hundred dollars to four hundred and fifty dollars, payable in goods. Wedding fees were in addition, but they might be paid in apples or vegetables. With his characteristic energy, the young pastor not only accepted the reduction, but increased his already heavy burdens by making his acceptance conditional upon the building of a church.

The young men were in the army; those who remained were practically penniless, but they enthusiastically undertook the task. One man donated the lots, a second gave logs, and a third sawed them into lumber. A "bee" quarried the stone, which Leander Smith fitted into a slanting wall. Since his knowledge of masonry came from experience with the fences of Massachusetts, it happens that the foundations of the church have the same inward pitch that he habitually used in New England. The Reverend Mr. Todd, a friend of Mr. Nutting's father, now came to the aid of the little church. A collection from his Sunday school at Pittsfield, Massachusetts, bought the finishing lumber, which was hauled eighty miles by wagon from McGregor. "And so," Mr. Nutting wrote, "we finished the building."

Meanwhile the words of the song "The Little Brown Church in the Vale" had already been written. They had been inspired by the beauty of the spot upon which the church stands, but the picture of the building itself was purely imaginative. Dr. William Pitts, while visiting Bradford in 1857, was impressed by the beauty of the valley that sheltered the little village. Leading from Bradford to Greenwood, a shaded nook on the Red Cedar River, was an inviting path that became the haunt of the young physician-musician. Nearly every afternoon of his visit found him following the trail up through the grove of oaks and out across the plain to Greenwood. Just where the verdure of the forest merged into the blossoms of the prairie was a little glade that Dr. Pitts described as "an attractive and lovely spot." And this broadening of the wooded lane into the more open country held for him an enchantment that found expression in his favorite song. The place was also a favorite with the people of Bradford, and it was here, a few years later, that they built the Little Brown Church.

The song was written at Dr. Pitts's home in Wisconsin, but it was first publicly sung in the church which it eventually named. A passionate lover of beauty, the young doctor carried home with him a vivid picture of the little prairie valley, and embodied this vision in what the world knows as "The Little Brown Church in the Vale." Five years later, Dr. Pitts moved to Iowa and settled in the neighboring town of Fredericksburg, but twenty miles from the Little Brown Church, then in the process of construction. In taking charge of the musical organizations of southern Chickasaw County, he became the teacher of a little singing school at Bradford. In the spring of 1864, Mr. Nutting, who was a member of the doctor's class, led the party to the church which, although enclosed, was as yet unfinished; and here, to an audience seated upon improvised board benches, Dr. Pitts sang from his original manuscript the song. Thus the bare unplastered walls that the lines immortalized were the first to echo their sweet melodies.

The song became immensely popular. It was sung throughout the country and before the royal courts of Europe. Bradford's little church, already closely connected with the song, soon became definitely identified with it. The building, dedicated on December 29, 1864, only a few months prior to the publication of the song in Chicago, had been appropriately painted brown. Whether this was due to the cheapness of brown paint or whether it is traceable to a desire to conform with the published poem will probably never be known.

The building that we know as the Little Brown Church expresses very well the sentiment of the lyric whose name it bears. It may be interesting to note just how the little church has fulfilled the statements and predictions of each stanza of the poem. Allowance must be made, however, for the fact that at the time of writing the nook selected by Dr. Pitts had never been popularly considered as the site for a place of worship, and that the church and graveyard of the song are the product of an idealistic imagination that felt no necessity for conformity with the real.

There's a church in the valley by the wildwood,
  No lovelier spot in the dale.
No spot is so dear to my childhood,
  As the little brown church in the vale.

The valley that shelters the church is charming in its simple beauty. The building stands at the edge of the break in the prairie. To the east, and yet really including the church within its borders, lies the vale, scatteringly wooded and appropriately set with the old-fashioned buildings. To the west stretches the blossoming prairie until it ends in the wooded skyline along the Red Cedar River. A few rods from the church, a wooden bridge spans the grassy-banked creek that courses through the valley. It all reminds one very much of an etching of an English landscape. Lofty oaks and stately pines still enshrine the little church, but the wildwood of the poems has gone with the life of the village that it surrounded. In the days when Dr. Pitts described the village as

"a veritable beehive of industry," Bradford boasted of two saw mills, and these were so busy that the logs for the frame of the church had to wait several months before there was room for them in the mill yard. The size of the forest monarchs that once surrounded the church is indicated by a black walnut timber, three feet square and forty feet long, which supported the top saw in one of these mills. A very pretty grove still clusters about the little building, and though it is but a suggestion of the former wealth of verdure, it forms a glade that at once secludes and dignifies the structure. This simple little church has sequestered itself among the protecting foliage, and there, enshrined in memories, it continues in its quite homely way.

> How sweet on a bright Sabbath morning,
>   To list to the clear ringing bell,
> Its tones so sweetly are calling,
>   Oh come to the church in the dell.

The praise of the bell is upheld in the love that the community bore it. Bells play a prominent part in many of Dr. Pitts's songs, but no other ever held for him the charm of the one whose soft enticing tones he immortalized. "The Bells of Shannon" may be as grand as the poet has pictured them, but you will never convince an old Bradfordite that they can rival the clear sweet tones of the bell that calls for the Little Brown Church. "The bell," it was called throughout the countryside, for it was the only one in the county and was the pride of all Bradford. Cast in Meneeley's famous foundry at Troy, New York, it was personally selected by Mr. Nutting because of its clear sweet tone. The bell was obtained through the benevolences of the young pastor's eastern friends; the inscription proclaimed it the gift of Mr. Thomas Cole and Catherine, his wife. Brought from Dubuque by wagon, the bell was rung almost the entire distance, and a considerable crowd gathered to view its entrance into the village, for the arrival of the "the bell" was an event in Bradford's history.

> There close by the church in the valley,
>   Lies one I loved so well.
> She sleeps, quietly sleeps 'neath the willow,
>   Disturb not her rest in the vale.

A pretty myth to the effect that Mrs. Pitts was buried at the Little Brown Church has grown around the sentiment expressed in this stanza.

To the rear of the church is a little swale that would have been beautiful as a graveyard. This is the mythical resting place of Mrs. Pitts, and here the willows still grow, just as the poet described them. But there are no signs that the spot was ever used as a burying ground. The writing of the lyric seven years before the dedication of the church accounts for the inconsistency in regard to the graveyard. At the time of writing, Dr. Pitts never suspected that a house of worship would later be built upon the very spot on which he erected his dream church. With his usual sense of aesthetic fitness, he not only created the church for which nature had supplied the setting, but he added the churchyard that completed the picture.

> There close by the side of the loved one
>   'Neath the tree where the wild flowers bloom,
> When the farewell hymn shall be changed,
>   I shall rest by her side in the tomb.

The sentiment of this stanza was fulfilled in the case of Dr. Pitts, though the burial did not take place at the Little Brown Church. In his later life, the Doctor moved to Clarion, Iowa, and then to Brooklyn, New York, where he died in 1918. The ceremony for him at Fredericksburg was fittingly simple; the singing of "The City Four Square" by his eight-year-old grandson was the only distinguishing feature. He was buried beside his wife in the local cemetery at Fredericksburg where at last he "rests by her side in the tomb."

The very simpleness of The Little Brown Church endears it to all who knew old Bradford. After all, it is only a little, very plain, storm-beaten church. But within it dwell the hope and love of God-fearing pioneers; around it cling the fondest memories that a scattered people cherish for their deserted village.

. . . Charlton G. Laird

·LITTLE BROWN CHURCH IN THE VALE — NASHUA, IOWA·

Ancestral Iowa

Jacob, Mike and Tom were my ancestors,
Tough old countrymen until they died,
Hands clever at holding knife or horse,
Good with a gun, tanning buffalo hide.

They knew the working of iron to a worn hoof,
Lay of ground for grain, the latch of leather,
Foretold if hay would fill a barn to roof,
Wise in breeding hogs, wary of weather.

From Eva, Alice, Rachel was I born,
Makers of buckwheat pancakes and bear broth,
Women who helped break earth and harvest corn,
In the long winter wove the homely cloth.

Suffered the prairie childbirth, bore their labor
Only by wolf howl and wan candle light,
Never any help but patient neighbor
Through the dread daylight-screaming hours of night.

While they brought tree to farm and built line fence,
Walked in withering sun, the winter rigor,
Ever the stalwart bone of common sense
Gave to the body a more stubborn vigor.

Here, in an unreal world of myth and mind,
What have I left of their great human will?
The field of fact to plow, the corn to grind,
My hand to learn old lightness in new skill.

                                        . . . Paul Engle

Friendly Persuasion

VILLAGES AND TOWNS DEVELOPED not only where there were mills or a cluster of log cabins, but also, at strategic points across the state, as market towns and cultural centers. Farmers needed a place, not more than half a day's drive distant, to bring surplus crops and other produce; they needed a source for necessary food, tools and clothing they could not produce on their own farms. And, if there were no rural church, they needed a place where they could worship God on Sundays and other occasions.

One consequence of the parallel development of urban center and farmstead was a friendly rivalry over the merits of each kind of life. An example of the fruits of such rivalry is in the following pair of letters. "Maggie May's" letter was printed in Manchester's Delaware County Union *on May 4, 1866. "Farmer's Wife's" retort appeared in print on June 1, 1866.*

Incidentally one notes the writing style of both letters. These were obviously well-tutored ladies, able with their pens, clear-witted. One can only wonder if this debate were ever continued face-to-face in a local parlor, or outside the general store or a local church of a Sunday!

Farming in 1866

I WAS TIRED of the old, lonely house opposite my east window—annoyed by the noise of the builders on the south lots, and disgusted at the proximity of the barn on the north side; so I concluded to leave care and trouble and rest a little while with Brother Carter, who is a farmer, and consequently (according to the papers) one of the happiest of mortals.

It took but two days to prepare for my journey: and I forgot all about the noisy carpenters and dismal house, as I, in imagination, feasted on Farmer Carter's "fat things," and wandered like a thistle into every pleasant nook and corner in his neighborhood.

Wouldn't I have the freshest eggs and the sweetest butter for breakfast? And then didn't the farmers always have lambs, and pigs, and turkeys by the dozen, and chickens innumerable?

And who ever read of a farmer's wife that didn't have the very whitest of bread, the sourest of pickles, and the best of fruit? There was the garden sauce too. Oh! I should have a delightful visit I knew. I started; I arrived at Sister Mary's gate; I wished to go into the house, but how could I? First was a broken, patched-up gate, hanging over a mud-puddle; then four yards of five inch mud; next a pile of wood, beyond which I saw the backs of three little pigs, that were seeking delicious tidbits in the bottomless mire.

I stood still in perplexity. I wondered if Sister Mary's folks had wings, or whether they walked on stilts. Presently a little boy came round the corner of the house, picked up a long board and came toward me, saying, "I guess the mud's pretty deep there," and down came the board, spattering my new cloak with mud and water. "There's a bridge for you now," said my champion, as he opened the gate, and bravely walked over the board to prove it trustworthy. I followed with fear and trembling, and landed safely on the chip-pile, from which I surveyed the next mudpuddle and my guide, wondering what would come next. "This is the way," he said, and I followed, stepping (at the risk of breaking my neck) on sticks, stones, and bits of board, until we arrived at the back part of the house. We entered a room filled with rubbish and grain of various kinds, through which we stumbled into the next apartment. This I soon found to be parlor and kitchen all together. Sister Mary greeted me warmly, and I know she was glad to see me. She presented half a dozen boys and girls to be kissed by aunt Maggie, and I went through the operation bravely, although I could not help wishing that they had washed their faces first.

Sister soon said it was time to get supper, and sent Tommy to get some wood, and Harry to look for eggs to make a custard. "For," she said, "I sent every one I had to town this morning. The teakettle was set on the stove, and a little three-years-old baby stuck his finger down the spout. Mary went into the rubbish-room and returned with a plate of fat salt pork (I had a barrel full at home), which she put to freshen, remarking that "Joseph had been talking of killing a pig for a week or two but had been so busy that he hadn't got at it yet."

Harry returned with one egg, saying that he "couldn't find any more, and guessed Smith's dog had been sucking the eggs, for he saw him running up the road."

Supper was ready, and we sat down to a plate of fried pork, a saucer of flat, flabby pickles, and a few little radishes that were "remarkably strong for their size."

Sister Mary said she was intending to bake some pies and cakes yesterday, but the baby was so cross she couldn't. I told her I was tired of such things, and had come into the country for greens. She laughed and said her "garden didn't amount to much, for the bugs and worms took everything as fast as it came up."

In the morning Mary asked Joseph to kill a chicken for dinner, but he forgot it and went to his plowing. After dinner we went to the garden to gather some currants for tea, but the birds had been there before us, so we got no more than a teacupful. I asked Mary why she didn't trim the bushes and set out more. "Why, I wanted to this spring, but I couldn't get time." *Next spring*, however, she was going to see if she couldn't work in the garden a little more. We pulled some stringy-looking pieplant stems to cook with our currants; instituted a search among some tall weeds for some young onions, and returnd triumphantly to find Susy screaming with terror, because the baby had swallowed a button, and Lizzy in a fit of sulks because we had not taken her ladyship with us.

Brother Carter soon came in, and said the cattle had broken down the fence and destroyed ever so much corn, and he couldn't kill the pig that evening, for he should have to mend the fence. Then he told me his best cow, that gave milk all the year round, had been bitten by a rattlesnake, and died in spite of doctoring; how five of his best lambs gave up the ghost, in contempt of care; how his wheat had musted and only brought half price; how his oats were so heavy that they all fell down and were half wasted, and that his best horse had been sick, so that he could not draw lumber to build his granary, and so had to keep his grain in the kitchen. Then, after he had gone to his work, Mary told me what a hard time they had to get their farm paid for. They had worked hard, and lived on the poorest fare, to lay by enough to meet the payments, and she had sold butter and eggs, cheese, chickens and turkeys. Then some winters the chickens would freeze to death, and sometimes the turkeys wouldn't hatch. She had set out ever so much shrubbery, but it was always destroyed in the winter, and—but that is enough. I no longer wondered that the farming community furnished more inmates for our insane asylums than any other class, but was astonished to find that my brother and sister were not candidates for one of those retreats. But then they were so hopeful. Their stock was increasing, the children would soon be some help, the farm was paid for, and now they were "going to fix up a little round the house." I returned home a sadder, but I hope a wiser woman. I found the carpenter's noise as pleasant as the squealing of pigs, an offensive barnyard as endurable as a dirty door-yard, and the clatter of loose boards and shutter no worse than the mending of wagons and plows.

... Maggie May

Farmer's Comforts

MR. EDITOR: Having seen a communication from Maggie May in your paper depicting the happiness of farmers' wives (as she calls it) in glowing colors, I think it the duty of some one of that class to say a word in favor of themselves and their calling. I have no desire to change my position, and would say to all young ladies they may do far worse than to marry a farmer. I *know* they do not all have mudpuddles before their doors, in fact I do not know of one that has, and Maggie May might sit down anywhere in my yard and not soil her nice dress or new cloak. Neither do we go over the chips or wood to get into the house. We have nice white bread and graham bread, pickles, and as yellow butter as one can ask, a very good garden, lots of currants, rhubarb, strawberries, and live in hopes to have all kinds of fruit in time. I have plenty of eggs, and chickens to kill when I want them, and among the farmer's families of my acquaintance they are all as comfortable, and more so in some respects. Most of them are getting started now, and in time they will have larger houses and ride in their carriages.

I have any amount of flowers, and it yields me many hours enjoyment taking care of them; and my husband is always ready and willing to assist me in any way that I ask him, and to spare a little money now and then to buy a choice flower or shrub for me. I have another source of pleasure on a farm I could not have in town—the live stock, from the tiny chickens to the great horse. I love to go out after sunset and smooth the sleek sides of the cows and speak to them; and have the sheep come and put up their pretty faces for a pat and pleasant words; and watch the cunning little lambs frolic, which the finest town lady could not help laughing at and enjoying. Take it all in all, there are many things worse in life than living on a farm. I do not think because one lives in the country they need to know anything. I enjoy reading as much as any one could, and nice dressing also. Town people are, many of them, like a young man in the *city* of Manchester, who made the remark about one of our neighbors in his hearing, "Oh, he don't know anything—he lives in the country." Now, my private opinion is, *that* gentleman knows more than that young man will ever know.

. . . Farmer's Wife

FAP Mural, 1930s

Oh Millersville!

IN 1940, CARROLL COLEMAN of The Prairie Press, then at Musca-
tine, later at Iowa City, published a most delightful book of topical verse
by "Fern Gravel." The authoress was said to have written the verses years
before when she had been a girl in the mythical Iowa town of Millersville.
The book was favorably reviewed in Iowa and across the nation. "We have
found the lost Sappho of Iowa," gurgled the prestigious New York Times,
whose myopic writers often failed to see anything of value beyond the Pali-
sades of the Hudson River.

Six years later, astonished admirers of Fern discovered, to their sorrow
it must be said, that Fern had never existed, that the poems had been writ-
ten by James Norman Hall, an internationally known Iowa expatriate
living in distant Tahiti. "I cried all day after reading that Atlantic *exposé,"*
said one Iowa City lady whose identity is safe with this writer. "But then
I decided that since I still believed in Santa Claus, I would continue to be-
lieve in Fern Gravel as well. It's less painful that way."

Here are four more of "Fern Gravel's" verses, all centering on her home
of Millersville. They are presented here, not only for the pleasure they
are sure to bring, but also because they present certain basic truths about
many Iowa towns. Iowa towns did have histories which paralleled Mil-
lersville's, there were debates over names for towns, and the Main Street of
Millersville was very much like the Main Street of many Iowa towns at
the turn of the century. "The Medicine Show" was a familiar part of the
entertainment scene in small towns even into the second decade of the cen-
tury. Finally, Iowa towns, then as now, knew the terrors of a tornado or
cyclone. So did farmers for that matter.

Millersville

I will tell about the town
Of Millersville to you.
The population is exactly
Eight hundred and thirty-two.

All around it
There are fields of waving corn.
We are still living
In the house where I was born.

My father is the agent
For a Fire and Tornado Insurance Company.
He drives all around the country;
Once in a while he takes me.

There is one business street
Where my uncle's drug-store is.
He owns the house they live in
But the store building isn't his.

It belongs to the Cragie Brothers
Who have their law office upstairs.
My father's Office is there, too,
Across the hall from theirs.

Doctor Born, the dentist, also
Has his office on the second floor.
The Cline brothers barbershop
Is close by, next door.

Millersville is on the railroad
Of the C.R.I. & P.
But some of the trains don't stop
At a town so small, you see.

I love trains
And I always listen for
Number forty-two. It goes through at night,
Whistling, with a roar.

From our dining-room windows
I can see its lights.
I like to see it best
On snowy winter nights.

Our principal grocery
Is Mack and Roberts store
They sell drygoods and groceries, both.
In that building, on the second floor,

Is the public liberry.
The liberian is Miss Addie Leach,
She has never been married;
She used to teach,

But she's too old for that now.
She is thin and very tall,
And very strict about the books.
I don't like her at all.

We have two doctors in Millersville,
Dr. Maybe and Dr. Gray.
In the Civil War, Dr. Maybe's
Right leg was shot away.

His wife died long ago
And he is getting very old.
I hate to see him driving
On the winter days so cold.

He lives alone in his house
And goes for his meals
To the Commercial Hotel
Which is run by Mr. Shields.

The largest church in Millersville
Is ours, the Methodist.
The Christian is the next in size,
And the smallest, the Baptist.

The Reverent Mr. Dotson
Is our Methodist preacher.
His daughter, Hattie,
Is a grade-school teacher.

My Sunday-school teacher
Is Miss Minnie King.
She is not of any use as a teacher
But I love to hear her sing.

There are other things to tell
About the town of Millersville.
I could write much more.
Maybe some day I will.

The Millers and the Dodds

Not many people know
How Millersville was given its name.
It was a long time ago
That two covered wagons came
To this part of the country;
They were two families.
In those days, on the prairies,
There weren't many trees.

These two families
Were named Miller and Dodd;
And they planted the first trees
And ploughed up the prairie sod.
And they lived in this place
Till the railroad came;
And then, of course,
It had to have a name.

Mr. Miller wanted it
To be called Millersville.
But Mr. Dodd said, "No we won't!"
And Mr. Miller said, "Yes we will!"
"I was here three months before you
And ploughed up the first sod,"
Mr Dodd said, "and so
We will call this place Dodd."
And when the railroad asked
"What are you going to call this town?"
Each one gave his name
And they wouldn't back down.

Then after a while
A railroad engineer
Who was helping to build it
Said to them, "Look here!
We can't have both your names;
You will have to choose
One or the other." And Mr. Dodd said,
"Oh, what's the use
Of quarreling and fighting
Over a thing like this?
Call it Millersville if you want to;
I don't care *what* it is."

And Mr. Miller was so glad
That he gave Mr. Dodd
One hundred and sixty acres of land
That was still prairie sod.
Some of the Miller family
Are living here still,
And they are very proud
Of the name, Millersville.

The Medicine Show

When the Kickapoo Indian Medicine Show
Comes to this town I always go.
They have it on the corner where the band
Plays on Saturday nights, near Barney Toller's popcorn stand.
They come in a wagon, and the show is free.
The Indian who made the recipee
For the different diseases is there.
He is deaf and dumb, and sits in a chair
On the wagon while the medicine is being sold.
He is a chief, and very old.
Doctor O'Keefe, the proprietor
Says he was famous in the Indian war
In Kansas. Four colored men
With banjos begin the show, and then
Dr. O'Keefe brings out the jar
Where some of the largest tapeworms are
That came from persons that didn't know
They had the worms, although
They were always tired and couldn't tell why,
And often felt as if they were going to die.
Some of the tapeworms are more than two feet long,
And now those persons are well and strong
Because they heard of the remedy
Of the Kickapoo Indians, and tried it to see
If that was their disease. It was a great surprise
To find they had worms of such enormous size.
Dr. O'Keefe sells other medicine, too,
That nobody but the Indians knew
How to make. Many people buy them.
They think that maybe they had better try them.
I don't blame them. I would too
If I felt tired and sleepy, but I almost never do.
My uncle says that Dr. O'Keefe
Is only a quack doctor and a thief.
He says that Millersville people are crazy
And the trouble with them is they are only lazy.

They will throw their money away to these quacks
When they have a good druggist right behind their backs.
But my uncle sells whiskey, and that is worse, I believe.
He hasn't any right to blame Dr. O'Keefe.

The Cyclone

I will tell about
The awful cyclone
In the town of Valeria
Whose name is well known.

I wasn't there
But I have heard people tell
Of that terrible storm,
So I know about it well.

There was a long black cloud
That came down to the ground,
And it tore up trees and houses
And scattered everything around.

A family named Kelly
Was not at home that day,
And when they came back, their house
Had been taken right away.

There were eight children
In the Kelly family,
And they were all away;
It was lucky as could be.

It drove an iron rail
Into the ground ten feet,
And it was hard to tell
Where was the business street.

Sioux City Riverfront, ca. 1870

The Cities of Iowa – Sioux City

IF ANY IOWA CITY can be said to be unlike its sister cities in the rest of the state, it is Sioux City. Where Des Moines, Cedar Rapids, Waterloo, and the Mississippi river cities of Burlington, Davenport, Muscatine and Clinton had looked back to the East where their roots were, Sioux City always seemed to be looking to the West where the country's future seemingly was. As a result, Sioux City became a "wild-west" kind of place, entertaining first the sorts of people B. Paul Chicoine writes about in his article, then later the cowpokes who brought their carloads of range animals to the city's vast packing industry. These men, off from a year on the vast grassy spreads of the plains, were rarin' to try a little city life after their long isolation from all but animal companionship. And Sioux City was more than a little willing to give them what they sought – sturdy shots of whisky in its bars, a stetson-raising game of poker in a gambling house, or softer feminine companionship in one of the bordellos.

Those days are gone now, just as are the days Chicoine talks about in his essay that follows. But it has always seemed to me – and I lived in Sioux City for a time and nearby in northwest Iowa for a dozen years – that on a windy, gusty night, walking slowly along Fourth or Pierce or Nebraska Streets, one might still hear, borne on the wind blowing up from the river or north from the old stockyards site, a "yippie-i-yippie-o" or a "heave ho, heave ho."

B[lair] Paul Chicoine is a free-lance writer living in Sioux City, but his roots are up the river a ways in South Dakota, where his French immigrant ancestors came to farm.

Sioux City's Steamboat Days

The rousters are rushing the cargoes on,
In the flush of the early dawn,
While the packets ride on the rocking tide,
And chafe to be out and gone.

THIS VERSE taken from Joseph Mills Hanson's *Conquest of the Missouri*, a biography of legendary steamboat commander Grant P. Marsh, captures only a fragment of the color and excitement that flavored Iowa's many river towns throughout much of the nineteenth century. The "heave-ho" chanting of roustabouts as they muscled cargo across muddy decks and levees, the thunder of unleashed steam valves, the swirl of woodsmoke and general uproar that marked a steamboat's arrival or departure—all provided a dramatic backdrop to daily life along Iowa's major waterways when steam and paddlewheels ruled the rivers and Iowa's great lakes.

Much of Iowa's steamboat lore has its focus on the Mississippi River, with its familiar images of Mark Twain and Huckleberry Finn, and memories of the giant paddlewheelers that once transported everything from Civil War troops to Wisconsin timber between such ports as Keokuk, Burlington, and Dubuque. Between the years 1856 and 1872, however, a steamboating drama of perhaps more rough-and-tumble proportions was being played out to its zenith on Iowa's Missouri River border, some 300 miles to the west.

Sioux City, then one of the few Iowa settlements along the Missouri, was the focal point in this chapter of Iowa's steamboating past. Indeed, from 1856 onward, an entire generation of river men, soldiers, settlers and other river-borne characters sallied forth from this outpost on Iowa's northwest frontier to do battle with the most treacherous water highway of them all.

Presumably the first steamboat whistle to echo off Floyd's Bluff near the present site of Sioux City was that of the American Fur Company's experimental steamer *Yellowstone*, during her maiden voyage up the Missouri from St. Louis in 1831. When the *Yellowstone* reached Floyd's Bluff (named for the ill-fated sergeant of the 1804 Lewis and Clark Expedition who was buried there), it was entering a stretch of the river that had long been a rendezvous for river travelers. Here, where the river's upstream course turns abruptly west, between the mouths of the Floyd and Big Sioux Rivers, a deep channel and stable shoreline conditions made conditions ideal for landing. For years all types of river men and their vessels—a flotilla that included dugout canoes, bullboats, mackinaws and keelboats—had stopped beneath the bend's protective bluffs to rest, refit, and trade with the local Indian tribes.

The first permanent settlers in the river bend area did not arrive until almost twenty years after the *Yellowstone*'s visit. Among them was a French-Canadian trader, Théophile Bruguier, who, along with his several Sioux Indian wives and other members of the tribe, established a fur-trading and shipment post at the mouth of the Big Sioux River. Other settlers and traders followed, and by the early 1850s, a scattering of cabins along the north shore of the Missouri marked the beginnings of the present-day Sioux City. A land office and post office followed in 1855, and a year later Sioux City, with 400 people and 90 buildings, became the county seat of Woodbury County. Indeed, by 1856, the town had become a strategic stop for virtually all fur trade and military traffic enroute up the Missouri's 2,600-mile waterway to the Rockies.

That same year, the *Omaha*, a St. Louis-based sidewheeler of over 300 tons burden, made its first visit to Sioux City. Chartered for what is believed to have been $30,000 by a Council Bluffs merchant, and commanded by Captain Andrew Windland, the *Omaha* arrived in Sioux City from St. Louis in June of 1856. It was the first boat up river that season, and the first ever to carry a cargo destined exclusively for Sioux City. The *Omaha*'s $70,000 worth of merchandise and materials included engines, bandsaws, and other equipment for the new town's first sawmill, as well as a number of prefabricated houses and store buildings. The *Omaha* also carried a full complement of passengers.

Because of its "first-charter" status, Windland's vessel thereafter became the favorite of pioneer Sioux Citians, who often referred to the *Omaha* as "our steamboat." Its arrivals and departures in ensuing years were always greeted by much fanfare in the local press, as exemplified by this 1858 announcement:

This elegant, speedy and popular steamer arrived at our wharf with a large amount of freight and upwards of sixty passengers. The Omaha *is the first boat to have loaded at St. Louis and come directly to this place this season . . . She has made more trips to this place than any other boat on the river. There are few if any swifter boats on the Missouri River than the* Omaha; *in fact, she made the best time between St. Louis and Sioux City that was ever recorded, performing the run in a little better than seven days.*

That same year, in a gesture often undertaken in other river towns, a delegation of Sioux City passengers and shippers drafted a resolution of appreciation to Captain Windland. Forwarded to newspapers throughout the country, it praised the captain for his "experience, skill, and urbanity," and commended the *Omaha* for its comfortable accommodations.

Captain Windland and the *Omaha* basked in Sioux City's favor until 1860, when the steamer burned and sank during a late-season voyage up the Ohio River. The *Florence,* another St. Louis-based sidewheeler, became the Omaha's successor.

The arrival of the first steamboat up-river from St. Louis after the spring thaw was always an occasion for celebration among Sioux Citians and their western Iowa neighbors. The event signaled an end to the long months of winter-imposed isolation with the arrival of fresh news, delayed correspondence, and badly needed provisions.

"They took the first census every spring in Sioux City when the first boat came up the river," wrote pioneer local historian Constant Marks, "as every man, woman and child went down to the levee to see it land. This landing was a complicated operation at high water, with a great amount of steam whistling and shouting, going forward and backing, and throwing of ropes. The boat always blew the whistle the loudest possible before coming into sight around opposite where the Floyd Monument now is. Soon the smoke could be seen, and the people commenced their march for the foot of Pearl Street."

In the early days, the alarm was frequently sounded by two local residents, Charles K. Howard, a druggist, and Bob McElhenny, a liveryman. Howard, a noted village baritone, would leave his apothecary counter at the first sign of smoke on the river and, with legs braced apart and lungs filled, would bellow a few long-drawn cries of "Stea-m-boat—Ste-a-m-bo-at!" McElhenny, a few blocks distant, would then pick up the cry and continue to echo it until the boat hove into view.

The *Omaha* was the first, but not the only boat in 1856 to unload its cargo at the Sioux City levee. Four others followed during that season, and by the next year, the tally had climbed to twenty-nine. The visitors included such noteworthy steamboats as the *D. A. Morton,* the *North Alabama,* the *Star of the West,* the *Spread Eagle,* the *Florence,* and the *Emigrant.*

To this latter steamboat, a sidewheeler commanded by a pilot known only as Tyrell, goes the dubious distinction of receiving the first negative travel rating awarded a Sioux City-bound vessel.

"For sloth, filth, niggardly fare, ill-management and inefficiency," blasted a *Sioux City Eagle* correspondent in May of 1858, "we think [the *Emigrant*] has no equal on western rivers. The Captain seemed insensible to shame . . . Especially is he unfit to command a boat on a thoroughfare where so many children and unprotected females are constantly passing. . . ."

The reporter was angered by the captain's approval of all-night poker games in the *Emigrant*'s main cabin—a popular diversion among passengers confined to a steamboat's decks for weeks at a time. The same columnist advised Sioux City-bound travelers "to be very cautious with whom you take passage."

Despite such periodic grumblings, most of which concerned lack of privacy, uncomfortable staterooms, and round-the-clock engine noise, the late 1850s and 1860s marked the golden age of steamboat travel along the Missouri. The opening of the nearby Dakota Territories to settlement in 1859, the Indian Wars of the 1860s, and a series of major gold strikes near the Missouri River's headwaters in what is now Montana sparked an explosion in freight and passenger traffic along Sioux City's crescent waterfront.

Most of this traffic was headed for Fort Benton, a major Missouri River outpost in Montana territory. During the peak of St. Louis-Fort Benton travel, more than 100 different steamboats called at Sioux City each year to take on added passengers and freight. Typical of these was the sidewheeler *Emilie*, which measured a generous 250 feet from stem to stern and advertised a cargo capacity of 500 tons. Built and captained by a well-known river man, Joseph A. LaBarge, the *Emilie* offered such refinements as spacious cabins, chandeliers, and a complete domestic staff—all of which helped dispel the usual complaints about the discomforts of river travel.

For these amenities, passengers traveling from St. Louis to Sioux City and beyond could expect to pay from $150 to $300. For as little as $25, a thriftier person might find himself sharing space with as many as 200 fellow passengers on a steamboat's cargo-jammed and unsheltered main deck. Fares varied according to the condition of the river, the demand for space (the report of gold strikes often brought a dramatic increase in ticket prices), and the degree of danger posed by Indian unrest.

The Indian threat, more than anything else, did much to heighten the adventure and risk of river travel. Because of the frequency of Indian ambush along the narrow Missouri River channel above Sioux City, steamboat owners were forced to adopt numerous protective measures. Among them was the common practice of sheathing, with boiler iron, the pilot houses and engine rooms of all westward-bound steamboats. Passengers, too, were expected to provide small arms support whenever needed. In one 1863 incident, a number of passengers aboard the steamers *Robert Campbell* and *Shreveport* added the fire power of three brass cannon to their own sidearms to repel a Sioux war party near the mouth of the Yellowstone River.

Until 1868, Sioux City served chiefly as an intermediate stopover for Missouri River traffic between St. Louis and Fort Benton, with the bulk of the northbound freight and passenger traffic originating in St. Louis. All this changed on March 7, 1868, when the first, long-awaited train of the Sioux City and Pacific Railroad steamed onto Sioux City's levee from Missouri Valley. Suddenly, the town was connected by rail to eastern Iowa and the world beyond.

Joab Lawrence, a brash and daring St. Louis cotton speculator and steamboat baron, was the first person to capitalize on this direct rail link between Sioux City and the east. Recognizing the advantages of short-cutting 860 miles of snag-strewn river, Lawrence, an aggressive organizer, had a year earlier begun to acquire Sioux City waterfront property and sell shares in his newly chartered Northwest Transportation Company. At the same time, he was busy in St. Louis, assembling a fleet of fast, shallow-draft steamboats to be based in Sioux City.

Throughout the winter of 1867, Lawrence supervised the extensive modification of three sternwheelers—the *Bertha*, the *Alabama*, and the *Barker*, eliminating all "frills and finery" in the interests of speed and lighter draft. Each vessel, according to the St. Louis *Democrat*, was equipped with a "twelve-pounder howitzer and twenty stands of rifles, with two thousand rounds of ammunition, for protection against possible Indian attack."

In the company of the *Deer Lodge*, another Lawrence vessel, the refurbished boats left St. Louis in March of 1868. The four traveled to Sioux City, then on to Fort Benton, then back to Sioux City, which thereafter became their permanent base of operation. So successful was Lawrence's enterprise that six more steamboats were added to the Sioux City fleet later that same year. These included the *E. H. Durfee* (named for a Northwest Transportation Company director), the *Esperanza*, the *Ida Reese*, the *Key West*, and two smaller sternwheelers.

To maintain his Iowa-based fleet, Lawrence, in late 1869, ordered the construction of a large drydock—the first to be constructed on the Missouri above St. Louis—at the foot of Jones Street. Situated a block east of the company's riverfront warehouses, the facility employed over fifty mechanics, carpenters, and caulkers, and was equipped with a battery of winches capable of lifting steamboats out of the water for repair and winter storage.

As business boomed, Lawrence brought an increasing number of steamboats into his fold, the best-known being the *Far West* and the *Nellie Peck*. Both fell under the classification of "Mountain Boats," a newer, faster, second generation of Missouri River steamboats that were then becoming dominant on the upper reaches of the river. Built in Pittsburgh for the Coulson brothers, partners in Lawrence's company, the *Far West* and the *Nellie Peck* were spoon-bowed sternwheelers. Each measured 190 feet long and 35 feet wide. Outfitted with the latest in high-pressure engines, they were capable of floating 500 tons of freight and 30 passengers on as little as three feet of water.

Like most Missouri River steamboats of the day, the *Far West* and *Nellie* also boasted "grasshoppers" — large wooden spars that could be lowered into the river bottom alongside a grounded vessel and employed like giant crutches to "walk" the ship into deeper water.

Just as on the Mississippi, captains of Missouri River steamboats often sought to establish records for speed. In 1872, the *Far West* and the *Nellie* paired off, much to the joy of Iowa and Dakota steamboat racing fans, in a race from Sioux City to Fort Benton and back. The winner, the *Far West*, covered the 3000-mile obstacle course of the upper Missouri in a record-breaking twenty-eight and a half days, edging out the *Nellie* by a slim four and one-half hours (a loss attributed by Sioux City wagerers to an inept pilot on the *Nellie* who accidentally steered his vessel into a sandbar.) Four years later the *Far West*, captained by the commander of the defeated *Nellie*, again attracted widespread attention. This time, as a supply ship for Custer's Little Big Horn campaign, the *Far West* raced down the treacherous Yellowstone and Missouri Rivers to bring the news of the Custer massacre to the world.

Throughout the 1860s and early 1870s, Sioux City prospered from the river traffic. By 1867, the city's steamboat landing, once no more than a half-block of muddy riverbank at the foot of Perry Creek, stretched as far as Jones Street, five blocks distant. What a decade earlier had been mostly a collection of waterfront shacks, interspersed with wood piles and cargo awaiting shipment, was now a congestion of shipping offices, warehouses, boarding houses, and saloons. In the lowlands above Perry Creek, a squalid cluster of log and plank gin mills, brothels, and gambling dens catered to Sioux City's transient population. Known as "Hell's Half-Acre," this low-life neighborhood prospered at the expense of giving the town an unsavory reputation. "Sioux City," commented one seemingly well-traveled observer in the early 1870s, "is one of the two worst hell-holes in the world — the other being Singapore!"

During the height of the steamboat era, Sioux City's waterfront teemed with violence. Street fights and tavern brawls were a near daily occurrence, with participants ranging from rival steamboat crews and striking roustabouts to ex-soldiers (both Union and Confederate); roustabout strikes, undertaken to protest low pay and often brutal working conditions, now and then flared into open riot. One such outburst, provoked by the Northwest Transportation Company's attempt to import 200 strikebreakers from Omaha, exploded for a time into a heated battle between gangs armed with knives and cordwood bats, before it was finally brought under control.

Between 1870 and 1872, Sioux City-based steamboat companies commanded a virtual monopoly over trade on the upper Missouri River. Although the gold rush fever of the 1860s had subsided, there was money to be made from lucrative government contracts for carrying soldiers and provisions up-river to the military outposts and Indian agencies of the Dakota and Montana Territories. A sampling of annoucements taken from the *Sioux City Daily Journal* of 1870 tell of a waterfront bustling with activity:

> The Far West *will load with lumber for the new military post at the crossing [Bismarck, N.D.]. The date of her departure is uncertain.*
>
> The Mary McDonald *left yesterday just after dinner for Fort Rice, with a load of freight and six companies of the Eighth Infantry. She experienced considerable difficulty in working around the first bend.*
>
> The Esperanza, *for [Fort] Buford, will clear this afternoon. She takes on at [Fort] Randall 100 recruits for Fort Shaw, who at Buford will be transferred to the* Sioux City.

In 1871, Joab Lawrence, the man who just three years earlier had established Sioux City's first steamboat company, sold his interest in his Northwest Transportation Company to Durfee & Peck, a large western fur trading and shipping firm. An enterprising outfit, Durfee & Peck combined with a number of former Northwest Transportation Company steamboat captains and owners in an effort to achieve near complete control of the Sioux City–Fort Benton trade. Later reorganized as the Coulson Packet Company, the firm included in its ranks such famous Missouri River boatmen as Commodore Sanford B. Coulson and his brothers, Captains Martin and John Coulson, Captain James C. McVay, Captain John Todd, and Captain Grant P. Marsh.

The new owners, unlike Lawrence, discouraged civilian passenger travel. There were greater profits, the line openly boasted, "in providing for the blanketed and uniformed sons of Uncle Sam," and in transporting furs–particularly the thousands of buffalo hides that were then being taken in vast slaughters on the western plains.

Because of Durfee & Peck and the Coulson Brothers, Sioux City became the receiving point for some of the largest fur shipments ever to travel a North American river. In 1871, the *Ida Reese* docked in Sioux City with a cargo of over 39,000 buffalo hides. That same year the *Nellie Peck,* running decks awash, nudged into the First Street boat landing with enough furs and hides to fill twenty-three railroad boxcars.

Despite this flurry of activity, Sioux City's prominence as a steamboating capital was on the wane. As had already happened elsewhere, the iron horse was swiftly and relentlessly putting an end to the glory days of the slow, plodding paddlewheelers. In 1873, the Dakota Southern Railroad completed a line from Sioux City to Yankton, some sixty-five miles upstream. A few months later Bismarck welcomed the Northern Pacific. With the break-up of the Durfee & Peck-Coulson Brothers monopoly and transfer of headquarters to Yankton and Bismarck, Sioux City became just a stopover and fueling point for steamboats serving isolated Missouri River towns in between rail centers. By 1900, railroads and packing houses had captured Sioux City's economic heart.

There were, however, occasional reminders of Sioux City's past steamboat glory. For many years the U.S. Army Corps of Engineers continued to maintain a small boatyard on the Big Sioux River as a staging area for the snag-pulling steamers and bank-stabilization crews that worked the upper Missouri. One of these "snag-pullers," the ancient Mountain Boat *Josephine,* remained based in Sioux City as late as 1906, towing rock barges and occasionally serving as an excursion boat for various local organizations.

Today, nearly all traces of Sioux City's colorful steamboat days have vanished. The once-crowded First Street levee is gone—the victim of first the railroads, and then concrete parking lots, motels, and auto dealerships. Although barge traffic still wends its way up the Missouri to Sioux City, the main artery of commerce has since become Interstate Highway 29, which today follows an almost straight-line course along Iowa's western border from Missouri into South Dakota.

The "Big Muddy," some Sioux Citians will insist, has changed little from its heyday as a steamboat waterway. On a warm summer's night, one can still hear the blast of a towboat's whistle as it salutes the last resting place of a Sergeant Charles Floyd, just as the *Yellowstone* did over a century and a half ago.

...B. Paul Chicoine

The Steamer Josephine

Iowa Corn Song

(1921 Version)

Let's sing of Grand old I-O-WAY,
    Yo-ho, yo-ho, yo-ho,
Our love is stronger ev'ry day,
    Yo-ho, yo-ho, yo-ho.
So come along and join the throng,
Sev'ral hundred thousand strong,
As you come just sing this song,
    Yo-ho, yo-yo, yo-yo.

We're from
    I-o-way, I-o-way.
  State of all the land,
Joy on ev'ry hand,
    We're from I-o-way, I-o-way,
That's where the tall corn grows.

Our land is full of ripening corn,
    Yo-ho, yo-ho, yo-ho,
We've watched it grow both night and morn,
    Yo-ho, yo-ho, yo-ho.
But now we rest, we've stood the test,
All that's good we have the best,
I-o-way has reached the crest,
    Yo-ho, yo-ho, yo-ho.

REPEAT:
We're from I-o-way, I-o-way . . .

Main Street, West Chester, Iowa

The Downfall of Elder Barton

JAMES STEVENS (1892-1972) was born in the farming community of Moravia, Iowa, halfway between the coalmining towns of Centerville and Albia. From 1925 to 1933 he published several tales based on his childhood in Moravia (he had left there for Washington state in 1900) which are some of the most delightful concoctions ever to come from the pen of an Iowa author.

This tale sets off an Iowa institution of the time, horse-trading, against another, debating the merits of the several town religious institutions, and, in addition, takes an occasional glance at morals and manners.

Stevens later became famous as one of the creators of the mythological hero of loggers and lumbermen, Paul Bunyan. It's too bad he didn't remain in Iowa—his fertile imagination might have given Iowa farmers and citizens of small towns their own folk hero!

The Downfall of Elder Barton

EVERY FOURTH SUNDAY there was preaching in the Hardshell Baptist meeting-house on the road to Hyattsville. When I was in my eighth year Elder Dewberry Barton of Tyrone rode our Southern Iowa circuit. Like all other preachers of his sect, he took no wages for his labors in the vineyard. Instead, he lived by horse trading. He was also a breeder of Morgans and an upright judge of rye whiskey, and in his youth he had traveled from Kentucky to the Territory of New Mexico. The elder was the first grand hero of my boyhood.

Moravia, a town of five hundred souls, was the trading center nearest the Baptist settlement on the Hyattsville road. On Summer Saturdays Elder Barton would ride over from Tyrone in his box buggy, trailed by a string of trading horses. He drove two snorting hot-eyed Morgans as black and proud as sin. The boys in my neighborhood always watched for the elder. It was the richest sight outside of a circus parade, as the coaly horses pranced down the street, with leather shining and nickel gleaming, with a flash of red spreader rings and goat hair plumes, a clink and jingle of harness rigging, a dazzle of whirling wheels. Sometimes twelve horses would be trailing with a fine thunder. Above all this magnificent motion, noise and color loomed the black-bearded elder. There was glamour in town.

The boys who were free of Saturday chores trudged through the heat and dust for Repp's livery barn when the hero had passed. The parade was over, and now the dickering was the show of the afternoon. Up from the hollows and down from the ridges of the rolling prairie country the farm people had driven, to bargain, swap and gossip in the Moravia square. Horses and rigs were still coming as we started for Repp's barn. Dust drifted sluggishly from the ruts, settled on the board walks, and grayed the leaves of the volunteer timothy in vacant lots. Where the walks were unshaded the boards blistered bare feet, and resin gummed unwary toes as we lazed on.

Generally the stricter Christian parents of Moravia prohibited their boys from loitering around Repp's barn. It was suspected as the town's lone haunt of the Old Nick. Pleas Repp himself had confessed religion; but he had backslidden twice; once from the Methodists, and again from the United Brethren. For two years or so he had considered giving the Holy Spirit another chance at him, this time through the Cumberland Presbyterians, but he was still holding back. Nearly everybody had lost hope for Pleas. People said he gassed with Jeff Biggle too much. Mr. Biggle was the one man in Moravia who came close to being an infidel. Stem Tracy was another sinful character who passed much of his spare time in Repp's barn. A boy was apt to hear profanity there and be tainted by a sight of cards and bottled beer. The Methodist boys yearned dreadfully for the lusty enchantments of the place, but they usually had to shun it as a pitfall.

II

The barnyard was the scene of the trading. There we might perch on the poles of the back fence, fairly safe from the sinful influence of the barn proper. Christian farmers congregated under the boughs of a great white oak, and the trader they dickered with was supposedly a holy man. So all the boys in my neighborhood were allowed to watch the trading. The elder charmed us like a circus ringmaster. I watched his performance with intolerable pride. I was the only Hardshell boy in town. Even the Rev. Pearl Yates, the tremendous Methodist preacher, seemed a puny and feeble figure when Elder Dewberry Barton strode forth to trade. The boys who sneered at the Hardshells at other times now thought of me as one related to a royal church.

Dickering went on in the oak's shade, which spread over a third of the barnyard. Below our perch ran a long wooden watering trough. The wet earth alongside it was a crazy pattern of horseshoe prints. Surreys, buggies, hacks and lumber wagons stood about the yard, with red and yellow spokes and iron tires shining. The trading horses champed, whinnied, snorted, stamped, switched flies and rattled halter chains from a feed rack at the right side of the yard. In the background towered the dull red wall of the barn. The air bristled with sharp smells. Gnats hovered over the trough. Flies buzzed viciously at our toes. Two sullen yellow hounds snoozed in the dust among the oak roots.

A row of farmers squatted on one edge of the watering trough, some of them puffing solemnly on corncobs and clays, all of them chawing plug. Every so often a straw-hatted head bobbed sharply, a whiskered chin jutted out, and then a thin amber crescent sparkled for an instant in the sunlight before cascading down on some mark—a bee, maybe, or a horsefly, or the tail of one of the hounds, or sometimes just the plain hub of a wagon wheel. A good chawer would always try himself on a live mark. A bee was hard, but a wheel hub was beneath contempt.

The dickering always started with a going-over of the elder's stock.

All along the string at the feed rack farmers sidled in between the horses, felt them down for sweenies and other blemishes which the eye might not catch, thumped their ribs, jabbed thumbs into touchy spots, hoisted hoofs, prying and testing for signs of stringhalt, spavin and ringbone. After such a ceremony a farmer would stand back and give the horse a general sizing up, nodding wisely, mumbling mysteriously to himself, plucking at a whisker, maybe, or else shoving up his hat and scratching under it. Scratching of some kind seemed to be a necessary part of sizing up a trading horse. The boys always did more scratching than anything else when they played horse trading. Pleas Repp was the one they liked best to imitate. He was fat, and his red face was as bare as a baby's. He had no hair to scratch, either, so he always scratched himself behind. Since he was considered the shrewdest judge of horseflesh in town, the boys figured that his system of thinking was the best one.

Every now and then a farmer would step up to the elder, point to a horse, and say:

"'Pears sound enough. But how's his wind and temper?"

"Sound of wind and a willin' sperit," the elder would declare. "You got the the warranty of Dewberry Barton fer that. And that there warranty means you can go the length and breadth of two counties 'thout findin' a Dewberry Barton hoss which is wind-broken or a balker."

Then, if the farmer asked any more questions, the elder would take him in hand and go on:

"Sta'nch as this yere white oak! Sound as a Bryan silver dollar! And that hoss has blood in him, sir! Look at his eye! You know a hoss has been *bred* when you see him roll a eye like that there one! Blooded, sir, blooded! Cash or swap, what am I offered?"

Any day during a week following Elder Barton's Moravia Saturday a mother of the town might look into her back yard and see her eight- or ten-year-old pointing pridefully at some smaller boy tied to the fence by a clothes-line and in a tremendous voice describing him as staunch as this here oak, sound as a Bryan silver dollar, and blooded, sir, blooded!

The elder's voice was so deep and rich it always somehow made me think of custard. He loomed mightily among the farmers, making most of them appear drab and mean. He wore a big black Bryan hat. A coal-black beard and wavy hair flowed over a red bandana knotted around his neck. A black cutaway coat flapped its tails above the tops of shining boots. But the elder's most glittering articles of apparel were the fringed and beaded Buffalo Bill gauntlets that he waved grandly in the heat of trading. The fringes fluttered and the colored beads sparkled in the sunlight as he made his fine mighty motions and expounded the beauties and virtues of his horses.

"A good man and an honest dealer," was the opinion generally expressed about Elder Dewberry Barton, "but jest a mite too gaudy fer a preacher."

From the first, indeed, there was considerable head-shaking in the congregation over his "soundness." He had buried his wife in Kentucky, so the story went, and had been a roving preacher ever since. He was still companionless and unsettled. In his home congregation at Tyrone there was some feeling against him because of his friendliness with the Irish colony there. The Irish were loathed as idolatrous Papists by all the Methodists and Hardshells of the prairie country.

But until he was actually convicted of traffic with Rome by the Rev. Pearl Yates, the elder had an unsullied glamour for all Moravia boys. He and his romantic trade were patterns for our play.

III

The Rev. Pearl Yates, the Methodist, was the main preacher of Moravia, and he kept hatred of Romanism going like a bonfire in the town.

He was a prodigious black bull of a man. Exhorting in the pulpit, he was a locomotive of the Lord, huge, sooty, steaming from every pore as he roared hoarse blasts for the salvation of the righteous and the damnation of sinners. The latter, he preached, were mainly drinkers of rum and members of the Church of Rome. When the Rev. Yates lit into rum and Rome his eyes would get a red-hot look under his smoky and bristling hair. In all his motions he spread the stubby fingers of his thick, hairy, swarthy hands like claws. He rasped and snarled when he was exhorting at top speed, and sometimes slaver oozed from the corners of his mouth and trickled on his black coat. I was fearfully afraid of him, for he made death and damnation seem just around the corner. Then I would forget Elder Barton and my bringing up as a Primitive Baptist, and wish I was a sound Methodist and safe.

When there was no preaching in the Hyattsville meeting-house many Hardshells would drive in to hear the Rev. Yates. As my grandmother lived in town, she generally attended the Methodist meetings. I would be lugged along, as I lived with my grandmother alone. The Rev. Yates often preached directly at the Hardshells in his congregation. He seldom shook their faith in their doctrine, but he did inflame them with hatred of Rome.

That hatred was already strong enough in all the Primitive Baptists by virtue of their own doctrines. When they called their church the True Church they meant that it was an honest daughter of the churches of the Corinthians and Thessalonians and others founded by the Apostles. They strove to maintain the practices of primitive Christianity. Their only ceremonies were communion and feet washing. Their elders took only thank offerings of food and shelter. No music profaned the church. The Hardshells chanted hymns exactly as the Negroes chant spirituals. Epistles were exchanged between churches. They had no Sunday-schools, Christian Endeavor societies, or missionaries. They regarded themselves as a little band of saints selected and maintained by the mysterious will of God through the centuries of the reign of those ministers of the Anti-Christ, the Popes. In His own good time He would overthrow Rome and bring victory and power to His true church. All was foreordained and predestinated. It was a faith of resignation. Only hatred of Rome gave it life and strength.

More than once I overheard the brothers and sisters of the Hyattsville congregation remonstrating with Elder Barton for his friendship with the Tyrone Irish, who were described by my grandmother as "all Romans, heart and soul, hair and hide." When he was rebuked the elder would only sort of smile through his beard and turn off the subject by saying that the Irish were good neighbors, and he couldn't hold their Popery against them any more than he could hold the affliction of sightlessness against a blind man. Somehow, that would shut up the remonstraters.

There were other black marks against the elder. He would get exalted and glorified while he preached, and actually appear to enjoy himself, whereas the usual prairie preacher would scowl, groan, tear his hair, thump the Bible and generally appear to suffer horribly through his own sermons. Even when the elder preached from Job and Jeremiah he would look as happy as though he were putting over a big horse trade. He would reel off yards of Old Testament Scripture without once looking at the Bible; he favored stories of warriors and kings above the warnings of the prophets; and his rich voice brought the stories grandly to life.

But his stern congregation wanted little of this rich stuff of Scripture; they hungered for the marrow of doctrinal bones; they yearned perpetually for reminders of their close kinship with the primitive Christian church.

"Elder Barton robs Paul to pay Abraham," my grandmother said. "The only hope he preaches for the True Church is of eternal rest in Abraham's bosom."

The Moravia Methodists, and the Hardshells who were with them in spirit if not in doctrine, got their chance at Elder Barton in the mortal sickness of the Widow Crouch. In that matter his traffic with Rome was brought to light, and the Rev. Yates convicted him of offending God. Even the boys were frightened into renouncing their hero. They had been brought up to believe in a God who would heave a soul into the pit of eternal damnation, not only for sin, but also for showing sympathy to a transgressor. The prairie Christian was convinced that his first duty was to make the way of the transgressor hard. So such hating preachers as the Rev. Pearl Yates won their power.

IV

In the eyes of the sanctified the Widow Crouch was the most sinister embodiment of sin in Moravia. They always called her the Roman widow. She was the town's lone Catholic, but that name of her church was never used by the local Protestants.

The Roman widow was also a first-rate hater. A high thorn hedge grew about her cottage and garden. No one ever visited her. Sometimes an Irish farmer from Tyrone way would fetch her a load of hickory stovewood, and once a month she would journey over to visit a cousin and to attend her church. Usually the only sign of life at her place was a gray drift of wood smoke fading up into the thick boughs of the old maples that shadowed the cottage and outhouses. Once a day the widow appeared with a wicker basket to do her trading. In all seasons she dressed in heavy black. Her face was lean and grim, with colorless tufts of hair sticking from her chin. Little gray eyes glittered venomously from the shadows of her dark sunbonnet.

Timothy Crouch had been an Iowa Central section boss who worked out of Moravia. He had come to a violent end while trying to thaw frozen dynamite in a can of water over an open fire. The widow had money from the railroad. She could have gone to Tyrone to live. Her cousin was also a lone widow woman and would have welcomed her company. But the Roman widow stayed on in Moravia, hated and hating, the Old Nick's own, and the Pope's.

Many believed that she was kept in town as a Papist spy. More suspected her of casting spells on the crops, the cows and the hens of sanctified Methodists. A belief in witches and in possession by demons was quite common in all the prairie towns. My grandmother was bold in it. I once heard her stand against Elder Barton himself in defense of this belief, supporting her arguments with quotations from Scripture. She silenced the elder and made him look troubled, though I could tell that he was not convinced. For a long time after that argument I had my own doubts about witches. But when the elder fell, the old tormenting belief came back. It meant something very real to a prairie boy of those days when he would hear: "Air you actually possessed?" or, "I declare, onless the boy's possessed, I jest can't figger what's a ailin' him."

Nobody ever openly accused the Roman widow of being a witch, for shortly after her husband was blown up she had gone to law with the Rev. Yates for scorning her name from the pulpit. The preacher was put to a tremendous lot of trouble and expense in settling the suit, and that gave the widow a malignant name. But there was back-of-hand talk going on about her all the time. My grandmother used to scatter salt and mumble charms around her garden, and I knew they were supposed to stave off the spells of the widow. I had learned long before that salt would melt the spells of a witch, if used with the proper charms.

There in my eighth Summer, however, I was getting fairly doubtful about the whole witch and demon business. It was against all the sense and reason that I'd ever learned at home for me to doubt, but I simply couldn't help it, the influence of Elder Barton was that strong in me. All sound evidence, it was plain enough, was for the existence of witches. There was Scripture for it. There were the facts of cows drying up suddenly, of a field of corn failing while the field next to it eared out, of hens molting and shutting off their eggs out of season. Such unnatural happenings surely had a reason back of them, and nobody had ever brought up a likelier reason than witches. But I let Elder Barton's doubts weaken my Baptist sense. Some wicked thing in me kept insisting that when the Widow Crouch went to bed at night she stayed there, sleeping like anybody else. I was naturally ashamed to confess my heresy to anybody. When a bunch of Methodist boys would hide arount the widow's hedge and yell out the song that started

There was a Romish lady, brought up in Popery;
Her mother always taught her the priest she must obey.
"Oh, pardon me, dear mother, I humbly pray thee now,
For under these false idols I can no longer bow";

I'd join in and sing on with them about how the Pope burned the good Methodist girl at the stake, pretending that I was still as sensible and decent as the other boys.

Perhaps to live hated and hating was what the Widow Crouch wanted. If so, Moravia appeased her hunger. She lived alone, loathed and abhorred by her neighbors, for ten years before she was taken mortally ill.

V

There were, of course, other sinners who plagued the sanctified of the prairie town. Every so often the Rev. Yates would steam up and roar down the whole line in one blazing sermon, from the Roman widow to the backsliding liveryman, Pleas Repp. The other churches in the town proper were the United Brethren, the Christian—always called the Campbellite by the Rev. Yates—and the Cumberland Presbyterian. The pastors of these sects were always trying to get ahead of him, but they invariably fell far behind, giving way to new aspirants, while he steamed triumphantly on. The Rev. Yates was the one real bugaboo of sin in Moravia, and he knew it. Every sinner in town feared him, though he never named names. He had a way of turning righteous wrath on a sinner without coming out openly against him.

When he blasted at the curse of infidelity in Moravia, for example, everybody knew he was hitting at Jeff Biggle, the shoe merchant. Mr. Biggle had resisted the working of the Holy Spirit all his life. Not once had he stood up and confessed religion or knelt in repentance at the mourners' bench. That was evidence enough for the Rev. Yates, though Mr. Biggle stoutly defended himself against the awful accusation by pointing to his standing in the Blue Lodge of the Masons.

"You can't be a Mason 'thout believin' in a Supreme Bein'!" he would argue. "And I'm a Past Warden. It's not the good Lord and His Word I'm ag'in, but yer dang' sec's. Yer dang' sec's! I say it agin fer I mean it! Jest chaw on that there till recess will you, reverend?"

The Rev. Yates tried every scheme imaginable to get Jeff Biggle into his church. One Monday morning little Luke Lolley, who was known as the brightest boy in the Methodist Sunday-school, traipsed into

Biggle's shoe-store, and began to talk in the style he used when he was making a recitation before the class.

"I seen you at church last night, Mr. Biggle," said little Luke, standing with his heels together and his hands by his sides. Mr. Biggle simply gaped as the boy raised his right hand and pointed like a picture in an elocution book. Then: "But you didn't come to Jesus, did you, Mr. Biggle?"

"You git, you whippersnapper!" roared Mr. Biggle, coming suddenly to life.

That took the starch out of the bright boy, and he ran out, squawling. Then the Rev. Yates came in. He had been waiting outside all the time.

"You ought to listened, Mr. Biggle," he said solemnly. "Might be the little feller was inspired. Out of the mouths of babes and sucklin's, you know!"

"Pap!" snorted Mr. Biggle, acting terribly put out. "That's all I ever knowed to come out of the mouth of a babe and a sucklin'! Pap!"

The next Sunday the Rev. Yates preached darkly about a man in town who had spoken slightingly of Scripture. Everybody knew that Mr. Biggle was meant. But he couldn't be budged. The only effect of that scheme of the Rev. Yates's was to fasten the nickname of Babe 'n' Sucklin' on little Luke Lolley.

Stem Tracy, the night depot agent, was perhaps the most brazen of the unsaved. He smoked what the Rev. Yates always called the vile cigarette, not only in the secrecy of the depot at night, but out on the public streets. Most of us boys were members of the Anti-Cigarette League, and we knew that Stem might go insane at any minute, and that in any event he was certain to waste away with a cigarette cough and die at an early age without a single lung left.

One day Dr. Prouty, who was a steward of the Rev. Yates's church, stopped Tracy on the street and gave him a free lecture about the ruin that threatened his health. The young depot agent listened with a sneer, then brazenly blew a cloud of the vile smoke in Dr. Prouty's face and went on about his business. The doctor had a bad temper. Tracy's impudence made him so angry that he swallowed his chaw. As he had a terribly weak stomach, he got sick right there on the sidewalk.

Stem was always held up to us as a horrible example, along with the Knapp boys and a few other young men who were known to play with cards, drink bottled beer, and attend the dances over on sinful Soap Creek. Yet even the Rev. Yates was generous in holding out hope for these young men. They had not offended God beyond repair by denying the authority of the church. Whenever they should come forward and be purged and baptized, the sancified would welcome them as sheep that had been lost and were found again. But they kept recklessly on in their sinful good times.

The influence of Elder Barton weakened my ideas about these wicked young men. In that eventful eighth Summer of mine I often speculated as to whether the good times of Stem Tracy and the Knapp boys were really sinful or not. Again it was the elder who turned me against all the Christian sense and reason I'd ever learned.

He did it in an argument with Brother Dolbeer, a tough little nubbin of a Hardshell farmer who had been powerfully moved by the Rev. Yates's preaching.

"It ain't in the doctern of the true church that we should set ourselves up as jedges," Elder Barton declared. "We like our mornin' nip and our bedtime toddy. You like yore chaw and I'm partial to my pipe. There's nothin' in the Word agin sech likin'. No more is there agin a likin' fer cigareets and bottle' beer."

"Not to hear you preach it, they ain't," snapped Brother Dolbeer.

"I preach. I don't jedge," said the elder.

When I got my sense and reason back I realized that it was the influence of Elder Barton that had weakened me all down the line. But salvation was at hand. The prairie God was looking out for His own. The Widow Crouch died. That event gave the Rev. Pearl Yates a chance to show up Elder Dewberry Barton in his true colors.

VI

The sun was so low that the oak's shade covered all of Repp's barnyard. Farmers were hitching horses to the rigs. Elder Barton was standing with Pleas Repp, talking about the stock dickered for during the afternoon's trading. Brother Dolbeer was swinging his team over the tongue of a lumber wagon just behind the liveryman and the elder. I slipped down from the fence and started to skedaddle home. My grandmother and I were to ride out with Brother Dolbeer, who was a neighbor of Uncle Harve Cate's. We would stall all night at Uncle Harve's, then go to hear the preaching tomorrow. I should have gone home a half-hour ago. So I hustled now.

But when Dr. Prouty came puffing out of the barn and wheezed up to the elder I simply had to stop and listen. The doctor was powerfully excited, and it was plain that something big had happened.

"Howdy, Elder Barton," he said, and then he had to stop and pant for breath.

"How air you, sir?" The elder was stern in his greeting. Dr. Prouty had often slurred him as a horse-trading preacher.

"I've a call in trouble to make to you, Elder," said the doctor, getting his breath and his dignity back at the same time. "It's account of the Widder Crouch. She's been on a sickbed for nigh on three days. Didn't show up to do her trading, and finally somebody looked in on her. It's typhoid fever, and it ain't the least likely she'll live out the night. You know that cousin of her'n in Tyrone, Elder?"

"Right well." The elder looked powerfully troubled as he spoke. "You want me to see she gits word, do you? Sho'. I'll go fetch Mis' Lennane myself. Typhoid—pore soul—laid sick fer three days, you say? Where does she live?"

"I'll show you, Elder. And—there's suthin' else." Dr. Prouty acted flustered again. His tongue seemed to stick on him. "Delirious," he managed to say. "But she makes out she wants a—uh—priest. I wouldn't want it said—of course, you could have somebody else in Tyrone fetch him—"

"Let's go right along," Elder Barton broke in, looking stern again.

I ran on ahead of them, tremendously excited, to tell my grandmother that the Widow Crouch was mortally ill. My grandmother had a fine neighborhood reputation for being good in sickness, and she grimly made ready to live up to it with the widow. In a few minutes she found the herbs which she favored in the treatment of typhoid, and she set out with them for the widow's house. I followed, shivering all over with the dreadful but fascinating prospect of seeing the widow in her own place, among the graven images. I had a dim idea that her room would look like the shop of Curry Grimes, who made tombstones. But I didn't have a chance to see if this was so. We were stopped at the gateway to the hedge.

Elder Barton, his expression still deeply troubled, was coming out with Dr. Prouty. His eyes lit up some when he saw my grandmother.

"Sho', Sister Turner," he said, "I might of knowed you'd come when you heerd. Ain't it a perishin' shame, though? That pore soul a dyin' alone and nobody to tend her!"

My grandmother spoke shortly, as she commonly did to Elder Barton, and started on for the house. But he stopped her again, to say that he was driving at once to Tyrone to fetch the Widow Crouch's cousin.

"I hope to bring her here before the end," he said. "I'll change hosses in Tyrone. I'll be out fer preachin' tomorrer, but o' course I won't git to Brother Cate's tonight. I wonder could you kindly send him my excuses?"

"And the priest," Dr. Prouty put in sharply. "Are you going to bring a priest like she asked?"

The doctor's eyes were squinted in a hard look which made me think of the Rev. Yates's fiercest preaching stare.

"I reckon," said Elder Barton.

"Mighty kind of you, Elder," said the doctor. "Mighty kind."

But that burning hardness in the doctor's eyes didn't lessen.

"Bub, you go wait for Brother Dolbeer," I heard my grandmother saying. "You tell him to leave word with yore Uncle Harve about the elder."

I ran back home. All the brightness of the afternoon was gone. The sun was still blazing, yet everything somehow seemed gloomy and cold. I had a queer feeling that Elder Barton's bringing a Roman priest right into Moravia was something more tremendous than just the plain fact that the Widow Crouch was dying.

People lying in mortal sickness and in the cold grip of death itself were a familiar sight to all prairie children. It was forced on them, as a warning not to get too sure and proud of themselves. My most vivid early memories are of pale people lying in rooms where all the blinds were drawn, of dead faces under glass and flowers, of burials in the rain. Perhaps it is a distortion of memory, but I am sure there was rain for every funeral in Moravia.

Anyhow, it seemed that the biggest thing I had to tell Brother Dolbeer was about a priest coming to Moravia with nobody but Elder Barton of the Primitive Baptist Church. Brother Dolbeer didn't remark upon it, but his expression told me plainly enough that this was also the biggest item with him. His eyes got like Dr. Prouty's.

It was the same with all the other members of the Hyattsville congregation and with the Methodists. When the elder showed up at the meeting-house all the brothers and sisters declared it was mighty, mighty kind of him to forget his enmity with Rome and be a good Samaritan to a poor soul who was dying. But everyone had that hard, suspicious look. Brother Dolbeer even put it into words.

"What did you and the Roman priest talk about, Elder, may I be so bold as to ask?" he said. "You had a good four-hour drive together. Mebbe you pried inter some of his sekerts?"

"Hosses," said Elder Barton shortly. "We talked hosses."

Elder Barton preached toler'ble porely, as my grandmother said. Even I could tell that he wasn't inspired. After the meeting he wouldn't stop for dinner. He had promised to drive the priest on back to Tyrone that afternoon, he said.

VII

Driving the priest back to Tyrone on a Sabbath afternoon was what actually finished Elder Barton in Moravia. I was getting my Baptist common sense and reason back with tremendous power, and I had to agree when the other boys talked about the scandal. The worst of it was that the elder had deliberately offended the Rev. Yates by driving the priest down the main street of the town and directly past the Methodist church and parsonage, when he could have taken a back road just as well. The preacher was just coming out of his gate when the Morgans came prancing down, with Elder Barton holding a tight line, sitting stiff-necked and proud in the buggy seat, and the agent of the Rome Harlot beside him. A crowd of young people were on their way to Epworth League. The Rev. Yates stood before them, and when the elder was well past he raised both fists and shook them at the back of the buggy, and thundered:

"To your tents, O Israel!"

Every Sunday from then on until Winter Rome got it hot and heavy from the Rev. Yates. And he certainly undermined Elder Barton with the Hyattsville road congregation. Brother Dolbeer was the first of the Hardshells to come forward to the Methodist mourner's bench. When three others joined him the congregation agreed to make a change in preachers, and Elder Detwiler, a stocky, bald-headed man with a bushy red beard, was brought up from Moulton. He preached nothing but Paul and primitive Christianity.

The Rev. Yates was always careful to declare that there was no prejudice in his fight against Rome in Moravia; he was just appealing to common sense and reason, he said; and nobody could ever accuse him of slinging mud at the name of any man. That was so. The Rev. Yates was always the first one to say that Elder Dewberry Barton had been mighty, mighty kind in the death of the widow Crouch. But he made it plain that there were plenty of Irish in Tyrone who had horses and rigs which their Roman priests could use when they were called in cases of sickness and death. The head priest had a fine span of his own, and a surrey and a sleigh. Good horses, too. Hadn't he bought them from a certain horse-dealer who also called himself a preacher? And so that same preacher had no call whatever to go hauling priests of Rome around the country.

"I expect I might falter in my own faith if I was exposed to the wiles of the Harlot all the way between Moravy and Tyrone," said the Rev. Yates. "We are all mortal sinners. That was mighty, mighty kind of Elder Barton, but could he have been teched and tainted? Could he? Only the good Lord and the wicked Devil know."

When Elder Detwiler answered the call of the Hyattsville congregation Elder Barton quit coming to Moravia to trade horses. By Winter the Rev. Yates got bolder in his holy fight. Finally it was rumored around that he had learned that a certain preacher of the Primitive Baptist church was preparing to marry a Romish woman in Tyrone, and that he would abandon his own church to permit a priest to join them in wedlock. Everybody knew that the Rev. Yates meant Elder Barton and the Widow Crouch's cousin, Mrs. Lennane. The talk created a powerful stir. Then it was announced that the Rev. Yates would preach a sermon on the subject. All of the Hardshells drove in that Sunday morning to hear him.

But Jeff Biggle spoiled the whole business. He proved for a fact that he was actually an infidel when he wrote word to Elder Barton about the projected sermon. And just as the Rev. Yates stepped up to announce his text Elder Barton swung into the center aisle, with Jeff Biggle marching behind him. The elder was dressed in his black preaching suit. With his flowing beard and his great mane of wavy hair he looked as grand as ever. But there was something in his eyes I had never seen there before, though it was a common expression in others. Hate was there, a hot, hard glare of hate. As he strode on, the people in the pews he passed drew in their breath sharply. The elder's right hand was gripping the black, snaky coils of a shotwhip.

He sat in a front pew, folded his arms so that the shotwhip lay coiled on his chest, and stared steadily up at the Rev. Pearl Yates. Jeff Biggle sat beside him, a curious expression on his wrinkled face. The corners of his mouth kept twitching.

Right then the meaning of the whole spectacle was dim to me, but I did expect the Rev. Yates to be taken aback. However, he wasn't. He gave Elder Barton just one look. Then he announced his text.

"My text for this mornin's subject. . . ." His voice shook into a hoarse mumble. The quiet in the rest of the church was awful. Then: "'Wine is a mocker; and strong drink is ragin'.'"

I was struck by the sight of Jeff Biggle. He had tucked his head down and he was shaking all over like a horse with the heaves. But I soon forgot him. The Rev. Yates was going it on rum. The rum demon never got a harder larruping than he gave it in that morning's sermon. I was sort of pleased. I was tired of hating Rome. Hating rum was good for a change.

That was my last sight of Elder Dewberry Barton. He came to Moravia no more. My Christian reason got stronger all the time, and the following Spring I was converted at a Methodist camp-meeting. Sanctification was at hand. My age was ample for it. At eight I had the perfect Methodist mind.

But even God's giant, the Rev. Pearl Yates, could not sustain my reason against the glamour that Dewberry Barton, the horse-trading Hardshell elder, had brought to our prairie town. The sinful light lasted in my memory, my first doubts bloomed on in its glow and caused my backsliding in the end. Above the most soul-shaking blasts of the Rev. Yates I would catch a worldly vision of trading horses, feel myself perched on the pole fence of Repp's barnyard once more, see the waving fringes and shining beads of Elder Barton's grand Buffalo Bill gloves, and hear his rich voice rise in praise of a beautiful black Morgan:

"Sta'nch as this yere white oak! Sound as a Bryan silver dollar! Look at the roll of his eye there! Blooded, sir, blooded! . . ."

. . . James Stevens – 1921

The Salt of the Earth

JAMES HEARST'S "The Movers" and Leo R. Ward's "New Neighbors in Search of Land" (which I have retitled "Newcomers to Irish Iowa") were both written in the latter half of the Depression years of the 1930s, one in northern Iowa, one in southern Iowa, a hundred fifty miles apart as the crow flies. I don't know whether Father Ward and Jim Hearst knew each other at the time, but it is not unusual that they would choose the same theme, the place of the tenant farmer in those years. Both would have been well-acquainted with the vision of the "movers" on the first of March every year. I include the two pieces here because they complement each other; Muck and Letty of Ward's story might well be the anonymous "movers" of Hearst's poem.

James Hearst was raised on a third-generation farm near Cedar Falls and taught creative writing at the University of Northern Iowa and its predecessors. Leo Richard Ward was raised on a farm near Melrose in Monroe County, a county hard-hit by drought and the Depression. He became a priest in the Community of Holy Cross and a teacher of philosophy at the University of Notre Dame.

"Ding's" cartoon of the tragedy of the sold-out farm family, as well as Ruth Suckow's "The Movers" (not reprinted here), also echo the plight of the under-capitalized farmer of an earlier period of Iowa agricultural history.

The Movers

The east wind whips the skirts of snow
with a passing shower,
and over Iowa on the first of March
wheels churn hub deep in the mud
or grit their teeth across the icy roads.

Home is only a shadow
flying down the wind in a
twisted whirl of snowflakes,
traveling down the road in an old lumber wagon
drawn by two shaggy horses
whose bones are too big for their flesh.

Even the wild goose
is not so homeless as these movers.
Peering ahead through the sliding curtain
of March rain they pass
with the furniture of home packed in a wagon.
Past corner, past grove, to the hilltop they go
until only chairlegs point from the skyline
like roots of trees torn from the earth.
And they are gone. . . .

This, the parade of the landless, the tenants,
the dispossessed,
out of their Canaan they march
with Moses asleep in the Bible.

Who will call them back, who will ask:
are you the chosen people, do you inherit
only a backward glance and a cry and a heartbreak?
are you the meek?

But the early twilight
drops like a shawl on their shoulders
and sullen water
slowly fills the wagon ruts and the hoof prints.

. . . James Hearst

Iowa Farmscape—Joan Liffring-Zug

Newcomers to Irish Iowa

IN THE EARLY DAYS, the great ambition was to get to Iowa where it was understood that the soil was strong and rich. *"Iowa Territory—* unsurpassed in the fertility of her soil, her resources endless." So ran a toast in honor of the Governor on September 4, 1838. The custom was for people to come all summer long. Men driving ox teams hundreds of miles could hardly gauge so much as the season of their arrival, and we know that it sometimes took them the whole summer. That was the case with my mother's people and the group that drove from Ontario in the 'fifties. My father's father came directly from Cleveland; they worked their way, perhaps mostly by canal, downstate in Ohio, then came down the river by boat and up the Mississippi. The journey took approximately three weeks. As was then the way, they settled first near the river, but after the War they came another hundred miles to our neighborhood because the church was being built.

That's what brought many of our neighbors. A stone church was being built. The men quarried the stone, a hard sandstone that is more brown than gray, and hauled it four miles in ox carts. My grandfather may have been a particular help, for he is said to have been expert in the trade of foundryman, and was also a well-digger and of course a farmer; and he was one of the four or five who had horse teams. The church had been started in '59, but the walls were left as they were, four or five feet high, when the men had to set out for the War; an old man whose family with one or two others was driven back from a non-Irish and non-Catholic settlement farther west says the bigger boys used to jump up and climb over the wall, but he, himself, was too little to get hold of the top. To this day, the logs of the earlier church, logs that were evidently squared with an axe, form part of the walls of a barn or shed that is now ready to fall down.

A man who came in 1870 has often said that the main road was a cloud of dust most of the summer, from the covered wagons going west. This man's brother, the Jackeen who is still plowing corn, came afoot and helped men to drive cattle.

But by our own time, that movement in wagons had totally stopped; never a covered wagon except a gypsy's, never an unknown mover's outfit. Any mover that came or went a distance made the trip in a box-car on the Burlington road which was completely built and double-tracked to Denver before I was born, though when my father came to the county it was, so he often told us, single-tracked and it stopped forty miles short of our town. After the turn of the century, not many new people came, just an uncertain dribble of settlers. The land was all taken, and for a long time no new claims were to be had; in fact, I talked to only one man, dead now a long time, who bought a forty directly from the government, a good sandy forty, too, but a little rough.

As late as 1909 a new family came to a farm just west of ours. In the first days of March, these new neighbors were moving into what was called the Dundon place; new snow was falling and drifting, and tufts of the old snow were yet on the ground. Because no one had occupied the place for three or four seasons, things were in a bad condition. Fences around the lots needed fixing, apple trees—and there had been good summer apples—had gone down, and burdock had grown up unmolested in the yard. Some of the people before the newcomers may have been good farmers, but a renter has to be much better than ordinary if he is to look after the soil or the improvements. Things had gone to ruin and it was not a fit place for people to live. Discs and corn planters had been stored in the room, and coal shovelled into the kitchen. No family could move into that house, walking with rats, the windows boarded up, the weather still like the worst of winter. Two babies actually had died in the house, and the rumor spread that it was of diphtheria.

So Mr. and Mrs. brought their stuff there from the freight car: three work horses, some heifer calves and geese, wagons and cultivators, tables and bedding. Then they came and lived three or four days with us.

My older sister and I had been reading a book (because we didn't often have a book to read, we usually read together; neither of us can say now what that book was). "See," she said, "how much Missus is like the woman in the book; watch the way she talks." That was true enough; but Mr. didn't look like a man in any book; on the contrary, a very good book might look a little like a chapter out of him. Mr. was a midwesterner, a hard old hickory, ready for splitting rails, fit for the plow. And we have to say that it must have been a very good book that had a woman like Mrs. in it. Mr. and Mrs. teamed up well together.

They had children. The youngest was a girl of two and a half. They had a white-eyed, red-headed girl of six or seven, a dark lean boy nearly ten, and they were to have a baby late in the spring. But to us as we first knew them, they were Mr. and Mrs. For a while, of course, they were the new neighbors, the new people on the Dundon place, then they gradually subsided into plain everyday Muck and Letty, and this is what they will always remain.*

All the time that we have known Muck, and it's a good while, his clothes have been in shreds and patches. He has always run right through shirts and overalls. Letty could not keep clothes on him, and we don't know that she has ever tried. He is only more or less covered. The shoulders and breast are half bared, and at times roughly scratched and bruised, as if he had gone naked through ripe cornstalks or hazel or along hedges. It is too much to say that he is slashed and gouged, or that he is perpetually letting blood; but he is like that; he leaves strips of the overalls and perhaps of flesh on wire fences. And like the rest of us, he is always in old gunboat shoes, old when he has worn them a time or two in the mire of cowlots and piglots. The shoes naturally go the way of the feet, push out at one spot, curl up at another like twisted sled-runners.

Often have I seen him walking on level land, his knees bent as if he were all the time climbing a hill or carrying a load; and it may be that he is. And when he does go up a hill, he appears to crawl on knees and toes. Winter and summer he has the same steadfast color, not a deep red but a kind of bay with a sprinkling of sand in the tangled brown hair.

Anything but a dapper little man, not nifty in gait or smooth in build, Muck has a slow, clumsy and genuine power. Once I saw him on a windy day in spring wrestling with pigs and steers in a muddy lot; he wanted to turn them out of the sloppy hog-yard and get them to a dryer spot, and he was as deeply plastered as they were. At last he had won; and the picture I have of him now, from that and other occasions, is one of rough strength: he is like a rusty hinge that creaks, and gives day by day, and yet stands for many a year; or he is like an unplaned barn-door that does not swing lightly or close at all points, yet stands strong and sure.

Muck and Letty came, lured by the promise of cheap rent, from down along old Crooked Creek, in Illinois; they thought they would be able to buy in a couple of years. Soon after Christmas, Muck had appeared unannounced and had rented the place when it was under snow and there was nothing to tell of its quality except the lie of the land and the word of neighbors, and a few hardy cornstalks and cockleburrs reaching up out of the snow, and the tumbleweeds rolled up against the

---

* "Muck" came in some roundabout way from Charles, and "Letty" from Loretto.

hedges. He could give credentials, but he himself did not ask any; he trusted land and weather and God and people.

Letty was, then and always, out of breath. She had sinking spells but she talked. At any instant, a person would swear she was ready to take the count and could scarcely be revived by a wink at the bottle, but she kept her feet and kept going. She could whip a mess of work out of her way. The two of them worked like horses, and turned out to be the roughest and best neighbors we ever had; at least, if the words roughest and best are taken together, no other neighbors could very well compare with them. And it is sure that we had many good neighbors, such as Big Man and Mary Ann and a dozen others, and some people would think almost any of them rough and ready.

When new neighbors came, people wanted to know one or two important things about them. Were they honest? They had better be! Were they friendly, and were they so friendly as to be pests? Sometimes people turned out to be dirty, yet surely the cleanness of people was something that could be taken for granted. Well, Muck and Letty at once qualified. They minded their business, paid as they went, and were careful not to wear out their welcome. Muck was what we call a born Catholic and Letty was a convert; in any case, we felt at home with them.

Letty had a new way of making cheese. It was not a secret process; her face as colorless as water, her body pulled down like the body of a mare with colt, she worked away; she wanted to teach everybody, and nobody could be displeased with her good will. Yet even a layman might suggest she had made no great discovery, and might claim that the curds were less risky than the new cheese.

Neither Muck nor Letty ever played cards, but she liked to dance, and they gave dances at which the whole neighborhood was welcome to dance, to play euchre, and to eat Letty's gooseberry and pumpkin pies.

They were wonderful to help, no matter how hard the work. It was as if that was what they came into the world to do. Before a neighbor asked at all, they would come and do any kind of work for him and with him; she would scald the churn and see after the incubator, with her soul set on what the result would be; and Muck would fix up a fence or a gate, and likely as not he would never say a word about it; the neighbor's need was chance enough for him. He was a strong, rough-bodied man, and he loved people. Whenever a neighbor threshed, Muck was there early, he opened the stacks, and he never let up until the grain was scooped into the bin and the straw-pile was covered with slough-hay and weighted down with poles or rocks.

It is true that he could get hot under the collar; everybody soon knew this and allowed for it. He broke out into living flame once in a while, but really it was nothing, it was only the spurt of a match; a moment later he was, though out of wind, gentle and kind, his voice deep and quavering and mellow, his light blue eyes soft. The worst thing about him, at least when we first knew him, was his discouraged hours, and even so he enjoyed being consoled, and the greatest good in his own day was in bringing comfort to people.

When a man fell from the fork-track of a new barn, Muck rose from a sick bed and went like a wild man across the fields on an old plug, bareback, to the man who as a matter of fact was then almost a total stranger to him. It was New Year's Eve, the ground was frozen solid, and the two of us were deputized to stay with Letty till we saw him come home at midnight and eat a gooseberry pie and drink a pot of coffee. He said, "Poor Stevie! To fall like that, there alone in the barn, and not a soul to help him out but his one sister!" The words shook up out of Muck and he used his favorite expressions: "By gol! And Stevie is such a g-good fellah!" Before daylight the next morning, Muck and Letty were on the road to Mass and to receive Holy Communion; they weren't going to miss, least of all on New Year's Day and when the poor neighbor was not able to go.

That's what they liked, not raising a bumper crop or shipping a car-load of hogs to Chicago, but helping a man who was out of luck. As they saw it, that was not only the right thing but the normal thing. Life itself was for this kind of neighborliness; the fact was as clear as sun and moon and stars.

We were all poor people, on every side of town, and those who were renting and moving needed no wagons to haul their money. Muck and Letty made no pretense to wealth. They came with their pockets slack; if they had a bit of cash, they may have kept it and actually have added to it in the best times, but with the times still good or ordinary and with themselves toiling they probably began to slip a little down the hill. Like all of us poor farmers, they dealt – if they dealt at all – in third-rate canners and feeders, and not as a matter of choice. And the Lord knows every calamity comes to poor farmers; the well runs dry, they get caught with land that sours or won't drain, the hog market starts down at the wrong time, the cash rent comes around much too quickly on them.

Now it is hard to way what odds and ends of misfortune hit Muck and Letty from one side or another. And the signs were on them. Clothes became skimpy, the house sometimes looked as if it had been robbed, and when they had produce they were so generous and whole-hearted that they did not run to sell it but to put it on the table. It was almost as if they were looking for someone on whom to bestow things. So money was gone before it came, and any tramp was welcome to a share of the food they had. Muck was always turning his pockets inside out to get half a pipe of tobacco, and Letty often had a time of it, after the middle of summer, to get enough cream together for a churning.

When they first came to us, and it's hitting around thirty-two years now, Muck and Letty seemed to us children an old man and woman. Well, they have grandchildren now this good while, but are not old people, not snowed under, not by a long way. Each of them can yet do a day's work, or a season's work. Of course, Letty is wind-broken as she always was, but she can climb a big hill if given moderate time, and though we may suppose she does not dance any more it is safe to bet she could do a turn or two. What is known is that on a summer morning not long ago she churned at five, walked a mile and a half to church, and after Mass appeared in the sacristy with a jar of the butter-milk under her arm. Neither the work nor the jaunt was too hard on her, because for a lifetime she has loved to do such things.

Muck appears like himself of thirty years ago. It is true that his face is now without the beard and is like a plowed hillside gutted and ditched with rains, and he is stooped at the shoulders and bent at the knees, but the rest of him stands fairly straight. When we see him ride an old white horse without saddle and with a kind of rope bridle, or hear him rattle along with team and rig, what we have to say is that he is not a knocked-out man. All his life long, he has known how to sit behind the kitchen stove on a winter day, or day after day, and rest up; but he never knew what hate was or is; so perhaps he will wear much better than men who were more neatly set up, but loved man less; he says that God means that every man should have something to suffer. In short, Muck remains a strong man hard to keep in clothes; he can raise good corn if he gets rain; his teeth are worn small but he has enough of them left to manage to munch at a mouthful of granger-twist. When in 1934 the lean times and the drought were combined and might be thought to be at their peak, he said that he had always had good neigh-bors and had no complaint to make against God or man.

Long ago, when Muck was already mature in years, I heard quite a young man tell him that no man ever need be poor: "not any more, old fellow." Muck was not tolerant of that idea, "need never be poor," and though he would be tolerant of it now, he still wouldn't believe it.

They were well met, as we used to say, the two of them, Muck and Letty. In many ways he must have seemed to most people a memorable person, and in fact a genuinely remarkable person; he had a hollow Lincolnesque jaw, a big chin, and a big mouth with the corners tipping up. Besides, he was probably boss of the farm. But there is no use saying Muck without Letty, or Letty without Muck, and none of their friends ever does say one or think of one without the other. They are a pair after all, a matched team, and if possible a person might not have said fifty years ago that they were simply born to go together, they certainly have gone well and happily together; neither one could have done much of the going alone; and it would seem strange now to any of their friends to think of them as ever having been for a week of their lives apart. At any rate, from the first day we ever knew them, they have smoothly managed their small cooperative.

Certain kinds of trees, such as running-oak and crab apple, grow, not in, but out of, our clay hills; that is the case of Big Man's rough forty, on much of the Mary Ann place, and on The Granger's poorer land. And yet it is hard to say. Maybe the hills grow out of the trees, the two are so close, so native to each other. Well, Muck and Letty have remained like that, and it is only half the truth to say that they are partners. For when a person met one, he certainly met the other, though the other might not be seen, especially by a stranger. And he wouldn't want to make up his mind too quickly which was the hill, and which the rooted running-oak or wild apple.

Muck was one person, and Letty another. But without the other, each would have been notably different, and likely would not have been at all. One of the good things of our life is to have known and still to know the two together, the two as one.

... Leo R. Ward, *Holding Up The Hills*, 1941

Davenport, Iowa, riverfront and first bridge across the Mississippi

The Cities of Iowa – Davenport

IOWA'S MISSISSIPPI RIVER CITIES, as Marquis Childs and Richard Bissell will insist a few pages on, are unlike other Iowa cities, because, say these writers, they are more a part of the River than they are of the land.

Certainly Davenport can be differentiated, as the authors of "Susan Glaspell of Davenport" show, by a statistical comparison of the number of wellknown authors it produced, as compared with the other river cities, Cedar Rapids, Des Moines, Sioux City and so on. Although these cities and others may have produced at least one wellknown author, none had produced even close to ten. (Iowa City does not count – most of the wellknown writers who have stopped over there have been either hibernating or estivating; they have little, if any, connection with Iowa otherwise.)

So here is Davenport, not as an industrial city, which it certainly is, not as a commercial center which it is also, but as an intellectual center which sent its sons and daughters forth to change the history of American writing.

Marcia Noe, an Assistant Professor of English at Black Hawk Community College in Rock Island, Illinois, is the author of an unpublished University of Iowa dissertation, A Critical Biography of Susan Glaspell *(1976). Part of her research was done in Provincetown, Massachusetts, and part in Europe, where, among other work, she interviewed Nilla, George Cram Cook's daughter by an early marriage.*

Susan Glaspell of Davenport

FOR A HALF CENTURY OR MORE the citizens of Davenport have speculated about the literary lightning which seems to have struck the eastern Iowa industrial city and produced so many important writers: Charles Edward Russell, Pulitzer-prize-winning biographer; his son, John Russell; Charles Eugene Banks, poet and author; critic Harry Hansen; Alice French ("Octave Thanet"); George Cram Cook; Floyd Dell; Arthur Davison Ficke; Susan Glaspell, also a Pulitzer-prize-winning author; Franc Wilkie Bangs; Blanche Fearing; and, later, Julie McDonald.

French was a major figure in the nineteenth-century genteel-local color tradition; Hansen, Cook, Dell and Ficke were participants in the Chicago Renaissance; Hansen was a literary critic, dying just recently—at his desk—at 92; Dell became a critic and novelist and edited *The Masses* with Max Eastman and John Reed. These writers, together with Carl Van Vechten of Cedar Rapids, played active parts in the intellectual and cultural movements of the decade 1910-1920 that revolutionized the arts in America. Cook and Glaspell founded the Provincetown Players in 1915, later took the group to Greenwich Village, first produced the plays of Eugene O'Neill, and helped change the course of the American theater.

During the next eight years, Susan Glaspell wrote, produced and acted in eleven plays which explored such contemporary topics as feminism, free speech and Freudian psychology and used experimental techniques in drama. In 1931, her play *Alison's House*, set in the Mississippi valley, was awarded the Pulitzer Prize for drama, and in 1940 her novel, *The Morning Is Near Us*, was chosen as a Literary Guild Selection. She died in 1948. On August 22, 1976, she was one of the first five Iowa women elected to the Iowa Women's Hall of Fame.

Susan was born on July 1, 1876. Unlike her husband, George Cram Cook, born three years earlier, she was not from one of Davenport's wealthy and prestigious families. "George Cram Cook grew up in a (Davenport) that had a Cook Memorial Library, the Cook Home, and a Cook Memorial Church," wrote Susan. Her own family seemed less important—"there (was) no Glaspell Home for the Friendless (!)"

Cook's great-grandparents, Ira Cook and wife, and Christopher and Elizabeth Rowe, came to Davenport by ferry in 1836. Susan's great-grandparents came three years later. There are still members of the

Glaspell family in Davenport. Susan's home on West Twelfth Street reputedly has Susan's name still visible, scratched on a brick inside the fireplace chimney.

It was a heady world in which Susan found herself. By the time Susan was twenty, Alice French had published dozens of short stories and four or five books. There had been literary magazines in Davenport since Hiram Reed's time (1856), and Charles Eugene Banks was editing one in the 1890s. The Germans had fled Europe in the 1840s, bringing their intellectual and dramatic traditions to Davenport with them; a German theater had been active in West Davenport for several decades. There were three daily newspapers, two weeklies, and a German-language newspaper. Local opera houses presented *The Mikado, The Pirates of Penzance, The H. M. S. Pinafore, Othello, Hamlet,* and *Macbeth.*

Floyd Dell has described the Davenport of this time as a town offering exciting cultural activities:

> *I suppose this is a respect for learning; but it is more due, I think, to the Germans who left home because they loved liberty, and brought with them a taste for music, discussion and good beer. There are so many of the Germans, and they have so much enthusiasm that they dominate the town. And for some reason they are not as solemn and stodgy as Germans often are—perhaps because of a slight but pervasive Flemish strain. Their robust mirthfulness is extraordinarily like the scenes in Flemish paintings. At all events, their influence has stamped the town with its own flavour. It is true they have never been able to convert the descendants of New England to gymnastics and choral singing; but they have laid out these magnificent parks and built our library—which, you will have noticed, is well-stocked with free-thought literature.*

Susan graduated from high school in 1894 and began work for Banks, then editor of the *Davenport Morning Republican*. A local magazine, *Trident,* said of her that "she wrote some pretty things." When Banks founded the *Weekly Outlook* in 1896, a magazine devoted to "Literature, Art, Music and the Drama," and other subjects, "Susie" K. Glaspell was its society editor.

In one of her columns, Susan showed an early interest in the theater as she set down, with tongue in cheek, "Rules of Conduct for Theatre-Goers":

> *Cultivate a bored look . . . look much at the audience . . . evince no interest in what is going on, but look politely and coldly condescending . . . If you are*

in a box make all the noise you can as your social standing is determined in direct proportion to the confusion you create . . . never fail to sniff at a leading lady . . . always come in late and make sufficient of a stir to detract everyone's attention from the play. . . .

Other columns are evidence that a free-thinking woman is developing. Often the new ideas that Susan is trying out are put into the mouths of factitious "society girls." One of these proclaims her weariness of "pouring tea for dead men, dancing with dead men, having dead men in our theatre box and at our table. The men in (our) three towns are nothing but floating logs on the stream of society."

Another complains: "I am like the flowers in the hothouse, a forced production. How would it feel to be free? To stay at home reading a book when you ought to be out calling, and be a free thinker and an eccentric generally?" Of the late nineteenth-century notion of the "new woman," she wrote: "She may smoke cigarettes, talk horse, and be a jolly good fellow all 'round, if she wants to, but she mustn't think with all that she can be set upon a pedestal and fed on sugarplums and roses."

In one of her last columns, Susan defended a rather unpopular view for the time, that women were entitled to a college education. Women college graduates were not "merely sexless exponents of higher education." Femininity is not destroyed by learning: "If I believed this it would make me most unhappy and I would feel compelled to start tonight on a holy pilgrimage to burn all women's colleges in the land."

Of her decision to enroll at Drake University, a reporter later commented: "(Susan) had the temerity to go to college. Before that, young ladies had been educated at academies and institutes and the finishing school was coming into vogue. This girl brought home a bachelor's degree. She was regarded somewhat askance, people wondered if it wasn't possible she was a little queer. For a time her health was said to be weak from over-study. . . ."

A classmate at Drake said of Susan: "Her personality was a flame in the light of the student body or at any rate in the group that felt themselves the social and literary leaders." Susan was literary editor of the college newspaper, won first prize in an oratorial contest, and unsuccessfully challenged Lucy Huffaker, life-long friend and fellow writer, for editorship of *The Delphic.*

With an 1899 Ph.B. in her possession, she went to the Des Moines *Daily News* as statehouse and legislative reporter, and wrote a column, "The News Girl." Out of this legislative experience came her earliest short stories, published in *Lifted Masks* in 1912. Many of these concern public figures who choose good over evil even though this choice invites political disaster.

Susan's best short story, "A Jury of Her Peers," was adapted from her one-act play, *Trifles,* "the best one-act play ever written in America." It was based on a murder trial she covered for the *Daily News.* A farm woman is in the county jail, charged with killing her husband. The Sheriff and the County Attorney go to the cold farmhouse to look for evidence. They take along their wives to bring back some items which will make the woman more comfortable. Because of the men's condescending attitudes toward women and their "trifles," they fail to notice the hard clues to the woman's motivation. Their wives, however, do notice the clues, and, out of understanding and sympathy for the woman, resolve to keep the knowledge to themselves.

Susan's newspaper career lasted less than two years. "I boldly gave up my job and went home to Davenport to give all my time to my own writing. I say boldly because I had to earn my own living." Two years later the *Daily News* reported "it is a great pleasure to many Iowans to know that Miss Susan Keating Glaspell is meeting with very flattering success as a writer of (magazine) short stories."

But most of Susan's short fiction is undistinguished. There was little of the experimentation with form and theme that would move Isaac Goldberg to praise her as ". . . a serious dramatist – one of the few Americans whose progress is worth watching with the same eyes that follow notable European effort. . . ."

In Davenport, where she "boarded" at her parents' home, she found a great deal of stimulus. Arthur Davison Ficke, recently graduated from Harvard in a class which included Franklin Delano Roosevelt, was practicing law with his father and chafing at the bit – he would rather have been writing poetry. George Cram Cook was also home from Harvard, where he had studied with Barrett Wendell and Charles Eliot Norton. After brief teaching stints at the University of Iowa and Stanford University, he returned to live with "Ma-Mie," his mother, and Ed Cook, his attorney father, in a log cabin in Buffalo.

It may have been a log cabin but Plato and Ruskin and Greek urns graced its shelves and its floorboards had felt the tread of Hungarian intellectual refugees. The cabin talk was of "Beethoven, the mysticism of India, old rites and the beginnings of art." "The (Davenport) community is today somewhat different because . . . one woman – very small, dark, quick, 'queer' – had a sense of values better than those of her time and place," wrote Susan of Cook's mother.

To Davenport also came Floyd Dell, a high school boy, much too mature and precocious for his schoolfellows. Soon he was charming Marilla Freeman, a local librarian, with his verse, reading Housman's poetry and his own to Harry Hansen on evening walks in Fejevary Park, and starting to make contact with Rabbi Fineschreiber, a liberal Reform Jew, and Fritz Feuchter, a postman, both with Socialist ideas.

Davenport was booming in the early years of the century's first decade, on the way to becoming the major industrial center it is today. German socialists in local brewing and cigar industries were arguing for the rights of labor. Soon Dell, and eventually Cook, who tempered these new ideas with the Greek philosophy he had learned at his mother's knee, became members of a socialist discussion group and founders of the "Monist" society, a group which believed in the unity of the natural and spiritual worlds. A newcomer to the intellectual circle was Mollie Price, a radical journalist from Chicago, with whom Cook immediately fell in love.

After spending some time at the University of Chicago, Susan came back to Davenport to discover she had become a celebrity. The *Trident* of July 30, 1904, called attention to her many short stories, one of which had been awarded a $500 prize. With Banks she presided over a meeting of literati at Winona Lake. In 1906 she was elected to the elite Tuesday Club, a women's study group, and was on her way to succeeding Alice French as the "literary queen" of Davenport.

But she was also attracted to a very different group. "Declining to go with my parents in the morning, I would . . . set out for the Monist Society in the afternoon, down an obscure street which it seemed a little improper to be walking on as everything was closed for Sunday, upstairs through a sort of side entrance over a saloon. . . . Suppertables of Davenport would be different that night because of the Monist Society."

The Society soon found itself embroiled in a public issue, the town library board's banning of *The Finality of the Christian Religion*. The Monists took up the cause of free speech and succeeded in electing a new mayor who promised to appoint a more liberal library board. One of Susan's short stories, "'Finality' in Freeport" makes literary capital of this event.

The attractions of the Monist Society were not merely intellectual. It was at this time that Susan became reacquainted with George Cram Cook just as he was marrying Mollie Price. The two fell in love, and it was not long before Susan was making excursions to the Buffalo estate under the pretext of soliciting Cook's advice on *The Glory of the Conquered*.

Dell had been shown how to criticize and revise his own work by Marilla Freeman. Now a hired hand at the Cook cabin and falling in love with Mollie, while Cook was publicly demonstrating his affection for Susan, he was able to show Susan how she might improve the novel. Cook, however, was the more important influence: "What (Cook) wanted was to shape life in a form most hospitable to the creative thing in us all," said Susan. And Arthur Davison Ficke noted that while Cook was a failure in his own work, "his inspired words in the endless talkfests, his enthusiasm always upon artistic integrity, made him in the highest sense the leader. . . ."

The Glory of the Conquered was published in 1909 while Susan, apparently concerned about her emotional state, had gone to Europe with Lucy Huffaker. She was not at home to read the Davenport *Times'* comment that "there is a breadth of thought and depth of feeling in its conception as a whole that is remarkable for so young a writer," or the *New York Times'* plaudits: *"The Glory of the Conquered* brings forward a new author of fine and notable gifts."

Susan's first novel may well have been a projection of her love for Cook. It tells the story of an all-powerful love of a couple with opposing ideas of reality, she an artist, he a scientist engaged in cancer research. Her philosophy degree, as well as her exposure to the ideas of Cook and his mother, may account for the novel's Platonic undertones and flavor of German idealism; her recent Chicago sojourn furnished its setting, the University of Chicago campus.

Because her first novel was both a critical and a popular success, Susan was encouraged to try a second, and the summer of 1910 she was again visiting at the Buffalo cabin seeking literary advice from Cook. Mollie was expecting a second child, and her husband and Susan were much together:

> Susan and I had a day of creative energy here about a girl going to the city to seek her social salvation—a questess. . . . We (asked) the model to . . . tell the story of her life. . . . Somehow the reality—graver, weightier than our incipient dream—overwhelmed us. Before that, Susan wanted to play with a socialist-individualist contrast between the girl and the man, and I suggested having them each convert the other and wind up on the other side. We rejoiced in that until our model arrived and then—her socialism is such a deep slow growth, having so many roots so far back in her experience, that we felt how shallow and unreal it was to try to uproot such a thing.

The man in *The Visioning* is a boat-mender who lives on a corner of the Arsenal Island; he seems to be an obvious projection of the ardent

Socialist Cook must have been at the time. Katie Wainwright, the socialite who becomes interested in evolution, socialism, pacifism and feminism as a result of his influence, reflects Susan's intellectual growth. Although Johnson Brigham, at the time dean of Iowa letters, preferred Susan's sentimental short stories and first novel to this sometimes shocking work, *The Visioning* is a much better novel than her first.

The scandal of the Cook-Glaspell relationship broke about the two writers as *The Visioning* went to press. This event provided Susan with an excuse to travel to New York, avoiding the censure of her friends and neighbors. Even Floyd Dell was unsympathetic. "How many times are you going to ask me to believe in your eternal love for some girl?" he wrote Cook. Rabbi Fineschreiber was equally distressed, calling Susan an "amateur vampire," and her lover "a child who tires of his toys too easily."

In the spring of 1911 Cook separated from Mollie and followed Dell to Chicago to become his assistant on the *Friday Literary Review*. Ficke was still trying to break loose from his law practice and become a poet; two sonnets which he wrote about this time appeared in the first issue of the new *Poetry*. Alice French's career was all but over, her fame behind her. Charles Eugene Banks had left Davenport for the West. Only Susan Glaspell was left, still "boarding" at her parents' home, facing, every time she went out, the disfavor of Davenport citizens.

Her feelings of frustration, longing and ambivalence appear in the last novel she wrote before the Provincetown period. *Fidelity* chronicles the development of an emancipated woman who frees herself of every kind of convention in an attempt to become a totally self-defined human person. Constructed so that no extraneous incidents of superfluous characters intrude upon its design, unmarred by the sentimental tone and clumsy sentences of her earlier fiction, *Fidelity* is Susan's best novel.

But the novel was not prophetic. *Fidelity* portrays a woman who elopes with her married lover, only to leave him after she realizes that their relationship is as limiting as the Midwestern conventions that prohibit their love. As the story ends, she is alone, faithful only to herself. Susan and George Cram Cook were married in 1913 and lived together until his death in 1924. Although she would live and write in Greece and England, as well as in New York and Provincetown, her thoughts were never very far away from her Iowa birthplace. Almost everything she was to write thereafter would have Iowa settings, characters or overtones.

The most interesting of these efforts is *Judd Rankin's Daughter,* published only three years before her death. In this book, Susan focuses on the conflict between the isolationist spirit and a more liberal, world-minded attitude, using setting as well as characters to dramatize this problem. Judd Rankin of Davenport is "Iowa stubborn" in his fight to conserve the values and traditions of his pioneer ancestors while his son-in-law, Len Mitchell, an eastern writer, battles fascism and anti-Semitism.

In the middle stands Judd's daughter, Frances, whose ambivalent feelings reflect Susan's ability to revere and criticize simultaneously her Midwestern heritage. "The Middle Western scene was for her not something to be lived down or forgotten," said Bartholomew Crawford. "(It was one) of her richest resources; and in every reference to the region of her birth, there is affectionate understanding and sympathy."

. . . Marcia Noe and Clarence Andrews, 1979

Susan Glaspell in her Davenport, Iowa, home

Dubuque—Bridges on the Mississippi

Remember Memorial Day? and
That Old-Time Fourth of July

WHEN WE WERE YOUNG in Cedar Rapids, Paul Engle and I, there were a number of special days—"holidays," in some cases—which brought long-remembered excitements—New Year's, St. Valentine's, Lincoln's Birthday, Washington's Birthday, Decoration Day, the Fourth of July, Labor Day, Hallowe'en, Thanksgiving and Christmas. On New Year's Eve we were permitted to stay up late and listen to the sound of church bells, factory whistles and gun shots. On St. Valentine's Day we had a special hour when Teacher drew valentines from a heart-decorated box and handed them around; if I got one from Helen Morrison my day was made. For the two President's birthdays we decorated our classrooms and dressed up for parts in brief pageantry, usually about Lincoln returning a few cents to an aged widow or George chopping down a cherry tree. Decoration Day (which became Memorial Day by the time Engle wrote about it) we went out to the cemetery and "decorated" the graves with flowers. And so on.

In the following two articles Paul Engle, in that pleasant prose style of his, recalls for us his own memories of a family's visit to the graves of its ancestors, and of Cedar Rapids, Iowa, Fourth of Julys.

Remember Memorial Day?

THE WAY WE CELEBRATED IT, there was little gloomy about Memorial Day; everything we did was gay and life-giving. Early in the morning my sisters and I would be out cutting flowers, wrapping the stems in damp cloth. It was important that we take our own flowers to our own people. My older brother would come out with his pocket knife, the big blade honed to an edge so sharp he would take a hair from my head and hold it up, and as he slashed at it like a scalping Indian he would shout proudly, "Couldn't feel it, could you?" Because he was tall, he would cut the lilacs with his knife, piling the blooms into my arms until their fragrance seemed as solid as the flowers themselves and the sprays reached as high as my head. I was allowed to gather some iris with the knife, and I can still hear the crisp, ripping sound as the blade severed the stalks.

By now my father would have driven up, our favorite chestnut horse, Alice, hitched to the light wagon. Alice was one of those gracious ladies with whom the world is blessed, gentle-mannered, sturdy, fond of children. On her patient and shining back all of us learned to ride. We learned to post in the saddle on her smooth trot and to rock smoothly in her rocking-chair canter. Now she was gleaming for the holiday. After all, you can curry and brush a horse in a tenth the time it takes to wash a car.

Into the wagon went our Memorial Day equipment; a lawn mower, a sickle, a picnic basket, all of the bundles of flowers, a horse blanket for spreading on the ground while we ate. The four children sat in back and our parents on the seat, my father trailing the lines behind him so that I could hang onto them and pretend to help drive.

Off we trotted in the bright sun, a wagon load of good smells, the fresh oat straw on which we sat, the flowers surrounding us with their mingled odors, the picnic basket with its fragrance of fresh home-baked bread, the tang of hot leather and the sweating horse.

We drove six miles to the small town where my mother's people were buried. The cemetery was a long wooded hill, very gay with people moving around and all of them carrying armloads of flowers and baskets. My father took the lawn mower, my brother the sickle, my sisters the flowers, while my mother and I shared the basket handles. There was a dense bush we called a snowball at the head of the plot, and thrushes had always nested there by the end of May, rushing out of the branches with an angry twittering when we approached, for after all, it was their place all the rest of the year.

My mother's father had been a Civil War veteran so that he had the little military marker with a tiny flag at his grave. We usually arrived just as the parade reached the cemetery, so that I could watch the few surviving veterans stand raggedly and proudly while a detail fired blanks into the air. I remembered my grandfather sniffing at the modern rifles, saying, "You ought to have heard those muskets we had. Didn't need to shoot a man. The *sound* would kill him."

It was a pleasant visit, with the tiny flags bright on the hill, the home-grown flowers adding their colors to all the shrubs in bloom, the slope full of the cheerful sound of whirring lawn mowers as families, under the old-fashioned custom long since changed, tended the graves them-selves. There was only one moment of sadness for me—when I saw the short grave of the one brother in my mother's family who had died young. For him I had been named, and often heard the story of how he went swimming in the creek one hot August day, came home, put his head under the pump while the cold water ran over it, and that night fell desperately ill, was paralyzed, and died two days later. He had been eight years old at his death, and as my own eighth birthday came closer I was scared of becoming eight, for did I not have his name, and might I not follow his brief career just as I followed his name? On the first Memorial Day after I had turned nine I came to his grave with a feeling both of relief at having lived beyond the fatal year and of sym-pathy for this uncle who from that time on would always be younger than I.

The graves neat and the flowers arranged on them, we would load up the wagon and drive out into the country along a curving sandy road where Alice would have to strain and the children would hop out and run alongside. We picked wild flowers, blue lupine, gentian, vio-lets, wild roses to add to the tame ones from home. We had a spade in the wagon, and now and then would dig up an entire bush of wild roses for planting in the rural cemetery we were going to.

This was country where both Mother and Father had lived as chil-dren, and they remembered every place. It was almost a homecoming as my father would point with his long whip and say, "Look at that, somebody must have bought the old Glass place." And my mother would look across the road and ask, with a light echo of homesickness in her gentle voice, "Remember when the Grieshabers moved in there? Couldn't speak a word of anything but German." And my father would reply, "There was an honest man. I never had to go out and smell *his* hay before I bought it."

So it was that this trip to the dead brought back to the living a heightened sense of their own lives. To the children, it gave an awareness of the ranging life behind them, of the very people who had made that road.

As a girl, Mother had walked down that road to the little schoolhouse which was our destination. She had walked it in the drifted snow of winter and in the bright, flowering mornings of May. As we drove into the schoolyard she would say with that wonderful gaiety she never lost, "This is the only place in the world where your mother was a second baseman!" There it would be still, the primitive baseball diamond where she played at recess with the Blass and the Grieshaber and the Shane and the Reinhemer kids.

My father would loosen the check rein on Alice and give her a nosebag of oats, my brother would go to the pump and rattle vigorously away at it until the water, cold from the deep pipe and tasting of the sweet limestone through which it ran, came splashing into his bucket. My sisters would spread out the clean horse blanket and help my mother unpack our lunch. We always had a jug with lemon juice and sugar and would fill it with the icy water, so that we had drawn our lemonade, as it were, from under the field where my mother had played baseball with the farm boys many years before. Under the white oak trees, on the grass so green and heavy it seemed to have grown a measurable height just while we sat there, we ate the cold chicken with crisp home-made dill pickles (there was wild dill growing along the edge of the field) and fresh-baked bread.

Rested, we would pack up and drive on to the country cemetery where my father's mother was buried. This was a tiny place where all of the graves were neighbors with whom my father's family had exchanged work when someone was ill. On all sides were cornfields and pastures, and when we arrived, cattle would come up to the fence and stare across, their brown eyes (they were always Jerseys and Guernseys) as deep as the wells and springs we had seen that day, as liquid and as alive. They stood there quietly and with the stolid poise of those who had come to pay their own friendly respects to the dead.

"This is nice," my mother said on the Memorial Day when I was eight, "this is nice." Sitting on the path, holding her large plumed and feathered hat on her lap, she watched the cemetery busy with people mowing and cutting and trimming.

Although my brother, older, larger, stronger, usually pushed the old lawn mower, I would be allowed to do so on such Memorial Days as I had the courage to walk over the graves. It always gave me a ghostly feeling to wander crookedly over the one mound we had come to visit. It felt as if the ground was unsteady beneath me, slightly pitching and tossing, and I would hang onto the handle of the mower for fear of being upset and pulled down below the grass.

The general mood, however, was bright and lively. We would put out the tame and wild flowers we had brought, set one of the wild rosebushes dug up along the road, and watch others moving about filling vases and calling warmly to each other. There would always be friends to come over and recall the cherished past. Some would have known my grandmother and would say enthusiastically, "My, she certainly would have liked the lilacs."

By now it would be late afternoon, the grave would be neat and gay, the fresh odor of cut grass, flowers, plowed field, pasture, and evergreen would be heavy in the air. So again we would load the wagon and settle wearily in the rustling straw.

When you start an auto and turn home, it is still the same mechanical process, but a horse is a revived and eager animal when you head it down a fine country road toward its barn. It steps out with liveliness, you can feel its anticipation carried up through the reins in your hand, and I could feel it even in the ends which I would clutch as Alice trotted off toward town. The sand would rise on the iron rim of the wheel and fall away with a tiny whispering sound. The wagon itself seemed to feel Alice's cheerfulness, and bounced along with a gayer motion. The straw gleamed more golden as the sun's light thickened in the west.

The children would grow sleepy with the jogging of the horse and the rocking of the wagon. My younger sister would curl up with her doll and doze off, while my older sister talked dresses with our mother. My older brother would argue the glories and disasters of the local baseball team, called the Bunnies, which leapt around the diamond with rabbits on their shirts. As we drove into the street by our house and tied Alice up to the horsehead hitching post, Father would slap her on the rump and say, "That's what she's needed, a real workout on the road." Alice would toss her head in a tired acknowledgment that the remark was probably true.

My brother had to go on to the barn to help with the horses, but I was small enough to be sent right to bed after a sandwich and a glass of milk. The whole long day had been a family affair and I hated to leave the human closeness which was so much warmer than on an ordinary day. The taste of water from the spring, the feel of cold water from the schoolhouse pump, the colorful brightness of tiny American flags, the smell of the sun hot on thorny rosebushes, the cud-grinding cows peering over the fence with animal curiosity, the farm families we met already tanned with working in the fields, these were jammed into my head as I trudged off to sleep.

Our Memorial Day was observed, not to remind the living of the dead but to assure the dead that life still went on in all its luck and wonder over the face of the remembering earth.

... Paul Engle, 1959

Memorial Day Observance

That Old-Time Fourth of July

WE WON THE AMERICAN REVOLUTION, but we lost the Fourth of July. I believe in the "safe and sane" Fourth, of course, and am grateful that my children are growing up without losing fingers to five-inch salutes or eyes to misfiring Roman candles. But in my heart I mourn that wonderful, mad, violent day. For a little while we shared a little of the risk that the old Continental troops had taken. Handling firecrackers, setting off rockets, blasting tin cans into the air, somehow we were close to that dangerous, original event.

When I was a boy in Iowa we started our short day, as those firm farmers at Concord Bridge had started their long war, with an explosion of powder. At dawn we sneaked off to the blacksmith shop, where the blacksmith, powerful in the pride of his brawny arms and his leather apron, would put a big charge of powder on an anvil. Then he would insert a fuse and put another anvil on top. When ignited, the powder blew up with a tremendous roar and a crash of iron, blasting indignant citizens from their beds, sending dogs howling under houses and bushes, terrifying horses in their barns.

Afterward we scattered to burn up in a few hours the fireworks we had bought with money painfully earned by selling newspapers and mowing lawns. All over town the debauch of our savings went on, a noise like the skirmishing of muskets, sounds our children do not know. What else booms like a giant firecracker lit and wildly thrown down a sewer, its long underground roar echoing through the pipes? There were "sons-o'-guns" which sputtered and crackled when rubbed over the sidewalk, or went tearing into your legs if you dropped a rock on them. We would light whole strings of tiny "ladyfingers" and throw them into the air, to catch in trees and carry on a private, spitting war at each other.

Sometimes the bigger boys would turn up with a crude cannon made from iron pipe plugged at one end. We would lie on the slopes of lawns like miniature Bunker Hills and admire their recklessness, dreading (and yet secretly hoping) that the whole infernal machine would blow up. Often it did, and those heroes would be carried home howling. The streetcars helped, too. We would put rows of torpedoes along the track and watch them shatter sideways with a ruddy flare. How patiently the motormen endured our follies!

Those noises are gone, and so are the smells—above all, the dense, brown odor of smoldering punk, used to ignite the firecracker fuses. Nothing in the world has that damp, persistent smell; mingled with burning powder, it made the air itself seem scorched. My grandfather always said that it rained so much during Civil War battles because the gunpowder explosions brought rain out of the clouds. I would stand there sniffing, to see whether our effort would not produce at least a shower.

The biggest event of the day was the parade, always with its Civil War veterans, my grandfather among them. He was a big, gentle man with a tremendous white beard, which he would trim before the mirror as he prepared for the parade. It was hard for me to think of him waving a saber and shouting in a cavalry charge. Yet when he had put on his uniform and braced himself for the march that he would not admit was exhausting, there would be in his effort to stand perfectly erect in spite of his farmer's stoop such a fierce determination that I could suddenly imagine the bloody and desperate young trooper. His jaw would set as I never saw it through the rest of the year, and he would step out with a hard look on his face that scared me.

I remember the Fourth of July when the family felt he was not strong enough to walk the distance. He shouted that it was bad enough for a cavalryman to walk like a foot soldier but, by the eternal, it was a disgrace to ride in a stinking automobile! But he gave in (his worst defeat of the war) and rode with a few other casualties of age, sitting grim and erect and ashamed.

Along with the risk to hands and eyes, there was one more menace on the Fourth—the public oration, delivered from the bandstand in the block-square park. The audience stood sweltering in the sun, unflinching in the face of volley after volley of murderous oratory. The speaker defended the Constitution fiercely, to an audience not precisely hostile to that noble document. There was fist-pounding praise of the sterling native stock which was the backbone of the country. This my grandfather took seriously, although his family came from Europe and he spoke German before learning English. Thanks were given to God for providing so few Indians to be chased from this fertile soil, and to the Milwaukee Railroad for sending a brass band.

While this fancy language held the crowd, there was always a handful of daring boys skulking on its fringes, throwing lighted firecrackers at each other, and causing horses to rear and plunge. Small children would crouch over little cones which, when the tip was lit, sent out twisting brown snakes. Usually snakes and children were stepped on as the crowd shifted, and piercing shrieks would ascend to heaven along with the speech.

Next came that furious trial by food called the Fourth of July picnic. On the banks of the Cedar River a collection of food was spread out as if a regiment were momentarily expected after a hard day's ride. All of it would be from the home farm: the fried chicken, the ham, the pickles (dill, sweet, watermelon), huge loaves of bread baked in the iron stove, butter churned that morning.

Best of all for the children was the ice cream, made on the spot. The can would be covered with chipped ice and salt and we would all take turns at the handle, enthusiastically at first and then wearily; but the rule was, "One hundred strokes after it gets hard to turn." Finally the great moment came when the dasher was pulled out, dripping with the best ice cream a boy ever tasted. But of course the other food had to be eaten first, and anything less than painful overeating was considered disloyal.

Night brought its own glories and dangers. Sparklers would dazzle the dark with their sudden light, and pinwheels would hiss and whir where they were nailed on trees. Some child always was burned by walking into a Roman candle. We'd use a section of rainspout for launching skyrockets, and it was a magnificent moment when the rocket burst from the end of the spout and tore into blackness with a trail of fire.

The day ended as the celebration of a time of danger and triumph should end: dirty, exhausted, bandaged and blistered, we struggled off to bed. A battle, in which only one side fired, had been won. The country was safe for another year and so were we.

. . . Paul Engle, 1958

Fourth of July Parades in Iowa.

Maquoketa, Iowa, 1919

The Cities of Iowa—Cedar Rapids

ALTHOUGH HE WAS BORN in the Wapsipinicon River town of Waubeek and educated in the public schools of Central City, Jay Sigmund, a business man turned author and poet, came to call Cedar Rapids his home.

As in many another town in Iowa and the United States, the 1920s were boom years in Cedar Rapids. The boom was particularly noticeable in downtown Cedar Rapids, with its new Roosevelt Hotel, Iowa Theatre, Capitol (later Paramount) Theatre, and its Merchants National Bank, the latter's 12-story granite-block building the "skyscraper" of the "loop."

And over on the Island, the governmental center of both the city and Linn County, there were two new buildings—the Greek-columned Courthouse, built after the county seat was "stolen" from Marion, and the City Hall-Memorial Building whose south tower, bearing at its very pinnacle a likeness of a soldier's bier, reached as high into the Iowa sky as did the bank's building.

That building became even more famous after Grant Wood's stained glass window, with its figures of the soldiers of America's wars, was added.

It was in this boom atmosphere that Jay Sigmund wrote his hyperbolic tribute to his adopted city, a tribute more poetic than accurate. But in those days, who needed reality—wasn't prosperity going to last forever?

Cedar Rapids

The glacier in its hungry mood crawled down,
Gnawing Earth's bosom into hills and swales —
Leaving the land a million scars and wounds
Before the suns of years could slaughter it
And send its fabric, liquid to the sea.
But when the monster ice-cap sunk to fog
It left a wealth of mellow, fertile drift,
Full of the very elements men need
To feed their sinews and to build their bones.

Here was the fertile loam which tall plants crave,
Here by the silver river where the stag
Came when the birds had scattered strong-germed seeds:
Here were the hills where giant red-oaks grew,
Kissed by the gifts of clouds for ages gone.
This was the land where hunger dared not come
Because of greening slopes which mocked at it!

And this is why beside this silver stream
The men of muscle with the dream-filled souls —
The men who loved the song of vernal winds
And held the red-wing's marsh-notes in their hearts
Came prairieward and stopped their sweating spans;
Spreading their canvas underneath the stars
Saying, "This land is good — Oh, we are glad!
Here is our journey's end — now we shall rest."

                          Their hammer blows
Came ringing down the morning, year on year:
The seasoned timber made their strong roof-trees
And limestone from the river cliffs their hearths:
Slowly, but with the sureness of the moon
As it goes swinging through the night's dark arch,
A city grew apace among these knolls —
A clean white city by a silver stream.

Across the seas
Went tidings of this place which strong men built
And those to whom the tyrant's yoke seemed harsh
Came, with a pulsing gladness in their breasts,
To lay their best gifts at this city's door —
The gift of manhood and of honest toil.

Year upon year
Trooped onward in their never-ending course,
As a regiment of soldiers march to war,
After the loosing of the first gun's wrath:
The silver river gave its flood of strength
To turning roaring wheels for bruising grain;
The hillside pastures brought their herds as gifts —
The sledge and droning saw were never stilled.
Though foes gave threat and blood was given up
From sons the city spared with tears and pain
The wings of gentle peace were close at hand
And in the main, through all the span of years,
Each breaking dawn has smiled upon a folk,
Who labored at their tasks until the dusk
Sent them across their door-sills with a song —
A song of gladness for the boon of toil.

Oh, spotless city by the wave-kissed banks
With hordes of singing workers on your streets —
With shirring wheels that grind the prairie's crop
And feed the children of a hungry earth:
Be proud and send your towers to the sky;
Be proud and spread across the fertile plains —
Send out your toiler's voice to summon all —
Invite the world to seek your busy marts
But keep your tulips and your cherry trees —
Your ordered gardens and your lilac blooms:
Guard well your cardinals and tiny wrens —
Let nothing rob you of your plots of green.

Yes, turn your wheel and windlass — shape your beams —
Be jealous of the power of your men
But never let your songs of joy be hushed
Or stain your beauty with the breath of greed
And keep your children happy . . . keep your soul!

. . . Jay Sigmund, 1926

Robert Nunn, 1930

A German Grandfather

IN THE NINETEENTH CENTURY, many ethnic peoples came into Iowa—Norwegians, Danes, Swedes, Germans, Italians, Dutch, Irish, English, French, Bohemians, Croatians, and others—and helped make Iowa the state that it became. At first many of these people settled near each other—Bohemians and Norwegians in northeast Iowa, Danes in west central Iowa, Irish in Leo R. Ward's rural section of Monroe County, the Dutch in Marion and Sioux counties, the Scotch in Tama and Jones counties.

There isn't room in this collection to look at all of these groups. So here, for a sample that might represent all of them, is Ruth Suckow's essay on her German grandfather, that touches many kinds of immigrant experiences—the reasons for leaving the old country, the long, hard sea voyage, the hard work to earn money to bring over a sweetheart or a relative, the journey westward, the belief that while the new world might be like the old, it was somehow better.

Ruth Suckow, one of Iowa's most distinguished authors, was born in Hawarden, Iowa, in 1892, then a new town on the western border of Iowa. As the daughter of a peripatetic Congregational minister, she spent her childhood in Algona, Fort Dodge, Manchester and Grinnell. She attended Grinnell College, then took bachelor's and master's degrees from the University of Denver. At the beginning of her career, she assisted John Towner Frederick at the University of Iowa; he introduced her work to the editors of American Mercury *and to Alfred Knopf; they began publishing her early short stories and novels—a total of thirteen books. She was married to Ferner Nuhn of Cedar Falls, a novelist and critic. She died in 1960.*

A German Grandfather

THE WAR WAS THE FIRST THING to make me realize that I actually came of German ancestry. Nearly every Summer of my childhood we had visited the farm where one grandmother and grandfather sat in rockers side by side, and the little Iowa town where the other grandmother and grandfather lived in a frame house painted in red and white to make it look as if it had been built of brick. But the ways of these old people were so different from any I had ever known that I had no real sense of belonging to them. There was nothing German in our home except noodle soup, a tree and frosted cookies at Christmas, and brown-covered copies of *Die Gartenlaube*. Our parents spoke German only when Christmas and birthdays were at hand; or when my mother, calling some queer old customer by a still queerer name, laughed and said, "Don't ask me to translate that!" We girls learned our German in school; and my sister (who, on a very fragile pretext, had always considered herself French) had so little talent for it that my mother read her lesson to her every morning while combing her curls. Years ago, in a pre-historic age so far as I was concerned, my father had gone over to the English from the German Methodist Church, and from that had graduated as far as the creedless Congregational.

At the time of the war, a member of our family objected to voting for a man who "had a foreign name." The names of our grandfathers were Suckow and Kluckholn. But the name of the German township, to which they had come as early settlers, had been changed to Liberty. At this same time one or two leading matrons of our city walked out of the Auditorium as a patriotic protest against the singing of German *Lieder* by Alma Glück. Our family was divided as to the necessity of this. I got out my sister's favorite old book of Schubert songs and picked out the air of "Du bist die Ruh" with one finger as my own private protest. I thought about the German songs I had heard my grandfather sing to his youngest grand-daughter, under the apple trees on the farm, to keep her out of mischief while her mother was at work. I didn't remember a great deal about either of my grandfathers—my mother's father, a minister, had died when I was a child—but what I did remember was singularly out of keeping with current notions about the Hun.

Later, my father and I visited my grandfather in Iowa. The war was over. He seemed to have been amazed by it rather than embittered. "Didn't de Germans help to settle all dis country?" he asked. "Why, den, are de Germans so bad?" He had come out to German township in a day when it was actually such boundless prairie that once, after wandering for hours at night, he knocked at a door to ask his way and found himself looking into his own house. This quaint little old man was so remote, now, even from the life of his own neighborhood, that I suppose few people had ever thought of the danger to the State from his existence.

We found him in a room with blue walls, attached to, yet separate from, the rest of the house. This was where he and my grandmother had spent their last housekeeping days together. The farm was the one that he himself had taken on the prairie. His son had worked it for years, but had now moved into town and left it to *his* son. My grandfather stayed. His reason was that Grandma had died in this room and he wanted to die there too. To me he seemed more like a figure in a German picture or a folk song than an actual old man. He gave me the same sort of delight as a finished work of art.

He gave me, too, an understanding of a statement by Einstein: Life tends to turn upon itself. When we visited there, it was perfect September weather. Stepping out of a landscape that seemed to be all blue and gold, we entered a room that was blue and silver. Against the wall hung my grandfather's big silver watch. He was sitting in his rocker in front of the open door that faced the blue sky. He wore a black skullcap and smoked a black pipe. His beard was silver and his eyes were as blue as those of very little children. One had a curious cast that added to his air of wistful drollery. Bees had found an entrance into the wall of the farmhouse years ago, and they hummed outside the open door.

He was too deaf to join very much in the conversation. Hearing, however, that we were planning a trip South, he begged us earnestly not to go. There were only two places in this country, he assured us, where human beings ought to live: York State and old Iowa. "Where you have lived," my uncle suggested. "Ja," he answered, and puffed smoke from his pipe. We all laughed and that pleased him. In fact, Iowa was even better and safer than York State. It was foolish to bother to take a trip out of Iowa. Hancock County was the best county, German township (he never quite got used to Liberty) was the best place in that county, and this farm was the best and safest spot in the world. We should all stay here. "But what would I do?" my father asked. He could sell old iron. That was a good business. Again the eye with the cast glanced off drolly askew and he puffed at his pipe. But most of the afternoon he did not attempt to talk with the rest of us. He rocked and smoked, and at times he murmured with a sigh, "Ach, ja, ja . . . dot was all so long ago!"

But he did have to move into town at last, like a good Iowa farmer. He still kept up his own establishment, however. When I saw him next he was living in a little one-room building called Grandpa's House in the back yard of my uncle's home. There were his own bed, his wooden rocker, his silver watch, and a kerosene lamp which my aunt came in to light every evening, since he now declared that he could not experiment with so newfangled a contraption. "What a big lady!" he exclaimed in astonishment whenever I came. But time, too, had turned upon itself. The past and the present were all intermingled. "*Ja,*" he would say then, "now I have a little girl again to hear my stories." He told me about wild happenings in the timber country in Northeastern Iowa. But when I left, he always warned me, "Be careful when you cross the railroad tracks!" The town where he now lived was a station on a little stub line of the railroad. One train went up in the morning and came back at night.

II

We all received these warnings. He begged us not to eat tomatoes for fear of the seeds, while he himself dined happily off cranberries and thick cream. Whenever the family set off on an excursion he went out to look at the sky and urged them to stay at home because it looked as if it might rain. He consented to an automobile ride only because "the rest of you are going to be killed and I want to be killed with you." My father was spending his vacation at a little fresh-water lake when he received word that my grandfather had broken his hip. The old man was suffering almost too much to talk with him, but he still could plead, "Willie, when you go back to the water, promise me never to go out in a sail-boat!"

But no one could get him to explain the discrepancy between these warnings and his own career. Many of his stories were concerned with the seven weeks of stormy weather which he had spent in a sail-boat crossing the Atlantic. "Ja, ja, those were fine times!" he said. He came to this country not knowing a word of English, and without enough money to pay for a berth when he took the boat to Albany. Later, with his wife and children, he struck out for the West and took a farm in the timber in Northeastern Iowa, where the woods were so thick that my father used to get lost trying to find the cows in the evening. My father told how terrified they all were during one of the annual floods of the Volga River, when the cows were carried off downstream and my grandfather on his horse plunged straight into the torrent after them. Later, my grandfather wanted to try still newer country, and they all set out again for the slough and prairie region farther West. "But to hear Grandpa talk," my father said, "you would think he was the most timid man in the world!" He could never understand why any of his children or grandchildren could be foolish enough to venture beyond the limits of German township.

His stories had now dwindled into stories about them. He always declared that he liked farming; but that he was never a real farmer was shown by the fact that he had wanted to stay on his land, would have considered California unfit for human habitation, and was more contented after his retirement than before. Then he had found a job that really suited him much better. There was a baby girl in the house and he took her in charge. All day long he sang songs and told stories. This was the only one of his various activities that he seemed to regret when it was past. "Ach," he said, "what shall I do? I have no little girls any longer!" While he was still on the farm, he had liked to gather the eggs. But when he came into town, this too was over. His eyes became too dim to read and he was so deaf that he could not talk much with people. So few came to see him that he had little chance to tell his stories. My aunt told him about what was happening in the world. But when she came to the radio, he threw up his hands and said that that was too much. His range of travel had narrowed down to an occasional excursion to the store for his tobacco. Then it seemed too venturesome to go out upon the one business street among all the automobiles. He stayed in his room and finally in his rocking chair, and he had very little left to do except pray and sing to himself. But he got great contentment out of these two things.

When he heard that his grand-daughter had published a story, he said that she ought to be given a title. "Ven de men do something more, dey call dem *von*, or dey call dem *bishop!* Why not den de ladies?" But he pondered over it. He said, "My mind is all de time so full of what happened in de old country, and here in de early days, why can I not write it into a story?" He had to tell his stories instead; and it was not until I was a "big lady" that I had a chance to hear many of them. More and more came back to him the older he grew. He told about the tall ancestor who had run away from Prussia so that he would not have to join the Emperor's six-foot regiment. "Schneiderlien, Schneiderlien!" the soldiers called. "Ja, come get 'Schneiderlien'!" he shouted back from over the boundary in Mecklenburg. He told about the molasses barrels that tipped over on deck in the storm at sea; and about Yankee Jim who shot up a town in Iowa and then stood on a hilltop just outside and shouted to a comrade: "Bill! Go fetch me my coat! I want to take it with me!"

In those days my grandfather used to get great amusement out of taking bachelor farmers around to call upon prospective wives. He would not permit them to give up, no matter how poor the prospects seemed. The success of one of these marriages was proved by the gift of a dollar from the bride every Christmas. One tale was an account of his visit to a Catholic church:

"First, in come de priest. He was a big two-story man but dressed up in skirts just like de ladies. He had a little bell. 'Ting-aling-ling.' A little boy come from de one side and bring him a towel. 'Ting-aling-ling.' A little boy come from de udder side and he take off de first towel and put on de second. All he said, it was in Latin. De people, dey can't know what. But before dey all went home, he turn around to dem from de alter. He say: 'On dat horse and buggy I buy me, I still owe eighty dollars, and de eighty dollars you must see dot I get.' Dot," my grandfather concluded, "he could say in English!"

III

When we came to see him at holiday time, he was mourning because he had a cold and feared that he could not sing his Christmas songs. His voice had the sound of a very old, very worn, still sweet wind instrument, and he kept time with his hand. Most of the time, he used his German Methodist hymnal, but he also sang me "Freuch Euch des Leben" and said: "It is good. It is not religious. But it is good." He liked "Der Himmel ist Schön" because it was Grandma's song. When his voice grew husky, he took to his pipe. Once he asked, "Do you ever see papa smoke a pipe?" I said that I had. "Ja, dot is right!" he answered with great satisfaction.

One more move was required of him. After he broke his hip, he had to leave his little house and take up final quarters in the guest-room of his daughter's home. He sat all day long in his rocking-chair. He was glad to have people come into the room but seldom demanded it. Even in the other part of the house he could often be heard praying and singing. He was now the oldest settler in German township, and he could not understand why he should have lived so long. He heard of the deaths of the sixty-year-old men and women whom he still called "de young people." Ever since Grandma had died, he had been ready to go; and whenever my father came to see him for the last ten years he said in parting, "Well, Willie, when you come de next time, I will not be here." After he had been sitting for a long time smoking, he would murmur, "Ach, ja, ja . . . dot was all so long ago!"

But to our surprise, since for years he had not ventured a mile from home without grumbling, there was a journey, when he was ninety, that he wanted to make. And he was willing to go in an automobile! He said that he would like to look at the farm.

My father and I drove over with the car and my father and my cousin carried him out to it. This, again, was in September. It was a fine day in which to see the country: sunshine, wind, a brightness over everything—the dry corn, the dusty road, the willow trees on which small scanty leaves glittered. Everything was quiet and just as usual at the farm. We stayed half an hour or so, and then he wanted to go still far-ther. He would like to call on "de old Mutter Meyer," he said.

We drove on to the Meyer farm. It had the usual well-painted house and red barns and dog running out to bark at the car. The Meyers came out to talk to us. There were the old lady, her daughter whose husband now farmed the place, and an elderly son who had such a great memory that he could repeat nearly every verse in the Bible and had room left for nothing else in his mind Mutter Meyer had a clean pink face framed in a small black silk bonnet, edged with white. She was the only one of my grandfather's old neighbors left – the only one of his contemporaries who had come out in the early days to settle German township. They talked in German together – saying "Ach!" many times, and "Ja, ja . . . " – and then they said, "Auf wiedersehen."

That was the first trip that my grandfather had enjoyed since he had definitely decided to give up roaming and settle down into being Grand-pa. It was the first that he had made except under protest. It was his last. A few weeks later, he died. His death was as peaceful as his age had been, without consciousness or suffering. He had been out of the life of the place for so long that people had almost forgotten him until they heard that he was dead. But they went away from his funeral say-ing:

"A few more years and there will be none of the old settlers left!" – as had happened in one community after another, since the first settlers had come to America.

When he was a young man, my grandfather had worked in Albany until he could send back enough money for his sweetheart to join him in America. They had kept traveling West until, across the Mississippi, they had found some country which my grandfather had said was much like that which they had left in Germany. But Iowa was "nicer country," he declared. He had never wanted to return to Mecklenburg. That was "de old country," but this farm in German township – the best and safest place in the world – was home. They had worked hard there, they had raised seven children, and when these were grown they had taken a little girl from an orphanage for fear of being lonely. During my childhood, I remember them sitting side by side in their rockers, contented to be with each other. Out of all their work and wanderings, they had only this farm to show. His small savings my grandfather had invested in a German Methodist concern and lost.

Nevertheless, their long journey was, in its small way, successful and fortunate. There are few men who can sing in their old age. Both lie buried in the graveyard of the German Methodist church in Liberty township – the church they had helped to found, where only English is now spoken, and which, even so, is fast losing its members to the church in town. Some day, no doubt, this will be another of those neglected and forgotten rural burying-grounds that are scattered over this whole country, and the names "Dorothea" and "John Joseph," still fresh on the shiny stones, will have yielded to the weather.

But the year after my grandfather died, we heard German Christmas songs in the house again. They came over the radio, on Christmas night, from records made in Germany. A prima donna sang "Heilige Nacht," and we also heard the "good will message" of the president of the Reichstag to the people of the United States. The war was over—a war which my grandfather could never really believe had happened. He had brought over from "de old country" nothing in his pockets, and the German heritage which he had left his grandchildren was only these songs.

. . . Ruth Suckow, 1927

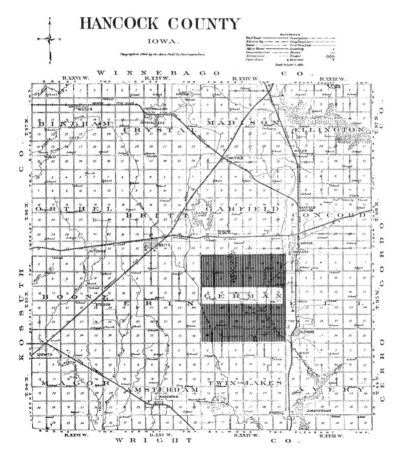

Harvest Time

THE TIME FOR BRINGING in the harvest of cash crops was an important part of the year for Iowa farmers, a time when a farmer could see how well he had done, could compare his crops with his neighbors, and a time when he could often cooperate with his neighbors in the social activities of the "threshing ring." Although there were independent custom operators who were hired by farmers to thresh their wheat and oats, the "ring," with its shared use of machinery and its trading off of work, was also important in the harvest scene.

Paul Corey, Frederick Manfred, Herbert Krause, and Phil Stong all made use of the threshing ring as part of the action of their several books about farming. In the following pages we see Phil Stong's description of one of the more memorable aspects of threshing time, the threshers' dinner. Stong focuses on the camaraderie of the occasion and the inevitable "horseplay," both verbal and physical, that accompanies many masculine work activities.

Grant Wood's 1933 Dinner for Threshers *manages to show all three parts of the dinner—washing up, eating (men and horses alike) and the women's work of cooking and serving.*

Herbert Quick's brief description shows an earlier era than that depicted by Wood. It was the time of the first "powered" threshing machine, the 1870s.

Phil[lip Duffield] Stong was born at Pittsburg, near Keosauqua, in Van Buren County (named for the man who was President when the county was founded), a fourth-generation Iowan. In If School Keeps *(1940), one of his more than forty books, he describes his education in the Keosauqua Public Schools and later at Drake University, where he graduated in 1919. After a short term as a journalist, he turned to fiction; his first novel,* State Fair *(1932), was so successful that it left no doubt as to his future.*

*Stong was married to Virginia Swain, who collaborated with him on his first book (*Shake 'Em Up!*, 1930) and was a novelist in her own right. Stong died in 1957.*

The "Buffalo Pitts"

THE PONDEROUS CYLINDER before him [began] to revolve, trying to gnash its polished steel teeth against those of the concaves, but
failing because they always passed each other by a hair's breadth. A
deep growl like that of a bulldog magnified fifty diameters, filled the
air, and as the cylinder gathered speed it rose from a bass to a baritone,
and then to a tenor of a volume which sang over four square miles of
haze-obscured prairie. The feeder looked up at the pitchers, saw the
man who pitched to the machine, with his next bundle ready to fall on
the table, saw Frank with his band-cutter's knife ready to slice softly
through the band of it, and then, he moved the first two sheaves gently
over between the open lips, deftly twitched their butts upward, and
the great operation was on. The tenor took a little lower note; the horses
felt the sweeps holding them back; the driver's shouts rose to a higher
and more peremptory tone; and if everything went well they were off
upon a half-day's run, during which the feeder's pride would be that he
would feed those four great stacks through the thresher so steadily
that not once would the thrashed straw in the straw-carrier fail to pass
in an unbroken stream, hiding the slats of the carrier; not once would
an inexpert handling of a bundle choke the thrasher down, even to a
baritone; to say nothing of a bass note; not once would the cloud of
chaff cease to rise from behind the sieves; not once would the stream
of wheat fail to flow into the half-bushel measures which would keep
the measurer and the man who hauled off in a perspiring hurry.

... Herbert Quick, *The Hawkeye,* 1923

High Noon at Harvest Time

EARLY THE NEXT MORNING a profane little tractor brought the great, boxlike harvester up the road toward the house and pulled it across the pasture to the wheat field. The crew was waiting for it. Farmers from three or four farms around in each direction had been arriving since six o'clock. At seven Thelma and Beatrice were in the kitchen roasting joints of meat, mixing dressing for the chickens, slicing cold meats, making bowls of cole slaw, opening jars of pickles, jellies, preserved fruits, pouring pie contents into crusts which were already half baked.

The pump handle turned, it seemed to Louise, continuously. Eager small boys, among whom she recognized Widdie, galloped in bareback on draught horses, pumped wildly and fled. Out in the wheat field a smoke of chaff began to rise from the machine, a pile of gold began to grow upon the ground where the bare straw was thrown down; by and by a wagon came in to the granary and Louise saw the fruit of many months and many acres shoveled into empty bins.

Louise was busy with preparations—setting the table; getting out basins and towels and pans full of soft soap, homemade of lard and wood ash, against the coming of the sweaty, straw-dusted men at noon. Occasionally one of the men on the wagons would pause at the pump

Grant Wood, Sketch for "Dinner for Threshers" (left section), 1933.

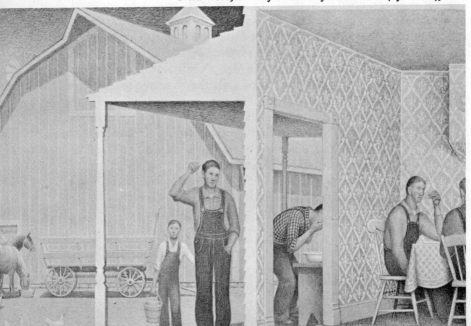

to shout a question about the identity of a smell from the kitchen. They did not shout at Louise. She was a stranger to nearly all of them.

The pile of gold grew—the wagons came and went—noon arrived. They came like troops rushing to mess. Suddenly the back yard was full of shouting men; if the pump handle had been turning before, it was spinning now; basins clattered.

"Purty damn good. It's going to beat Old Man Pearson's."

"Aw, the hell it will. It's harder grain, though—"

"My God, Jeff Slutts is a-washin'! First time since we started out this year!"

"Hey, Ancy, that soap ain't to eat!"

"Yay, Simon, boy, how you hold that stack down!"

And she heard Simon's familiar voice, "It's nothing to do with a bunch of paralytic old women like you."

"Paralytic, huh—"

She looked out of the dining-room door just in time to see Simon turn a man over his hip and slap him on the ground. There was a chorus of cheers. "He'd ought of known better, the damn fool—"

And the victim, brushing himself, said, "Well, if I wasn't before, I'm paralyzed now. Geeze, Simon, I'd ruther take on the threshing machine."

Simon was not magnanimous. He growled, "And I've been workin' all morning while you Ladies Aiders were watchin' the wheels go 'round."

Sketch for "Dinner for Threshers" (right section), 1933.

It was the first information she had had that Simon was a formidable person and was so regarded about the neighborhood. She made a swift readjustment of her conception of Simon as a laconic clown. The first of the farmers, an elderly man with a scraped face which showed prominent blood vessels, came and seated himself at the table. Louise waited at the kitchen door. And then they began to come in, two by two, one by one. Thelma hissed from the kitchen:

"You better begin taking things in!"

She carried in the platters of beef, chicken and pork; then she brought in a heaping bowl of mashed turnips; mashed potatoes; parsnips; boiled cabbage; a great pine-tree trencher of blanched lettuce and onions jellied with beef broth, to be sliced into salads; pickled beets hot from the stove—the preserves and jellies had been placed long before—creamed cauliflower; young gourds like oysters; brown gravy and cream gravy; mint sauce and pepper sauce; celery; young radishes; stuffed peppers containing mushrooms and calf's tongue; beet-top salad limp with hot mayonnaise—

"When you coming with the food, young lady?"

It was the veteran, the first arrival, who inquired. It was so notorious in Van Buren County that Storrhaven always fed threshers better than any other house that the customary competition between housewives had almost disregarded the place. The family recipes and the family menus were unassailable.

Louise looked up at the old man with a slightly concealed grin. "I didn't think I'd come with it until people began to get here. . . ."

"Uh!" He pulled his long mustaches and affected to be crushed. He moved his mouth slightly and phrases came from it like "impudent little whelp," "young upstarts," "little town brats—"

"Here," Louise said finally, "for God's sake take this gizzard and if Beatrice ever hears about it, Heaven help us all."

"That old devil has got the gizzard at Claytons', Bakers', Duffields', Bill Crothers', Pearsons', and now at Storrs'," said one of the younger threshers bitterly.

"I'll give you a gizzard too. Will you cut the beef, Grandpa?"

The younger thresher muttered something about the elder member of the company—"Stalling all around. Get everything that's fit to eat—damn shame—shoot off a lot of these old idiots—" It amused Louise to see that conversation could be orchestrated—that the strings and words of ideas could be made to fade and appear as impressions, nuances, by these strong and perspiring men.

There were a dozen of them at the table now and more coming from the yard. Louise busied herself at passing various bowls and platters; in keeping the dishes full from the kitchen; in refilling water glasses and maintaining the corpuscular movement of the food about the table. And yet a kind of etiquette obtained. Within their metes these men were more soft-voiced and gentle than any Louise had ever known.

The young thresher, his mouth full of food, complained softly, "Once Old Man Gilbert gets the gravy, you can't stop him till he's fished out the livers and everything."

Louise hurried in with fresh gravy. "Doesn't that make you feel better?"

"—we do all the work and they get all the gizzards—"

Another thresher looked up with a dry grin. "Say, Miss Storr, you going to let Arch Manning have all the buttered beets? I been sitting here a-waiting and a-waiting."

Louise secured the bowl for him. She did not smile. "I'm sorry you broke your arms this morning. What were you doing, fanning yourself? Or scaring away flies?"

"He rolled on them," one of the elder men said.

There was a tremendous clatter of silverware and chomping. "This little sliver of chicken ain't so bad. I know meat's expensive."

Grandpa handed Louise the platter and she took it around to the protestant. He served himself half of a fowl. "What they do these places," someone observed, "is not give you any water, so no matter how hungry you are you can't swallow."

Louise realized that she was being hazed, but she brought the water pitcher quietly. The joint of beef was down to the last slices; there were still chicken and half the roast of pork. A prolonged and hearty sigh was relayed around the table. Men nibbled at the salad.

"A good big hunk of pie would go mighty nice now—if there happened to be any pie around," the old man of the gizzards remarked hopelessly.

"—and another cup of coffee—"

"—and some more water—"

"—I think I could do one more drumstick—"

"Hellions!" Grandpa growled. "Ill-bred, lousy clodhoppers. Bet there isn't a one of you has had a square meal since last harvest."

Louise danced about the table and in and out of the kitchen, in an apparently hopeless race with the threshers' wants—real or invented. She was pink with heat and she could feel her hair clinging damply about her forehead, but her eyes were twinkling, and once Grandpa had so forgotten his patriarchal dignity as to look up at her and wink. Guy took his food as it came to him and grinned. She understood that this was an initiation; that these men were signifying that she was part of the community—a friend.

At last there was silence, except for sighs and the occasional rattle of an empty coffee cup.

At last there was silence, except for sighs and the occasional rattle of an empty coffee cup.

"If I could just have got to the blackberry pie before that old devil did," said the young thresher, indicating the old one. "I sure do love blackberry pie." He looked at the empty plates with exquisite longing. Louise had seen him eat two pieces of pie. She stopped before him sternly.

"You want more blackberry pie, do you?"

He shook his head dolefully. "I sure do love blackberry pie with lots of good, rich cream on it."

"You're sure you want another piece?"

"Oh, I wouldn't want to be no trouble."

Louise's eyes narrowed. "There's plenty more blackberry pie in the kitchen, but if I go and get it for you, you're going to eat every bite of it, or I'm going to push it down your throat."

The young thresher looked seriously disconcerted. He wriggled and glanced about the table, but there was no diversion. He knew that if he stumbled now the pack would be on his back in a minute.

"You better have a piece of pie, Homer," Grandpa said hospitably but firmly.

"Well, not too big a piece," Homer said weakly. "I don't want to founder this afternoon even if I do love blackberry pie."

Louise marched to the kitchen and returned with a generous piece of pie richly smeared with whipped cream. Homer had been steeling himself for pie, but at the sight of the cream a little moan escaped him. Louise placed the pie before him and stood back with her hands on her hips.

"I think that cream's turned a little," Homer said, brushing it back from the point of the wedge. He cut off a very small bite and ate it.

"That cream was perfectly all right five minutes ago," the older thresher said innocently. Homer shot him a mortal glance. The boy managed another infinitesimal bite. He gave Louise a piteous look, but her face was hard and merciless.

Homer slumped back in his chair and his arms dropped at his sides. "I guess my eyes was bigger than my stomach—"

"—you might have let me get them shut," he added a second later from the midst of a crimson ruin of blackberries and cream. There was a roar from the table. Louise, gurgling with amusement, handed Homer a dish towel.

"Wipe it off with this till you get out to the pump."

The old thresher rose and shook Louise's hand. "That's a mighty fine lesson for him ma'am. Now maybe the rest of us will get a bit to eat now and then."

"Do *you* want another piece of blackberry pie?" Louise inquired.

"No, ma'am, thank you just the same," the old thresher said virtuously. "I couldn't eat another bite."

The threshers rose and filed out to the lawn, laughing. "You might wrap me up a piece for supper, though," the old thresher shouted from the safety of the gate.

"Coward!" Louise called back. . . .

At five o'clock the faint bellow of the harvester suddenly stopped and the last wagons of grain came into the barnyard. The threshers were driving back across the farm by twos and threes and disappearing up the river road.

"G'by, Miss Louise," the old thresher shouted from a rattling wagon as he crashed through the drive on his way to the road. "You're a first-class thrashin' hand!"

It was an accolade which was completed by Homer. "Thanks for the pie. Save some for me next year."

. . . Phil Stong, Stranger's Return, 1933

Threshing in Iowa, 1890s   --Midwest Old Threshers

Feet in the Grass Roots

FROM THE FRIENDLY HORSEPLAY of Stong's threshers to the grim determinism of economic reality underlying Josephine Herbst's early depression article may seem like light years to those who did not live through the 1920s and 1930s, but for those who did, the sudden change from the halcyon days of the third decade to the stark psychological darkness of the fourth was akin to facing the grim consequences of an unexpected head-on crash during an otherwise ordinary Sunday afternoon drive.

"Feet in the Grass Roots" actually happened; Miss Herbst was there, returning under rather unpleasant circumstances to her Sioux City roots. Anyone who might doubt the accuracy of Miss Herbst's reporting in this January 1933 Scribner's article is invited to turn to Mary Heaton Vorse's "Rebellion in the Corn Belt," Harper's, December 1932. There the skeptic will find almost a word-for-word documentation of the present piece.

Miss Herbst was the author of several highly respected proletariat novels of the 1930s, one of which, Rope of Gold *(1939) treats in part the same farm strike which is the subject of this article.*

Josephine Herbst was born in Sioux City in 1897 and attended three schools—Morningside College, the University of Iowa and the University of Washington—before taking a degree from the University of California in 1919. For a while she worked for H. L. Mencken's Smart Set *—about the time he began publishing the short stories of Ruth Suckow, whose literary style Miss Herbst disliked. She then spent three years in Europe in the company of America's other expatriate writers, including novelist John Herrman, whom she married in 1925.*

She was the author of numerous short stories and nine novels. She died in 1969.

Feet in the Grass Roots

YOUNG MEN COMING TO IOWA in the eighties used to sing a song about the land of the free where the mighty Missouri rolled down to the sea and a man is a man with the freedom to toil. That these rich Iowa acres have been worked by men who toiled is plain to the eye. Only the paint wearing thin on barns and houses this year hints of the disease that is making the farmer feel all his toil so much folly. A blight more bitter than drought or grasshoppers has fallen upon him, a drop in prices below cost of production, coupled with plagues of high taxes, mortgages and falling values of farm lands.

The farmer has listened to a good many quack cures for his ills. News that he is at last treating himself only becomes real on the Denison Highway when we pull up beside a red lantern, a red flag, and a sign, STOP — FARMERS' HOLIDAY. A group of farmers on the steps of the Golden Slipper Dance Hall outside Sioux City convinces more than any boiled-over comments in papers east. The farmers are striking. They are big men, in overalls, stubbly faces, not so slack in the pants as the farmers I remember, not so shy or ingratiating. They look at us without smiling and we look at them.

A car drives up and an old farmer comes out to it. The man in the car, sitting hard back on the seat, stops as if pulling in a team of horses with a "Whoa, there." "Going to shut 'em up tight as a drum, boys," he says. A movement among the boys, quick excitement, the positive feeling that something is about to happen.

We move on toward town with its dingy red-brick buildings that now seem to hold the excitement of a barricaded place. The town people are chattering about windshields being broken, produce withheld from market to force the price up, milk spilled, highways picketed. One minute they talk of their sympathy for the farmer, burdened with taxes, liens, mortgages, feed and seed loans, deficiency judgments, bank waivers, and prices below cost of production. The next they hint that if something isn't done the militia will be brought in, and then bloodshed. There are the excitement and timidity that war brings in their analysis. A lot of them aren't sure the farmer isn't getting just about what he deserves. They mutter that he was "extravagant" and wasted his substance following high prices during the war. The farmer's dumb, the town man likes to think, he's getting it in the neck, but what of it? The fictitious farmer who craves a fancy education for his children is the one the town man thinks he knows.

Coming back to Iowa is coming to the State where I was born and raised. As we roll along the hilly green fall country, the fat barns, good houses and good crops make the towns seem negligible. In the eastern part the old trees and houses, squares, and prominence of churches make living seem a little plush and stale. In the western part the towns stick out, ugly, from the fat countryside, the homes up-to-date, suggesting Sears Roebuck and a quick, raw method of getting and spending. This industriously tilled soil has brought trouble to the men who work it.

My father sold farm implements to these men in northwest Iowa, Nebraska, and the Dakotas. He was a kind of family doctor to their machinery too, when it began limping in threshing season. As a child I drove all over this country with my father, eating fried chicken and chewing corn on the cob, and when the crops were in he and I would take the team and drive around to see what cash we could pick up on old debts. They put him off oftener than not, and we would drive back in the violet evening with the hills dark and lovely and beneficent and he would point out the fields quietly with his whip. My father lost his business trusting farmers who could not pay their debts. Land prices climbed during those years. Yet he went out burdened with outlawed debts of farmers who year after year didn't have cash to meet their payments. Some farmers sold out and came to town, but I never saw a farmer living "high." Most of his family worked hard a long day. The town man grumbles more than any farmer I ever heard of, but he likes to talk of the bellyaching farmer. He's talking now, half sympathetic, half critical, because he's not sure his bread isn't buttered by the farmer.

Buying a paper, eating in a coffee shop where the old corn crib is glorified in frescoes, we hear traveling men talk of bad business and the farmers' woes. This town has been stoned to life by farmers throwing spiked telephone poles in the path of deputies. The streets here look very much as they used to, but the cheaper red neon light has almost wiped out the white electric sign. The day before, four governors and representatives of four governors broke up council about the farm situation. No one was stunned by their presence. The talk is of the farmers' big parade piling through the street backed by their "demands." Not requests, demands. Thirty thousand crowding the streets and the governors' recommendations passing the buck to Congress did not even bring disappointment. Who had really expected anything? Not the farmer.

Someone tells me that Milo Reno, nominal head of the Farmers' Holiday movement, is a smart man. He was saying three years ago that the time to go on strike was before an election. For a smart man he gets very little comment from the farmer. Out on Highway 20, known as Bunker Hill 20, where the first picketing brought success to the milk strike, winning a rise of one and one-half to three and one-third cents a quart, sitting around the fire with the picketers that night we heard Reno's name mentioned only once.

But first we drove around the town where I lived most of my life. The thing has mushroomed out into comfortable homes. It is evening and the lights are on full blast. There is a great deal of light in this town, and the red neon lights of the downtown streets are curiously fitting for it, with its flavor, never lost, of a frontier town, where good women and mothers rouge higher than in Eastern cities and obscure murders and rape crowd the front pages of respectable daily papers because people demand such news. On this very night as picketing is somberly going forward on dark roads, a rocking-chair contest is limping along in town and little high-school girls are entertaining at parties, very conscious that their efforts will flash on the society page the next day. The town man has had his salary cut, many have lost their businesses, but the lights are still bright. Only in farm homes have the electric lights been turned off, the telephone wires cut. The farmer is filling the old kerosene lamp to his paper by.

The road to Bunker Hill 20 is full of curves. The tall corn grows to within a yard of the pavement. The night sky is very deep blue with a moon almost full. Then the top of the hill and on the swing downward a fire burning under a canvas shelter, a ring of men on the ground, two tents with lanterns in doorways, a long bare table. The talk as we come up dies down, then as we squat by the fire, comes up again. A few look at us curiously, we at them. Some fine-looking strong fellows in overalls, blue shirts open at the neck or loosely tied with a stringy tie. Stout men in this group and stout sticks in their hands. As the farmer talks he stirs his stick quietly in the dust.

I ask a farmer near me if he knew my father. He is too young; my father went out of business fifteen years ago. An old man with a white mustache and fluffy white hair slides around and says: "Better sit on this piece, you ain't sitting comfortable." He points to a bigger hunk of wood and I say I am sitting all right. He says, "I knew your father. He had a partner who was a great horse swapper."

The tight ring around the fire seems to open, the eyes looking down look up, a rumble down the road at the foot of the hill, a cry "truck" and every man is on his feet, moving toward the road with stick in hand. A big fruit truck heaves up, stops, and then passes. The farmers are after only farm produce. They drop to the fire again and the old man with the white mustache, eager and complete with the kind of rare quality of a person who has had a good life in spite of disappointments, this old man lolling by the fire talks of the old days when all you had to do was to buy land and sit on it and the price would rise. He names a dozen farms I used to know, all heavy with mortgages, some ready to foreclose.

"The farmer's got his back to the wall. He can't go on like this. Some of the boys are hard to convince at first, they're so used to muddling along by themselves. You have to reason with them. But all we need is to hold together; we can't lose then. At first there were only a few. Every idea begins that way. That first day when the deputies drove through, the boys scattered through the corn. They wouldn't do that so easily now. Look how tall that corn grows. It's as good to fire from as to hide in." His voice is slow and quiet. At that moment he believes what he says and every other man around the fire believes it. When one talks the others listen with a civilized courtesy that belongs to people like them, or to the stage, not to the town and its nervous, interrupted chatter. It is all orderly, like a play.

There is another cry of "truck" and they amble into the road. The night is set like a stage. The deep blue sky, the fire, and the lanterns burning, the strong shapes of the men in their loose overalls, slouch hats and caps, impressive sticks. An argument begins. You can hear the appealing tones of the driver, who admits he has been closed out of Highway 75. "Now, boys, I don't know why 75 wouldn't let me through. I reasoned with them."

"Don't you know you can't get through without a pass?"

"No, boys, I never had a pass before and I came through this very road." The challenger peers at him and turns to the boys. "Any of you boys seen this fellow before?" No one speaks up. The challenger says, "None of the boys ever seen you before."

"Now, boys, I didn't know you had to have a pass. I've been through here and never had one. I talked to one of you boys."

"Who'd you talk to?"

"Now, boys, I don't know his name, but he was wearing a brown coat." He is pleased with his identification and leans forward. The boys bunch together and talk low. The challenger leans forward and says, "Well, you can't go through here and you know it. We ain't letting anything by on this road. What he's doing, boys, is bootlegging milk from Lemars."

The old man comes up. "What do you do that for? Don't you know the milk agreement? All of us have milk we can't sell. Why don't you buy from us? Why don't you deal with the men who signed the agreement?"

"Now, boys, I've got all my milk bottled right here. I wanted to deal with a square shooter; but you take those fellows, they will hook you for every hook in the road. They'll knock you off."

"What about us?" says the challenger. "We're knocked off. Why don't you stick with us boys so we can hold our prices and sell."

"Boys, I'll go half way with you. I'm ready to do what's right. I'll go to the office tomorrow and fix it up and one of you can go with me and see I do, but this milk will be wasted if I don't get it in." He gets out and comes toward the boys, a little man with an anxious, apologetic face, not a producer, just a milk deliverer, crushed between the two stones. The boys are now showing signs of relenting. There is a split among themselves and there are no leaders. They are proud that they have no leaders. They bunch together now to argue it out and you can see their kindness—the civilized ability to put themselves in another man's place—working on them. Against this is the tough quality of the upstanding old man, who is sure that nothing can come of benefit to anyone without some hurt to someone.

"Now, you all have a say here; come up and let's decide this." They huddle together and you can hear the arguments against letting the man through gradually downed by a rising desire to let him through this once, for the last time. After all, he isn't a scab, he was on the picket line himself three weeks. They turn to him, and, relieved, he gets his truck going slowly up the hill. But the farmers are dissatisfied with themselves. They sit around, and two who held out for not letting him through have gone home disgusted. The talk goes back to their woes and unequal struggle. To the hogs that ought to go to market, but what's the use with the price two cents?

"I say, let's see how big a hog can grow. I got some 600 pounds right now, eating their heads off. I've got the corn and can't get a price for it, the hogs might as well have it."

Most of the men sitting around the fire own their own places. One is a farm hand. I know the names of these places and it is all good, ample land. One of the men is talking of a mortgage on his land for fifty dollars an acre. It is good land and able to raise sixty to seventy-five bushels to the acre. He can't pay his interest and they want to take his machinery, his crop, and his household goods in payment. He had better let his land go but if it was put upon sale it would only bring twenty-five dollars an acre. They could then get a deficiency judgment and sell up his household goods and his livestock to square the difference. He has fought this move. The farm is worth $20,000 but the $7000 mortgage is going to get it down.

The words "international bankers" leap out and every man responds to those words. They can see their farms ironed out by the big chain farms, the insurance companies capturing their land, themselves sold out as cheap farm labor.

"We shouldn't have let that fellow through," one of them says. They begin to talk of the night they drove back the deputies. Hundreds of cars lined the road in a few minutes. "The telephone girls are with us, they put the calls through. We can rouse the whole countryside in fifteen minutes." The tense way they talk, the cool night air, their determined faces, give you the feeling of Paul Revere rousing the countryside. They themselves bring in references continually to their own American Revolution. "We aren't so different from the Boston Tea Party, boys. Those fellows weren't keeping the law. If they had kept the law we would be tied to the skirts of Mother England now."

They like this argument because the talk of the town people piously saying that the picketing was not legal got under their skins. They had to find upstanding precedents for their action. They found plenty. They are not so sure that what the town people call "legal" means anything to them. Charley Dawes got his $80,000,000 in a legal way. The banks get their holiday in a legal way. A sheriff's sale down the road would have sold up a farmer and turned him out in the cold, and they saved him by getting around legality. They shook hands on it, turned out at his sale and the whole works didn't bring more than $14.75. They turned the money over to the bank and the bill of sale to the farmer. He didn't even have to move a stick of his furniture.

In the darkness they are looking ahead. They talk about perhaps picketing until the snow flies. They aren't going to give up without getting somewhere. "Partner," says the old man, "we are at the T in the road. We can't go back now." They are very sure at this moment that they will keep their stand and their sureness is not the excitable cockiness of men going off on a tangent. It has the reasonable quality of men who are calm because they are desperate.

A picket line out by the big Sioux Bridge is near the place where we used to picnic when I was a child. The fine road was gumbo then and it was commonplace to go up over the hub in rainy weather. Farmers came to lodge picnics at the park near the bridge. In those days every family was equipped with fried chicken in white cardboard shoe boxes. One farmer has a house near the place where I once stayed during the threshing season. The woman there set a pretty table with two kinds of pie at every meal. While the threshers ate at the long table, she walked behind them waving the fly chaser over their heads. One of the young fellows asks if I knew the postmistress at McCook was dead. We don't spend much time on memories.

The young fellow explains that the yeast of this movement is the young men. There are a number around who got some education, they've got a Notre Dame man and several Ames men. They won't stand for what the old people stood for, not that old people aren't coming in on the strike in a surprising way. They are the very meat in the broth.

Everybody is worried about foreclosures. Not a fellow there isn't tied down with a mortgage or feed and seed loans. The government has them hand and foot. It compels them to pay off the loans in full before they can dispose of any of the crop. They need cash for taxes and where is it coming from? They need cash for interest to the banks. Everywhere the cry for cash.

They discuss the attempts at legislation for the farmer but without any belief. Someone has just said that their vote isn't worth anything but their economic power is. It is the young man talking and the older fellows, crowding close, nod soberly. One man asks what I think of the expensive harness they have ordered for the Missouri. The rest laugh and the young man says it is a lie that fixing the Missouri will give work to any of them. "It will be like the roads. They brought in machines and we didn't get to use our teams even. They brought in men from the outside and nobody made anything but the construction company. It's all for the construction companies." Again as they talk you get the hint of a combine against these men and their definite feeling that they are up against a wall.

These farmers are good company and back in town, afterward, the talk sounds shallow. The town people are milling around getting sore because they say their city alone is being discriminated against. Quietly, under the surface, business men are beginning to put pressure on the proper spot. In the name of law and order they are pussyfooting to the governor. The threat of militia hangs in the air. One paper, out for the farmer, has its advertising sharply cut. The business barometer has gone down all over the country, but the local men prefer to think that if picketing is ended things would take a sharp upward turn.

Their plots against the farmer are in sharp contrast to his open concern for them. "We are all in the same boat," the farmer says; "what is bad for us is bad for him." During the milk strike the strikers brought in milk confiscated on the highways to give away to the unemployed. Many well-to-do families were not ashamed to drive up in cars to gobble up free milk when they could. In the beginning, restaurants shared food with the strikers and bakers contributed stale bread, but now that the movement shows signs of power they have withdrawn this support.

We would rather visit picket lines than see the inner workings of town life with its stale, corrupt hints. The Republicans want to think that the entire Farmers' Holiday movement is subsidized by the Democrats to break the Republican vote. They hint at paid pickets, with the curious doubt of anything done without pay. Money, that moves the town man's world, or political gain, must be back of every act. They crow at the dumb farmer, just the tool of parties and power.

They even explain the centralization of the strike area around Sioux

City from the standpoint of petty politics. The proudest battle of the picket lines was fought at James. A thousand farmers turned back truckloads of deputies with guns leveled to shoot. In this spot the grasshopper and drought had hit hardest.

Look at the map and see that around Sioux City is the highest percentage of tenant farming. Rich State that Iowa is, its rate for the State is 54.6 per cent, but in the northwest area it is over 60 per cent. In that area also banks were most active in declaring arbitrary holidays and demanding waivers over deposits. Some have demanded five-year waivers. Such sound economic reasons do not satisfy the mind used to juggling with politics and deals. The town man will tell you that James was a hot spot because Milo Reno had a spite against Sioux County. Of course the town men rarely talk to farmers and did not visit the picket lines. They really believe their little fables and live by them.

The fighting men at James were more in earnest and more grim than anywhere else. They had faced guns and tear gas and only one had fallen, their dog Rover. His grave, rounded in yellow clay, was by the road. A fence was around it and a sign over it. *"Here lies Rover, he died for the Farmers' Holiday."* A James farmer is standing by, a little grim. "If I fall by this road, I want to lie right there, too," he said. Another said, "That's the place for us all if we fall." "Looked like we'd all fall last week," a third said.

A dilapidated horse and buggy crossed the road in front of them. Someone yelled to stop him and laughed when he saw a kid driving the shaky structure. "Soon we'll all be going around in rigs like that," he said.

Another said, "Good thing is we had all stayed like that." But a third speaks up, "Why, they can take that thing away as soon as they can a farm." Across the road is the station of James and back of the station is a dirt road leading into the country where I taught school one spring. It was rich farm country and its school had been exploited by lazy teachers from the city. The teacher before me made the kids sing "Here We Go Round the Mulberry Bush" for forty minutes until they were ready to drop while she wrote letters to her beau. The farmers were anxious to give their children a good education and ready to raise the salary of any teacher who could teach. In the farm home where I boarded, the women and children all worked long hours. We all went to bed early every night. But the farms were rich, and a good, self-respecting living went on in those houses, warmed by growing things around it.

Between the town of James and the bigger city there is hardly any country now. It is all town, spreading out to meet the country, like a huge sprawling spider. It lies there waiting to grab what the farmer brings to town, and many in that town have waxed fat on the farmer and have built brand new homes in new additions. The Chamber of Commerce tells you Sioux City is the shopping center for eight times the number of people in it. It is the biggest hog-trucking center in the world. The town has grown with tradesmen's homes reaching into the country, eating it up to the north of town, where a huge golf course awaits the leisured. Many of these houses are mortgaged, and new additions have flattened more than one man taking a flier. The brand new houses are houses of cards in this period of depression.

Men picket roads all day and night, and in town busybodies are at work, honestly thinking their town is in danger, their business getting worse than it is, and all on account of the obstinate farmer. Papers begin to print misleading news about the roads, claiming that most of the roads are open. Picketers take time and investigate. But something soft is beginning to work from the top downward.

When 3000 men meet at The Golden Slipper Dance Hall you see their united protest against any weakening. A thousand crowd into the hall, and the overflow outside listen to speeches. They begin balloting as to whether picketing should continue. None but actual men on the line votes. Each is identified by two from his line; 420 votes are cast for continued picketing as against 210 opposed. This method keeps out the stockyards boys, who are said to have come to break up the meeting.

I didn't hear a man talk against picketing or the movement that night. A man told me he and his wife couldn't starve, no matter what happened. They had put up 500 quarts of food that summer, but they had fifteen to feed. He sold cucumbers around and took what he could get. No one had money, and he would even take an old pair of shoes. Other day he took a corset. He didn't know what he could do with it, but he took it.

During the evening one of the committee men tells me he could see this coming ten years ago. The banks were after you then to take bigger loans. If you asked for $500 they urged you to take $1000. They were always suggesting new barns or silos. Now it looks like a plot had been cooked up against the farmer, and the government was in cahoots. This solid landowning man believes what he is telling me and he is mad clear through. He has been in the red for twelve years. He farmed 160 acres and just made ends meet. They were always talking production and so he got the idea that if he had more land and produced more, he could make something, so he reached for another 80. He could just clear the slate with that by being stingy and watching the pennies. So he tried for another 80 and now had 320. Now he had to have bigger machinery and he could still just make ends meet. So he reached out for 280 more. He was now farming 540 acres and last year had as pretty a field of wheat as you'll see. He took 260 out of his own pocket to get that wheat to an elevator and he might as well have thrown a match into it. He finally ground it up for his hogs.

He looks out the window and admires the sight of farmers getting together for the first time in history. A dozen times I am asked if I ever saw anything like this. Their delight in their solidarity, in numbers sticking together, is new. Or is it so new? The pioneer needed the help of his neighbors. Before the automobile a kind of group social life had sprung up among them. There were dancing in barns and big picnics in ravines. The automobile did away with a good deal of that. The farmer seemed heading toward prosperity, and a man on the make is always a lone wolf. In disaster he sticks to his kind. All of them? Well, a wealthy conservative farmer near Moville estimated that more than 80 per cent were with the Holiday movement. Around his place 24 per cent of the farms have fallen under the axe this last year. In twelve months, if something isn't done, all but thirty per cent of the farms will be foreclosed.

We talk to this man at the Moville Fair as the kids lead their sheep and beeves around a ring for judging. The kids have been taught to raise the finest animals. The farmer has learned to get the most from his soil. And he can't sell it for enough to pay for raising the stuff. This college-bred farmer also mentions that bogy, the international bankers. "If they try to take their homes, they will fight," he says. Farmers are already planning ways to circumvent the sheriff. These people will stick together; even those who are still clear of debt see the handwriting on the wall. The farmer is not trusting the government much. His Farm Bureau has always prated more of his duties than of his rights. The only advice his State Agricultural College can give is to use gunny sacking for the lining of clothes.

No wonder that when Milo Reno at a meeting of 3000 farmers at Fremont, Nebraska, sharpens his speech to include remarks like this, "Don't let people scare you about a strike or being radical. If a man isn't radical today he hasn't enough red blood in his veins to stain a handkerchief. Take steps or lose your homes. This is your last stand. You'll either win or put on the wooden shoes"—they applaud fiercely, and you can be sure if Milo Reno has put that much in a speech it means that farm opinion is strides ahead of him.

The empty oratory of the governor's representative following him is flat in comparison. A farmer with pale blue eyes presses forward and raises an eloquent imploring hand. You feel his place is about to fall under the axe. "Can the governor do anything about a moratorium *now?*" The spokesman, face empty as a tea cup, says the governor can recommend a moratorium for mortgages and interest and he has every confidence that his recommendation will be respected. "But *now,*" the farmer says, insisting, and you know his farm is tottering. He is too old to wait. It must come Now, not Tomorrow. Against that *now* the ambling vacant promises fall and the farmer and the audience move away from them. They are trying to get out from under the threat of politics waiting to gobble their united strength.

They move off and in a meeting of their own, voice their suspicion of leadership. It is an organization meeting, and a minor issue of whether they shall charge dues of fifty cents becomes major in its import. A farmer with blazing eyes makes a speech.

"We thrashed that out in committee and we gave it the best thought we got. The best is none too good. We are dead set against dues. Twelve cents don't look like much but get a lot of men paying it and it amounts to a good deal. We don't want the money coming in to tempt someone to set up a good office and a fine desk. First thing you know you've got someone you can't get rid of. Those fellows wear good clothes and I can't buy new overalls. I tell you I'm ready to fight. Fellow on the Farm Board says to me, 'What do you think of Friend Hoover now, course you're prejudiced.' I says, 'I ain't prejudiced, I'm damned mad now.'" He sits down. Why does the place ring with applause?

Suddenly, clearly and certainly you realize their scepticism in leadership, their belief in the dirt farmer and the rank and file. Now their continual assertion that "there are no leaders, we all got a say," takes on the most unmistakable meaning. A second farmer in a checked suit rises and urges that none but dirt farmers be admitted to membership. "Beware," he says, "of the wolves in sheep's clothing." Again you get their dread of leadership such as has weighted unions. These farmers are not pushed by anyone, their phrases are their own, and they mean to keep a grip on their own business.

How will they succeed? As I write, Brookhart is already muscling in to capture the Farmers' Holiday movement. The leaders of that movement called off the picketing, but no one knows where the deep, spontaneous mass indignation against their loss of rights will spring up again. The shush-shush of town folks, the play of politics, the fear of militia have tamed the first expressive warning down. The town man is even trying to make out that the picket lines were manned by bums and paid agitators. The police, hauling in some hundred picketers, couldn't locate one bum. As for agitators, the farmers are themselves agitators now.

The town man would like to put the farmer back in his place, humbly serving. It will not be so easy. The affirmation of thousands of farmers at the Golden Slipper, at Fremont, at the big parade, at every picket line, wherever farmers meet together, will be too much for a politician's craw. At this minute the farmer is quoting Lincoln in behalf of his own cause, which he feels to be righteous. He will point out to you that it is not only himself, it is the unemployed, and the hundreds of thousands of boys and girls, admitted by the Children's Bureau of the Department of Labor to be roaming the West in search of food, children out of work, riding trains, homeless. Where are these straws blowing? The farmer knows that his picketing was more valuable as a demonstration than as an actual means of raising prices. He is talking of another demonstration in an American tradition, the covered wagon again on a migration, but this time to the East. In Washington he thinks his plight may seem more dramatic. And he will refer you to the demonstrations made by the now honorable John Brown and by members of the Boston Tea Party, for the farmer is a proud man and likes historical precedent for his actions.

... Josephine Herbst, 1933

Farmers block stock truck on Iowa highway, 1932

SOLD OUT
. . . Jay N. "Ding" Darling (ca. 1932)

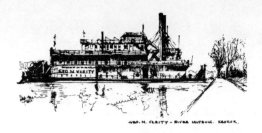

GEO. M. VERITY - RIVER MUSEUM. KEOKUK.

The Cities of Iowa — "Winslow"

After the Fair is over,
What will Chicago do
With all those flimsy houses
Put up with sticks and glue?

SO CHICAGO SKEPTICS mocked that greatest invention of Chicago builders — the "stick house" or "balloon-frame house." Later, of course, the same critics were to mock those Chicago builders who invented the "sky-scraper" — which we now call "high-rises."

But it was the "stick" or "balloon-frame" house that made possible the building of economical farmsteads on every quarter section of fertile Iowa land, and the rows of frame houses on all the Main and Elm Streets of every Iowa village and town. There weren't enough trees in Iowa for many people to have log cabins — which, in any case, were not easy to build. "Soddies" were all right until one erected something better, and caves were practical only when a tornado or a cyclone roared into sight.

The balloon-frame house was practical, relatively inexpensive, simple and easy to put up, its materials easily carted across primitive roads. And the materials needed were close by. Just to the north there were vast pineries of tall straight trees, the Mississippi flowed down out of those forests to Iowa's front door, there were thousands of men looking for work, and there were entrepreneurs . . .

But this is Marquis Childs's story and I'll let him tell it. He was born in Clinton, one of Iowa's Mississippi River cities, took a degree from the University of Wisconsin in 1923, worked for a while as a journalist in the midwest, then came to Iowa City for graduate work in the University of Iowa's English Department.

For almost sixty years he has been a prominent American journalist and has also written nearly a score of books.

If you need any clues as to the identity of "Winslow," you might count the letters in the name of Childs's imaginary town and in his birthplace.

River Town

THERE IS A SPECIAL PROVINCE which belongs to the Mississippi, carved out of the States through which it flows. It can be cut in two at St. Louis to form two distinct domains, one of the upper river, the other of the lower. The latter is well known and frequently celebrated; it has certain picturesque advantages and two great books to its credit; although Hannibal is geographically above St. Louis, Mark Twain in *Tom Sawyer* and *Huckleberry Finn* was writing about the lower river, where his interest was.

The province of the upper river does not deserve its obscurity. The life along its reaches was the life of the Mississippi with a special quality of the Northwest added; a defiant, reckless courage and arrogance that the stream in the south lacked. Even today a river town is a special kind of town. It is only technically in Wisconsin, Minnesota, Illinois, or Iowa. By virtue of the Mississippi, the extravagant commerce that flowed for so many years on its broad surface and the incorrigible human cargo that came along with this commerce, the river towns escaped the blighting respectability of the mid-western Main Street.

Many of the upper river towns that flourished in the days of the great lumber boom have disappeared altogether; visible now only as moldering ghost towns. Others are dying, shrinking slowly into a pale semblance of the past. Galena in Illinois is shut off from the Mississippi, its tributary Fever River choked with sand. Bad Axe in Wisconsin has become the hamlet Genoa. Dubuque, Iowa, dwindles, and so do Clinton, Burlington, Muscatine. Beef Slough in Wisconsin, once the center of tempestuous life, with a hundred raft crews charging in and out of saloon and brothel, has disappeared. So has West Newton, across the river in Minnesota.

II

Winslow is a town such as Clinton or Dubuque. It is in Iowa but it has no more to do with that rural state than has Tombstone, Arizona. In the beginning Joshua Winslow, a hard-bitten Yankee from northern New York, came with his ailing wife and built on a rise of ground where the river was open, free from sand bars and towheads—the small islands which clog the stream. That was in 1826. Considerably before the Civil War Joshua and his wife had died of ague and chills and fever and the other miserable diseases that attended pioneer settlement in the valley.

By 1865 Winslow was a thriving town of more than three thousand population. It had eighty-six saloons and a subscription library. The

Winslow Young Men's Association, which fostered the library, organized in 1865 a lecture series and brought to the town Emerson, Horace Greeley, P. T. Barnum, the freed slave Douglass, and two or three others of almost equal note. The Association also gave a Promenade Festival at which the sum of three hundred and forty-two dollars was raised to buy books; one of the local wits offered a humorous monologue in the person of "Professor Agassick" of "Cambridge University" [a pun on Alexander Agassiz, world-renowned naturalist of Harvard University, at Cambridge, Massachusetts], discoursing on Adam and Eve and the revised story of the Garden.

Already there were half a dozen sawmills at Winslow. In that year old Rizen Abbott paid a [Civil] war tax to the government of ten thousand dollars of his income, and J. L. Westbrook is shown in the published lists with almost as much. But they were pikers still, buying the logs they sawed in their mills from timber contractors in the pineries to the north or from chance raftsmen who came drifting down the river to barter logs. As the West came to demand lumber and more lumber, Abbott, Westbrook, and the Devines began to realize that God had indeed been very good to them. To the north were the incredible fine stands of pine, so large that man could never exhaust them; to the west was the treeless prairie, with the railroad beginning to push in; and the river was at their door, a free highway for northern lumber.

Scarcely a town on the upper river between St. Paul and St. Louis but had its mills. They were called sawdust towns. In the spring when the river opened and the first rafts came down the muddied, drift-laden flood to Winslow, the great circular saws set up their shrieking whine again—the sawmill sound that carried so far on still hot days in the summer. The shift was twelve to fourteen house a day, the pay eighty-five cents to a dollar and a quarter. There were numerous accidents. Often men were ripped in two; the saws stopped for a few minutes, and the undertaker had a difficult job. There were many Germans and Irish in the mills. On Saturday pay night no good woman stirred out of the house without a strong man at her side. Two constables were required to keep the drunks on Main Street from falling under the buggy wheels. There were sixty-three saloons on the six blocks between the levee and the Randall House at the corner of Sixth Street. Iowa's prohibition law came early, but to Winslow and the other river towns it made no difference. The proprietors of the saloons were brought into court once a month to pay a fine of ten dollars and costs, which was the equivalent of a license fee.

But it took a raft crew to make the town really lively. In the early days they were all from the northwest; Wisconsin woodsmen who turned to rafting during the summer, French Canadians many of them. Later on boys from along the river took to rafting, and there were Winslow men on almost every raft. And there were the bums who came back each season, starved, ragged, eager to get a berth for a single trip, enough money for a drunk. They were known to captains up and down the river by their nicknames, "St. Louis Blackie," "Sliver," "The Tomcat." They had no other names. A captain would walk along the levee and prod one sleeping bundle of rags after another. "Here you, Bat-Eye, and you, Mugs, go on aboard the *Fanny Harris* and report to the mate." When the season ended in the late fall they migrated by some circuitous and difficult route to the deep south, where they worked on the sugar plantations. All raftsmen had in common a proud, willful independence. They took the town when they turned to pleasure.

The floating brothels, rigged on small barges, knew them. Often these pleasure craft would follow a raft, or two or three rafts, to the mills at Winslow, sure of patronage when the crew were paid off. The roosters, which was the name the raftsmen acquired because of necessity they roosted anywhere they could during the strenuous down-river trip, loved a brawl. They went often to the German beer garden, the Schüt-zen Park, on the edge of town. Sometimes they were admitted, some-times not, depending upon the state of the Schützen Verein's treasury. But always they fought, and the Germans almost invariably lost and swore never again to traffic with such brutes. After a particularly vio-lent battle, Heinrich Schenk, lawyer for the Schützen Verein, had twenty raftsmen haled up in the justice of the peace court. The small room would just accommodate the hulking defendants and two or three con-stables. The complaining witnesses had to wait outside. At intervals Heinrich would lean out of the window to call, "Send up another black eye," or "Another one with teeth out, if you please."

Certain of these roosters acquired highly colored reputations in Winslow. Big Jack Manville had been a Winslow boy, but no one was so feared. Once he smashed a dozen windows on Main Street before the constabulary could control him. He appeared in court the next day, sober and subdued, tall and dignified, looking like a kindly colos-sus. Two or three merchants had come to see that he was at last put in jail, but they lost their courage when they saw Big Jack in the flesh. After waiting a while, he said, "If there's not going to be any action here I'm going home," and went out.

You could tell when a neighbor had come off the river: his clothes would be decorating the back fence in order that they might be de-loused by the sun and air. Men were compelled to shed their river clothes in the barn or woodshed before conscientious wives would allow them to step into the house. Sometimes raftsmen bound down-river to a mill below Winslow would steal an hour or two at home. A ribald story passed around that Shady Ashcraft kept his little boy on the river bank watching for his return. At the approach of Shady's raft, the youngster was required to run like hell and bear this warning to his mother, "Go on to bed, ma, because pa's just about to step on shore." Many raftsmen spent the winter at home in pleasant idleness, slept late, danced, played cards, called on the girls, bought a Stetson hat and a pair of box-toed shoes. There were boat yards at Winslow, busy through the winter, employing skilled caulkers and woodworkers, who made good wages and spent freely. In the spring there were two or three launchings that called for all the rancid butter from the county round about to grease the ways.

Respectable mothers in Winslow despaired of their children. Little girls who wore white aprons to school came home in tears. Some big girl or loutish boy had pulled their braids. In summer, despite the vigilance of the raftsmen, most boys lived on and along the big rafts that were tied up by the mills, waiting to approach the log chute. It was a wonderful place to swim and dive, but dangerous; slip under that unbroken carpet of brown logs, and it was ten to one that you would never come up alive again.

The sawdust piles had become small mountains. Rizen Abbott—called Goat Abbott for obscure reasons—was already a rich man. On Abbott's slough he had three great mills topped by three tall stacks, and the square piles of sweet-smelling lumber covered acres of ground in his yards. He was a broad, thick man. When there was good sleighing, he often gathered all the children of his neighborhood into his big sleigh, took them for a swift ride, and then bought them boots with red tops and copper toes and a box of candy all around. Each day at six o'clock he was all but stationary. He would take more whiskey, but it would not stay down. He was full of whiskey; he carried in four or five pockets half-pint flasks which contained what was for him a single drink. But his vigorous mind was apparently never dimmed. Mrs. Abbott was a proud woman. She had few friends and even they said that she was distant, cold. She wanted their one son, Will, to be a gentleman and go to Harvard College. Goat Abbott wanted him to go into the lumber business.

III

Abbott and Westbrook and the Devines were all in the pool, the combine of lumbermen which dominated the entire upper river and a good share of Wisconsin and Minnesota. It was common talk in Winslow that they stole as much of the forest as they bought. J. L. Westbrook was a hard man. He was godfearing, and he wore a little fringe of whiskers, like a half moon around his face. The stern tenets of his Methodism would not permit him to work his men on Sundays. On Saturday at midnight it was his custom to order his steamboats which were to return north for rafts restocked with provisions. The Westbrook foreman turned over to the grocer a long, long list of supplies, and the grocer and his two brothers and his wife toiled until midnight Sunday to fill the orders and get the supplies aboard. Westbrook was obviously not responsible for the souls of the grocer and his family.

It was in this custom that the hatred between the grocer's family, the Sewells, and the Westbrooks originated. Once when J. L.'s younger son, Philomen, was eighteen, J. L. became enraged at something the boy said and there in the street he thrashed him with an axe handle until he broke his arm. It was late at night, and only a few men gathered. When J. L. strode away, the onlookers picked up Philomen, carried him into a saloon, and went for a doctor. It was in this way, they say, that the old man broke Philomen's spirit. But J. L. had an older son, Horatio, who was just as mean as his father.

The Devines were milder. They were French-Irish and they liked to live in pleasant, easy style. Old man Devine came to Winslow with only his shirt on his back, but as soon as he began to make money he let his family spend it. They built a house on Fifth Avenue, young Bernadotte and Paris went away to a military school, and Antoinette, Louisa, and Fanny were sent to Ferry Hall in Lake Forest.

There were others whose fortunes were mounting upward as the logs flowed in a ceaseless brown web down the broad stream. There were the Tollivers and the Bradleys and the Gardiners. But Goat Abbott, Westbrook, and the Devines ruled the roost. Sometimes their mills and their lumber piles burned—burned for days—and all the town was black and reeked with smoke and all the women made sandwiches and coffee for the fire-fighters. They built up the mills again and spurned the insurance which cautious underwriters held at fabulous rates.

These three families were expanding rapidly. They were making money in undreamed-of sums. They were not the biggest on the upper river; they were under the domination of old man Weyerhauser. But they had long since become the richest men in Winslow, outstripping pompous Peter Van Hewitt Smith, who came west with six hundred thousand dollars and a number of grand ideas, which he slowly and painfully relinquished. The pace on the river had become faster, harder. During the open season Abbott and the others lived on their boats between Winslow and Beef Slough at the mouth of the Chippewa River. For three weeks, during the big fight over the Beef Slough boom, Goat never took off his clothes. The rafting crews worked fourteen, eighteen, twenty hours a day. The rafts crowded one on the other so fast at the rafting booms that time and again men slipped beneath the treacherous, shifting surface of the logs, and there was no thought for them, because a man was so cheap. For one entire week the river before Winslow was covered with logs for seven miles, and people came from round the whole county on a Sunday in mid-June to see the spectacle.

Goat Abbott, when at last he wearied of his wife's nagging, built a huge house, all turrets and towers and porches and three upstairs balconies and a stained-glass window on the stairway twenty feet high. Goat had them panel one room in white pine with a low polish. He said he liked the smell of the wood and, after all, it was the way he made his money.

A little later Louisa Devine married Philemon Westbrook. The two families built for them a handsome house on the bluff back of the town. From the wide window of their drawing room (Louisa, who had lived in New York, said it was not a parlor) you could look over the hills and the flat roofs of the town to the shining river. There were separate quarters for the servants in the stable. No one had ever called them servants before, to say nothing of having special quarters for them. Later on, old man Devine built another big house for Antoinette and Billy Rickard on the bluff and another one for himself; so that the three houses dominated all Winslow.

The Devines were living high. It was Bernadotte Devine who built the first houseboat. It was called *The Princess*, for his sister, Fanny. That had been Fanny's name since she was a child with long, carefully curled golden hair. The Little Princess. And the towboat that pushed *The Princess* was called *The Duchess*. Those first boats introduced a grand, lazy, blissful sort of life. The logging business was almost at an end; they were all rich, they could take time. Or at any rate the Devines could. *The Princess* was fitted out by Marshall Field's [of Chicago] eight bedrooms, five baths, a main saloon, a dining saloon, the master's library, and a verandah deck that ran the whole length of the boat, tricked out with blooming plants along the rail and with hanging baskets of fern. There were no cares, no worries, no smoke, no vibrations – just drifting along on *The Princess*, scarcely aware of the puffing *Duchess* which pushed behind. It was a great life while it lasted.

The best of the Devine crews, the crack pilots, were always assigned to *The Duchess*. And the colored stewards on *The Princess* were chosen for their musical ability, as much as for anything else. Toward the late afternoon *The Princess* and *The Duchess* would head into some quiet slough, and the whole party would go swimming along a sandbar, then picnic there, and in the moonlight listen to the colored people singing on the deck and the strumming of the banjos. On the verandah deck there were hammocks that held two, a hammock for each couple, and the official chaperon was not too watchful. The Devines had friends all up and down the river, and before each trip hampers of the finest imported champagne and claret and liqueurs and whiskies were carried on board. Stop at Burlington and have a party; it was there that the new Brussels carpet in the main saloon was initiated with spilled champagne; that was the trip on which they made the distillery towns from Peoria to Louisville, up the Ohio. Nothing to do, nothing in the wide world to do, through long lazy afternoons; the green, mysterious shore slipping gently past the rail.

Soon there were other houseboats. The Tollivers built and equipped *The Chaperon* and *The Summer Girl,* and old Westbrook was at last pried loose from the cash for *The Eva* and *The Uncle Tom.* But the Devines managed to lead. They initiated the Outing Club. Paris advanced the money to build the big gabled clubhouse on a point of land at Weehasket, five miles below Winslow, where the river makes a great bend, sweeps by in all its swelling might and majesty. The *Winslow Gazette* said, with considerable justice, that no verandah in the Middle-West could boast a finer view. There were twenty suites, bedroom, bath, and small sitting room; card rooms, three dining rooms. The ladies spent long, carefree weeks there; husbands drove down in the afternoon in smart turnouts, with a groom up behind. Visitors from Minneapolis and Chicago liked to stop at the Outing Club.

How they dominated the town, the Devines and the Westbrooks. Goat Abbott was away most of the time; he had branched out into railroads and timber on the West Coast, with his son, Will, who had gone to Harvard and was a gentleman but good at business. Mrs. Abbott had shut herself away entirely; she lived with an old servant in the big house and sometimes you saw her sallow, withered face at the window. She refused to meet her oldest friends; they said it was because she was so unhappy with Goat. The Devines and the Westbrooks had it all to themselves. They were like the ruling families of some small middle-European principality.

Each detail of their life was discussed. When Paris Devine was drowned off *The Princess,* three thousand people packed the levee to see them bring his body ashore. The town knew that Antoinette didn't get along with Billy Rickard; the report of a separation hovered in the air for years. The very appearance of their children, riding in a high-wheeled wicker pony cart, with a watchful, British-looking governess, was enough to set every curtain along the street to fluttering. Other children stopped their play to stare with awe that was not unmixed with envy at sight of the smart Shetland pony and the smart little cart and the youngster who held the reins with such casual pride. On their second trip to London Louisa and Philo bought a Daimler and brought it back to Winslow; it was the first car the town had seen nearby. Billy

Rickard drank too much and ran with women; that was established. Louisa and Philo and their children traveled between California, New York and Europe, with brief stopovers at Winslow. Old man Westbrook was dying of cancer; he got scant sympathy from the town; everyone knew that Horatio would get the money and conserve it as meanly as his father had.

All the mills were closed now except one that Goat Abbott kept open to saw the few logs which still came down from the north. The sawdust mountains were brown and discolored; they had begun to settle into the river. There were great mines of rotting lath and waste lumber where the yards had been. The tempo of the town was slower. A number of the best pilots had gone to the Yukon; a few found berths in government service; others settled down to loaf away their lives or they took to modest farming. Iowa was dry in earnest, but Fairview across the river in Illinois was dripping wet, and a stream of thirsty Iowans poured through Winslow and over the high bridge. Returning very drunk, they gave to Main Street a semblance of the wild and bloody past. The high bridge had never paid before; it now became as the mines of Ophir; liquor was smuggled across in wheel-barrows and baby-buggies and push carts, anything on wheels.

The old-timers were dropping away. Jumbo Bradley committed suicide. Goat Abbott had a stroke in Seattle; but not before he had made sure of proper entry into heaven. "They may be right, you can't tell," he was often heard to say as age crept upon him. "These Christians, these church folks may be right. Anyway I can't afford to take such a big chance as that." He gave to the Episcopal church handsome carved choir stalls, an altar, and a communion service of handwrought gold; a new organ, a new roof, and an endowment. He left an estate of $17,000,000, and when his son, Will, died six years later, it had appreciated to $33,000,000. Mrs. Abbott lives on, more withered and yellow, seldom venturing from the house, never from the big yard and the protection of the high cedar hedges around it; intruders are turned away by Anna, who has been with the Abbotts for thirty-eight years. The Westbrook fortune went, when the old man died after incredible months of torture, to Horatio, who was to administer it for Philo, the two sisters, Ella and Jennie, and himself.

It was strange how quickly it ended. Horatio Westbrook, closed away in his massive, fortresslike house on the little park off Fifth Avenue, occupied himself solely with preserving the great fortune he had inherited from his father; administering the income to his family with all the niggardliness the law would allow; dominating the town by the cold threat of his personality. The Devines, upon the death of the head of the family, ventured into Southern pine and high finance. Within a few years they took such severe losses that their way of living had to be curtailed in drastic fashion. Louisa and Philo and their children came back for a month or two in the summer, but the rest of the year they were at Pasadena. Antoinette divorced Rickard, supporting him in a sanitarium for alcoholics until his death. Fanny terminated a romance long frustrated and married Captain Henry Robaire of her father's fleet; he had one-eighth Chippewa Indian blood. As Mrs. Robaire, she developed a giddy streak and was given to becoming tipsy, a foolish smile on her foolish face, beneath the absurd crown of graying yellow curls.

IV

Although an air of quiescence and decay hangs increasingly over Winslow, its character persists, stubborn and unregenerate. For many of the figures of the great past live on; like figures from some heroic frieze buried under wind-blown sand and lost to time: difficult and un-understandable. Big Jack Manville, Captain Cameron, Mr. Jabez, and many more survive. They are not unlike certain houses which a pre-tentious generation has covered with a thin coating of stucco, a meager surface that does not conceal their sharp, uncompromising angularity. Big Jack lives alone in a small yellow cottage; he can see the river from his front door; his mate's license hangs in a gilt frame over the radio. Mr. Jabez sits on the rotting remains of a shiere boom and talks of the past in his fine Irish speech. Captain Cameron is eighty-six, but he looks as though he were carved out of hickory, as tough and as limber, with the fringe of stiff-looking whiskers that encircles his face.

Winslow bears a resemblance to the dying New England coastal towns of a generation ago. There are many spinsters, odd crustacea cast upon the beach by the receding wave of energy. Some of them are so old that they were brought to the West by their fathers, as little girls, from Boston and Gloucester and New Bedford. The river attracted these New Englanders. Winslow was destined to be a great town, one to rival Chicago. Wilda Cranch's father came west to start an insurance company in Winslow. It failed swiftly, and Mr. Cranch died of the galloping consumption. That happened in 1857; Wilda was four years old; but when she speaks of it today there is the shadow of forgotten emotion in the parchment of her face. The Monday girls must be seventy—yes, seventy-five—but to Winslow they are still the Monday girls. Olive Read lives alone in the big shuttered house at the end of Chestnut Street; children play in the tangled undergrowth and shrub-bery of the lawn until she comes to drive them off; the neighbors leave custards and small loaves of newly baked bread on her doorstep. Effie Law was with her father, the Captain, when he was killed in the explosion of the *Silver Wave* near Bellvue. She has lived on the charity of her neighbors since that time, repaying their generosity with the mild humors of her imbecility. Until a recent date a whole tribe of idiots lived and bred in a cluster of squalid huts along the river bank, beside the deserted button factory; one family's reputed ignorance of the laws pertaining to incest was the source of three or four of the more furtive jokes in the town, the kind told in a shocked whisper at the Winslow Ladies' Literary Society and to the accompaniment of guffaws of laughter in Frankie Jonas's pool hall.

The young have gone away. It is a confession of failure to remain in Winslow; an occasion for apology to return for more than a weekend or a few days. Winslow's younger generation lives in Chicago and New York, St. Louis and Minneapolis. When they meet afar they agree that Winslow is dead; they speak with pity of Fred Craddock and Georgia Hensley and others who are caught there. Returning for a brief visit, they are depressed by the very absence of change; by the fact that houses and people seem quite the same. It is only after a longer interval that the processes of withering decay are apparent. Certain faces have disappeared; here a house has fallen into ruin, gaping and black; and age is seen like a thick film upon all familiar things. Even those industries that grew out of the lumber boom are passing. They are dismantling the sash-and-door factory and selling it for junk.

The only new life has no real relation to the town. The Lincoln Highway runs along Main Street, and in summer there is a constant flow of cars. Winslow happens, too, to be a distributing center for one of the large alcohol rings. Alcohol for Iowa, Nebraska, a part of Minnesota, and the Dakotas crosses the river at this point and comes within the jurisdiction of an Italian with a soft voice and soft yellow-white face. This young gentleman, dressed expensively, slouched down in the seat of a long low car, waves his hand to police and townsfolk along Main Street with a fine impartiality. It is not difficult to identify at least ten members of the ring stationed in Winslow. They make the Dew Drop Inn their headquarters, coming and going in an indifferent, easy way or pausing for a whispered consultation. Nick, the local head of the syndicate, sometimes boasts, pays off his drivers with a flourish from a showy roll of bills for the benefit of hangers-on in Jonas's place. Two or three Winslow young men have gone to work for Nicholas. It is a great temptation, as he pays $25 a trip to Des Moines, $60 to Lincoln, and furnishes a big car with a built-in, concealed eighty-gallon tank. There is a mild risk from hi-jackers, less from the law, but the poorest driver makes $50 a week, others as high as $100.

The alcohol is not taken across the high bridge. The trucks from Chicago stop at the Illinois shore, arriving there always at night. The ten-gallon containers are transferred to flat-bottomed skiffs and ferried over the river. Sitting on his porch through long summer evenings, Mr. Jabez has learned to identify the brief, flashing signals of the truck drivers across the river. He counts the skiff loads that come over on dark nights. "Well, by Jesus Christ," he says with a sudden flare of indignation, "you can't beat a country like this one." But his anger subsides to philosophic contemplation of the spectacle of lawlessness at his doorstep, and he reflects that Winslow has never in its history been law-abiding. "It's a river town, and you know what they are," he adds.

The death of the Little Princess the other day gave the righteous in Winslow the opportunity to write a very moral epitaph to a whole long period of history. Fanny was found drowned in her bathtub, whether accidentally or not will never be known. Captain Robaire had departed three weeks before with the contents of their joint safety deposit box. It had not contained very much, the town said, but at least it would have given Fanny a decent burial. As it was, Horatio Westbrook and four others put in a hundred dollars each for a modest funeral. Fanny had quarreled long before her death with those members of her own family who had retained any part of the original Devine fortune. They telegraphed to Louisa, but no one was certain of her address, and no answer came. Antoinette Rickard, living obscure and forgotten in the south of France, cabled an appeal to Horatio. That was all.

Because so much has gone on there, the town is full of tales. Not one person who walks down the street but has a history that the rest of the town can furnish on demand. People seem to live more and more in the past, feeding upon reminiscences of the great days. There are times when Mr. Jabez dwells completely in a world that has long since disappeared, speaks of friends long dead as though they might come round the corner to question his story, and refers to landmarks obliterated years ago as though they stood shining and new to the gaze of the smallest child. Beneath the present weariness, the film of decay and age, lies the memory of this stirring past. Winslow is a river town if only in the dim reflection of ancient glory.

. . . Marquis Childs, 1932

The Trail of the Hawkeye

IN 1938 IOWA CELEBRATED the Centennial of its organization as a Territory of the United States (it became a state in 1846). Among several formal and informal observances of the anniversary, the Library of Congress set out a summer-long display of books related to Iowa, the Post Office issued a rectangular purplish stamp with a representation of "Old Capitol" on the campus of University of Iowa, and Wallace Stegner's article "The Trail of the Hawkeye" appeared in the Saturday Review of Literature *in July.*

Stegner, who spent his childhood in Iowa, chose to focus on Iowa's development as a cultural and literary achievement in a land of pigs and corn. The achievements he describes have, unfortunately, not been equaled in Iowa in the more than four decades since this essay.

Stegner was born on his grandfather's farm near Lake Mills in north central Iowa, spent his later school days in Saskatchewan and Salt Lake City, then returned to Iowa for a master's degree (1932) and a Ph.D. degree (1935). His short stories, literary essays and some twenty-odd books, as well as his directorship of the Stanford University Writing Center (since 1947) have made him internationally famous.

The Trail of the Hawkeye

THE YEAR 1938 marks the hundredth anniversary of the formation of Iowa Territory by the dissection of the previously existing Territory of Wisconsin. It also marks the passage of one hundred and fifty years since Julien Dubuque, a French Canadian, obtained a lease of twenty-one acres from the Indians and brought in a company of lead miners to found the first settlement of whites in the state, on the site of the city which now bears his name. Iowa has been a State since 1846.

Anniversaries are classic times for the taking of inventory. But an inventory of Iowa's development tells us little that we didn't know. There has been a tremendous growth of material prosperity. The Iowa legend of tall corn has matured; Iowa hogs have reached a point where one of them could be made the hero of a novel by Phil Stong. Twenty-six colleges and universities have taken root and survived. More than this, there has grown up in Iowa a society probably more rural in its philosophy than that of any state in the union. Ninety-six percent of Iowa is arable farm land, as fertile as any on earth. With a population of two and a half million, the state has no city larger than 175,000, and that city, Des Moines, is almost three times as large as any other Iowa town.

It is a region of villages and farms, and its people are villagers and farmers. The fantastic prices to which Iowa farm land soared until the depression knocked it down again are only one indication of the extent to which land and crops are basic in an Iowan's thinking. And people whose principal interest is the land are likely to look peculiar and backward to other sections of the country where mercantile and industrial interests predominate.

Iowans do. The state has been ridiculed as the home of the original hundred-percenter, a place where violent patriotism, both national and local, is a prized and widespread virtue; a place marked by the survival of Independence Day oratory and lavish produce fairs, a place whose greatest boast is the production of taller corn and huger hogs than any other region in the world.

It has been said that Iowa took pride in little else. Ellis Parker Butler (who incidentally is one Iowa writer with a large and enthusiastic audience in his own state, and whose "Pigs Is Pigs" seems likely to become an enduring minor classic of homely humor) expressed an almost universal opinion of the corn belt's cultural ambitions in his classic motto for the state:

> Ten million yearly for manure,
> But not one cent for literature!

When people spoke of Iowa culture they spoke mirthfully, having in mind the (Little) Old Lady from Dubuque, or the combination literary and sewing circles where Iowa housewives, freed by prosperity from household drudgery, hunted the arts in pack. Josephine Herbst, a rebellious Iowan herself, had a great deal of fun some years ago in an *American Mercury* article, lampooning the culture clubs which sought sordid realism with bated breath, and buzzed with indignation when they found it.

But the very existence of the culture clubs should indicate that Iowa has long been proud of other things than corn and hogs. Those same societies over whose prostrate frames Miss Herbst trod so triumphantly still take patriotic pride in pointing her out as an Iowa writer. Why are they proud? She is successful. Her name is known outside the state. "Nothing Is Sacred," "Money for Love," and "Pity Is Not Enough," although they may titillate the moral indignation of many Iowa readers, are yet too well known elsewhere for the state to repudiate them. So, read or not, Miss Herbst takes her place with the long list of Iowa artists expatriate from the motherland, but cherished in innumerable files of pamphlets, lectures, clippings, reviews, which almost every public library in Iowa keeps handy for the patriotic historians of local literature.

There have been many writers of importance in the past forty or fifty years who can more or less justly be claimed by these patriots, but whose lives and works have wandered away from the corn belt, and who frequently, from Greece or New York or Tahiti, let loose barbed shafts against their native state. Yet they cannot shake their connection with Iowa. The patriots hunt them up, hide the horrid fact of their antecedents how they will, and utilize them as one more prop to local pride.

The revolt from the village, and the corollary revolt of many Iowa writers against their home, needs no explaining. The reason why Iowa readers embrace the serpents who sting them perhaps does. Iowa is, and has been from the beginning, a provincial state, a hick state. Iowans were rubes and they knew it. Until very recently most of them, including the writers, were ashamed of it. In the general selling of civilized birthrights that accompanied the settling of the land, the arts were lost except to a few jealous guardians, women and schoolmasters and preachers. That doesn't tell the whole story, but in essence it holds, and it has been the history of every frontier community. The culture these people preserved came, as Ruth Suckow pointed out some years ago, from the Eastern centers of the higher life, particularly Boston. For generations, therefore, the culture hounds looked nostalgically Eastward, turning up their noses at the life around them, which, though certainly crude enough, was a great deal more genuine than the watered Neo-Anglophilia they cherished. Iowa, like its sister states of the Middle West, has suffered from the colonial complex just as surely as New England suffered from it until the middle of the last century.

Glenway Wescott has described the Middle West as, among other things, "a state of mind of people born where they do not like to live." The twenty-five thousand bona fide Hawkeyes who jammed an Iowa picnic in Long Beach, California, a few years ago are one gauge of that statement. But in many other ways the state where the tall corn grows is the very middle of the Middle West, the quintessence of Middle Westernism. Its ruralism is little relieved by urban and industrial life, its society is extremely homogeneous, despite the variety of racial stocks that flooded in with the settlement. Intellectually and spiritually it awoke later than any of its neighbors, and it is only the last two decades which have witnessed any appreciable diminishing of the colonial complex.

The temptation to regard Iowa's literary history as a kind of miniature reproduction of the literary history of America, to see it as an unformed and hesitant thing at first, groping its way toward maturity and confidence, outgrowing its dependence and timidity and mean opinion of itself, is a great one. But though tempting because of its simplicity, the pattern does not apply absolutely; there are foreshadowings and throwbacks which confuse the lines of development. And if it is hard to find a pattern into which Iowa writers will fit, it is equally hard to know just what an Iowa author is. Ted Robinson, in an article on Ohio writers in *The Saturday Review,* has detailed his difficulties. There is no need to repeat them: they are the same as my own. But in general it has seemed expedient to classify as Iowan those writers who were born and grew up in Iowa, or those who spent so considerable a part of their early lives in the state that they were indelibly marked by their environment.

Probably the earliest writer of any prominence who can by these lights be legitimately considered Iowan is Emerson Hough, born in Newton and educated at the University of Iowa. His first success, "The Mississippi Bubble," appeared in 1902, and his last two, "The Covered Wagon" and "North of Thirty-Six," in 1922 and 1923. Rancher, traveler, historian, conservationist, Hough wrote in all more than twenty-five books and hundreds of magazine stories and articles. He fits no pattern, and he left no recognizable legacies to authors of his state and region except his keen interest in the western migrations of settlers.

The next two in line, however, have both had a profound effect in molding Iowa's opinion of itself and in stimulating other writers.

Hamlin Garland seems to me rather more Iowan than otherwise. Though born in West Salem, Wisconsin, he moved with his family to Iowa in 1868, and spent the whole formative period of his youth, from the age of eight to the age of twenty-one, in Iowa. His books deal with the life of several states, and any consideration of Garland's significance cannot be confined to one or another of them, but the author of "Main Travelled Roads" and "A Son of the Middle Border" certainly belongs in any discussion of purely Iowan literature. As a member of the gifted Midwestern group that gathered in Chicago, and as a forerunner of the many writers who now profess cultural regionalism as a literary creed, Garland is of the first importance.

So is his contemporary, Herbert Quick, a Grundy County lawyer who took to authorship in 1902. Less talented than Garland, and cursed with less social conscience and less burning zeal, he produced for almost twenty years a series of comparatively innocuous books, but he kept in his mind an ambition to write in serious and appreciative terms about his native state. Publishers objected that there was no interesting material for fiction in Iowa (the same complaint had been made about America in general as late as 1820). It was not until 1921 that Quick brought himself to the writing of "Vandemark's Folly," to be followed two years later by "The Hawkeyes." Those two books gave Iowa a history. They spoke of Dubuque and Waterloo without apology, as if they were as worthy a place in fiction as Paris or Versailles. Melodramatic and over-heightened as they are, Quick's Iowa novels took Iowa a long stride out of the colonial wilderness.

But Quick was an old man when he wrote those books. They represent one phase of the broadening interest in local subject matter and the local way of life that took place after 1915. Before the war most of the writers the state could boast of were either in absentia, or clustered in a few literary centers, and they were interested in other things than exploiting the natural resources of fictional and poetic material immediately around them.

There were such groups early in the century in Iowa City, in Des Moines, in Davenport. Of them all, Davenport produced and attracted the most first-rate figures. Within the space of ten years there were born in this Mississippi River town George Cram Cook, Susan Glaspell, Arthur Davison Ficke, and Harry Hansen. When they were still young and in the first experimental throes of creation, there came to them from outside Floyd Dell, who by working for a few years on a Davenport paper got himself adopted as an Iowa writer, though he was born in Barry, Illinois, and has spent most of his creative life in Chicago and New York. To them, also, from Bryn Mawr, came Cornelia Meigs, an English teacher of almost native antecedents, since she was born just across the river in Rock Island.

At the core of this cluster of people later to be well known was a woman already established and successful as a writer. This was Alice French (Octave Thanet), who had been brought to Davenport at the age of five, and had made her permanent home there. Her writings, even at that time, had experimented with Iowa backgrounds, and as she was a woman in her fifties when her young satellites were in their twenties, she exercised a great deal of influence.

But if Davenport could collect a brilliant group of young writers, it couldn't hold them. College, travel, newspaper work, took all but two. It may or may not be significant that those who left all achieved bigger reputations than those who remained. Whether brilliance was a cause or a result of their migration I leave to the scholars. Certainly cross-fertilization and exchange of ideas are essentials for any sound artistic growth, and even though Davenport was by all odds the best place in Iowa for writers to find a favorable environment, it couldn't compete with New York or with the brilliant spirits gathering in Chicago. By 1908 both Dell and Hansen were Chicago newspapermen. The careers of Susan Glaspell and George Cram Cook are sufficiently well known. Susan Glaspell's plays, Cook's brilliant conversational ability and magnetic personality, their elevation of the Little Theater into something live and strong, belong not to the literary history of Iowa, but to that of the United States. Nevertheless, the works of these two are among Iowa's proudest possessions, and they will still show you the place where George Cram Cook had a vision in the library stacks at Iowa City. "The Road to the Temple" begins, Iowans will tell you, on the banks of the Mississippi.

Here are two important writers and an original idea out of Iowa. They come out of Davenport, but they don't happen there. In that generation the Iowa writer was still a migratory bird, laying her eggs a long way from her birthplace.

One might add to these any number of other wanderers, of the Glaspell-Cook generation and later. Carl Van Vechten was born in Cedar Rapids, but has spent his mature life in New York. When he finally, after numerous books on cats, Spanish music, theatrical history and appreciation, and the like, returned to Iowa for fictional material, the result was "The Tattooed Countess," banned from the Cedar Rapids library. That book, like many another, is a satirical picture of the dullness, stupidity, smugness, fatuity, and all-around clod-hopperishness of the Iowa town. It is part of the revolt from the village.

The sun never sets on wandering Iowa authors. "The Able McLaughlins," Harper Prize novel in 1923, Pulitzer Prize in 1924, stems from Traer, Iowa, via India, where Margaret Wilson spent several years as a missionary. And the whole stream of James Norman Hall's books, ending in the Bounty trilogy and "Hurricane," is a product of Colfax, Iowa, by way of England, France, the Lafayette Escadrille, and the South Seas. Josephine Herbst I have already mentioned. Rupert Hughes, by virtue of a boyhood spent in Keokuk, has had his five-foot shelf of writings placed in the Iowa collections.

Of the post-war generation of writers in Iowa it is possible to say this with confidence: they consistently choose to utilize the materials of their local environment for fiction and poetry, and they show an increasing willingness to live in the state they were born in. Iowa has become as fit a subject for books, and as reputable a state for a writer to live in, as any other. If there is a slight hysteria accompanying the liberation, it can be understood, and it will pass. Cultural regionalism is the philosophy of many Iowa writers today, but the movement is liberalizing rather than the reverse. In a society moving toward complete industrial regimentation there is a profound need for the preservation of healthy provincialisms, as Josiah Royce pointed out as far back as 1902.

Properly to understand the background of the writings of Ruth Suckow, Phil Stong, Tom Duncan, Paul Engle, Winifred Van Etten, James Hearst, Jay G. Sigmund, and a good many more, we must go back to 1915, to Iowa City. In that year and that small university town, John Towner Frederick, then an undergraduate, conceived, and with the help of professors and others brought out, a little magazine called *The Midland*, dedicated to furnishing an outlet for honest and serious writing about the Middle West. This, the first of the little magazines with a regional aim, achieved in eighteen years a reputation far out of proportion to its expensiveness or appearance. In an article in *American Prefaces* some weeks ago Charles Allen lists a few of the "discoveries" made in the height of *The Midland's* career. Among the Iowans Mr. Allen notices MacKinlay Kantor, Paul Engle, Phil Stong, James Hearst, and Marquis Childs (the latter a student at Iowa at the time). Others include James Farrell, David Cornel De Jong, Albert Halper, and Clifford Bragdon.

In effect, John T. Frederick and his friends on *The Midland* did for fiction, through the little magazine, what Susan Glaspell and George Cram Cook had done for drama through the little theater. But the regional flavor not only of Frederick's magazine but of his own novels ("Druida," "The Green Bush," "The Stockade"), and the fact that his work had been done in and for Iowa and the Middle West, have made this unselfish and helpful critic and editor the greatest single force in Iowa letters in the past twenty-five years.

I have mentioned some of the writers who owe to John T. Frederick much of their confidence in dealing with local materials. There is another man, Lewis Worthington Smith, a professor at Drake University, to whom a whole group of Des Moines youngsters owe much. Smith, a poet, critic, and editor himself, kept alive an interest in writing at Drake for many years, until it finally flowered in a number of nationally known writers. Phil Stong, whose "State Fair" was a kind of triumph of simple localism, is one of that group, and though he chooses to live in Connecticut, his choice of Iowa as a locale for stories and novels has been consistent and sympathetic. Similarly Tom Duncan, author of "Oh Chautauqua!" and several volumes of sturdy verse, made use in his novel of the rural entertainments of Iowa. State fairs and chautauquas, Iowa hogs and Iowa countrymen in their square-toed Sunday best, belong to the same category as Ruth Suckow's "Iowa Interiors," "The Odyssey of a Nice Girl," "Country People," and "The Kramer Girls." They are part of the literary awakening to which James Hearst's "Countrymen," Paul Engle's "American Song," Winifred Van Etten's "I Am the Fox," and Margaret Wilson's "The Able McLaughlins" belong. Artistically, this awakening in literature is paralleled by the regional painting of Grant Wood, now professor of art at the University of Iowa.

One other writer, properly a member of the Des Moines group, must be mentioned. He is MacKinlay Kantor, who, though never a student at Drake and never under Smith's direct influence, associated himself with Tom Duncan and the other writers of the capital. Kantor has never exercised himself too much over Iowa materials. From his youth upward he has been fascinated by Civil War stories, and his writing has leaned in that direction. But he got his start by winning a short story contest sponsored by the Des Moines *Register;* he worked on newspapers in Webster City and Des Moines; he lived for a time in an abandoned farm house and wrote furiously. "Diversey," "El Goes South," and "The Jaybird" gave him something of a reputation. "Long Remember" and "The Voice of Bugle Ann" clinched it. Without ploughing as earnestly as Phil Stong and Tom Duncan in the Iowa soil, Kantor is an integral part of that Des Moines group.

And this brings us to a second literary "movement" in Iowa—or rather, to a continuation of the one begun by Frederick, Edwin Ford Piper, Frank Luther Mott, and others. This movement, centered like the first in Iowa City, is built around the School of Letters, directed by Norman Foerster. Aiming at offering a broad education in the humanities, the School of Letters from its inception in 1930 has encouraged creative writing. One result has been the development of a group that may in time become as well known as the Davenport group of a generation before.

Even in the twenties, it was possible for students at Iowa to obtain higher degrees with imaginative theses. Only one, however, tried it. Josephine Donovan offered her novel, "Black Earth," as a Master's thesis in 1929. It was accepted, but before she could finish the degree the novel was bought for publication, won a two-thousand-dollar prize, and was being dickered for by the movies. So Miss Donovan lost interest in the academic M.A. But after 1930 the creative thesis was expanded into a planned system. Edwin Ford Piper began to be flooded with volumes of verse, collections of stories, novels. Paul Engle and Richard Maibaum were among the first experimental cluster of student writers. In all, there have been something over forty imaginative theses offered and accepted for both M.A. and Ph.D. degrees.

In 1935, feeling an increasing need for a magazine like the old *Midland,* the School of Letters and the Graduate College subsidized a periodical called *American Prefaces,* edited by Wilbur Schramm. *American Prefaces* has taken up where *The Midland* left off. It has maintained a high standard, has been flattered by Edward J. O'Brien as one of the best fiction magazines in the country, and has offered an outlet for the shorter work of the group of writers congregated in Iowa City, as well as for the good work of unkowns from outside. Here is an example, a unique one, I think, of the creation of a favorable literary environment within academic halls.

As additional stimulations the School of Letters imports men of national reputation as lecturers or "tame poets" or conductors of round table discussions. Such diverse people as Stephen Vincent Benét and Vardis Fisher have been in residence. There are two practicing poets of distinction, Piper and Paul Engle, on the staff. Grant Wood's studio is open to visitors and his conversation is free—and freely given. In the past two years four novels, a volume of verse, and a collection of essays, all of them offered as theses, have been either published or accepted for publication by Eastern houses.

The emergence of Iowa as a conscious intellectual and literary region gave rise some years ago to the phrase, "the Iowa Renaissance." It has not been a renaissance in any sense of the word: there has been nothing to be reborn from, but only a long and slow awakening, through three generations of writers, to maturity and self-sufficiency. The environment of Iowa no longer looks stifling. There are definitely spots in the state where literary people congregate. The rather general tendency of those who a generation ago revolted from the village to reverse themselves and revolt from regimented industrial cities has accelerated the growth of literature in Iowa. Cultural regionalism is the dominant creed, not only of Grant Wood and his satellite artists, but of many writers, but there seems little of the aggressive sectionalism that has colored the literature of the South.

Iowa has had no literary renaissance, but it has definitely come of age. And the homogeneity of the state, the stability and conservatism of its society, the unbroken tradition of people living in much the same way for four generations, gives a solid cultural earth for the artists to dig in. That seems to me the one profoundly essential element in lasting art. That, plus a congenial intellectual environment for the artist such as the state university is offering, ought to be sufficient reason for a good deal of hopefulness about the future of Iowa literature.

.... Wallace Stegner

John Towner Frederick

Phil Stong

MacKinlay Kantor

Ruth Suckow

Clock Tower, Dubuque City Hall

Sigourney Between Depression and War: 1940

DALE KRAMER, THE AUTHOR of this Forum *essay, born in one Iowa small town (Batavia) in 1911 and died in another (Sigourney) in 1966. But in between he got around a bit: he was a newspaper reporter in Elkader, Sigourney, Iowa City, Cedar Rapids, and Des Moines; editor of farm-labor leader Milo Reno's "Holiday Farm News," an experience that led to his* The Wild Jackasses *(1956), a book about rebellious farmers, including those Josephine Herbst described; national secretary of the Farm Holiday Association; the Minnesota State Miller; free-lance writer in New York City; staff correspondent for* Yank *in World War II (Hartzell Spence was* Yank's *first editor); staffer on the* New Yorker *(an experience which led to his* Ross and the New Yorker *[1951]); and journalism professor at the University of Iowa (where the present editor was his successor).*

So Kramer was eminently qualified to do this first detailed study of what he always thought of as his "home town." His second study appeared in the Des Moines Sunday Register Picture *magazine November 11, 1956. Of the two I like this one better.*

Sigourney Between Depression and War: 1940

DURING THE 'TWENTIES a whole school of American writers gained a comfortable living by the relatively simple process of ridiculing American Main Streets. Sinclair Lewis, a native of a small Minnesota town, was discoverer and a chief exploiter of the vein (Carl Van Vechten did the same for Cedar Rapids in *Tattooed Countess*), his works being largely responsible for the assumption that America's commercialism sprang from the small town. H. L. Mencken agreed but added a bitter charge of responsibility for Prohibition.

Doubtless the arraignment was not without some justification on both counts. A success itself, Main Street, like any self-made man, was willing to advise others on the proper conduct of their private and public affairs. And it was but natural that the pioneers, since prosperity came only through hard work and sacrifice, frowned on such time-wasting frivolities as whisky-drinking, dancing, card-playing, and over-indulgence in the reading of books.

But when, through Prohibition, Main Street succeeded in at least partially forcing its code on the rest of the nation, the intellectuals of the cities rebelled, and were joined by the less inhibited sons and daughters of Main Street who had fled their environment. The fight became so extensive that the loudest anti-Main Street gun, Mencken's *American Mercury,* became the 'twenties' symbol of sophistication, and the founders of the *New Yorker* established the urbanity of their venture by simply casting an aspersion or two on "the little old lady from Dubuque."

Unfortunately, most of the anti-Main Street crusaders turned to political and economic pontification after the stock market crash of 1929, leaving the small town and its affairs largely unreported these last ten years. What, for example, was the effect of the Depression itself on Main Street civilization? Of the repeal of Prohibition? Of Roosevelt's New Deal? In short, how does the Main Street of today compare with that of the 1920s?

To answer this question, the writer has examined the business, social and cultural—with slight excursions into the political and religious—life of Sigourney, Iowa. Sigourney is a Midwestern town, county seat of Keokuk County in south central Iowa, untypical only in that it was named after a poetess, the now almost forgotten Lydia Hunt Sigourney (1791-1865), sweet singer of the middle nineteenth century.

The business houses serving the town's two thousand odd inhabitants and the surrounding farm population are set in a square around a neat, green park in the middle of which rises a three-story stone courthouse, with a six-foot town clock in its tower—the traditional courthouse square. Other essentials of Main Street life necessary for the survey—neat Carnegie library, prosperous movie theatre, the dozen odd bridge and study clubs, a new liquor dispensary—are present, and a touch of color is lent by the community's proximity to two favorite place names of the old Main Street baiters: What Cheer, twelve miles to the west, and Oskaloosa, twenty.

II

Main Street's economy—the manner in which it gets a living—is properly the first segment of its life to come under examination. Here one is struck by three major circumstances: the small community's relative prosperity, dependence for the latter on a myriad of federal agencies, and last but not least, the decline of what was loosely known as Babbitry (after the business man Babbitt of Sinclair Lewis's second novel about Main Street).

It is only necessary to glance around Sigourney's square to see that businessmen are once again feeling good after the dark years of the early 1930s. At night one may count no less than twenty gleaming neon signs, and a surprising proportion of the business houses have been remodeled inside and out. The visual impression is confirmed by local bankers, who declare that a majority of businessmen are making a living out of their establishments and that a few manage to put money aside. The percentage of merchants who are solvent is about the same as in the 'twenties, but profits are generally less.

The reason put forward by these local observers for recovery is increased business efficiency. Not so long ago there was talk of the local merchant's being driven to the wall by chain-store competition, but now he fears the chain unit no more than any other rival—although confident that his profit would be larger if the combination were legislated out of business. Careful buying, excellent display of goods, and strict cash selling have largely solved this phase of the small-town merchant's problem.

The effort to dissolve another difficulty, that of out-of-town trading, has been less successful. Shopping is a major pastime of women everywhere, and those of small communities have more and more taken advantage of the automobile and hard roads to visit the larger stores of nearby cities. As trade slackens, the stocks of those Main Street merchants most affected—dealers in dry goods, wearing apparel, and furniture—narrow, accelerating the trend.

Fittingly—though it is considered a none-too-healthy development by most economists—the place of leadership formerly held by these businesses has been taken by dealers in the commodity chiefly responsible for their decline, the automobile itself. Sigourney has four-teen garages and service stations, some of them the best money-makers in town. Even lawyers, the writer was informed by a prominent local attorney, find a chief source of income in a motorcar by-product—litigation over highway accidents.

Thus Main Street merchants showed courage and adaptibility in meeting the impact of depression and the encroachment of outside competition. But, speaking generally, they refuse to recognize the extent to which the federal treasury is responsible for lifting the black fog which enveloped them at the end of 1932—an error not indulged in by such a conservative guardian of the public purse as the *Saturday Evening Post*, which often speaks bitterly of Iowa and other hinterland States which draw more money out of the national treasury than they pay in.

There have been the AAA, CWA, PWA, WPA, CCC, FSA, FCA, SSA, SERA—a mouthful for any anti-New Deal orator. They com-mandeered all available extra space in the courthouse, including the old Assembly Room, crowded the offices under the new post office, and finally overflowed into private buildings. But each has done its bit toward priming the town pump, and more than a little of the water flowing from the spout still comes through the top rather than from the bottom of the well.

Most important, of course, are the AAA and the other agricultural agencies, for Main Street merchants are naturally dependent on the patronage of farmers. The "gentle rain of checks"—averaging about $300,000 yearly for Keokuk County—has stimulated buying, while loans from the Farm Security and Farm Credit administrations have liquified mortgages in banks and furnished capital for purchase of operating equipment.

Fewer funds have gone directly to town residents, but even these sums have not been inconsequential. Sigourney was one of those many communities which, in the dark days of 1931-1932, attempted a public works program of its own. Men were employed to crush road-surfacing rock in a local quarry and were paid in scrip which eventually was re-tired by attachment of stamps representing 2 per cent of its face value. In theory, of course, business was to be stimulated by increased buying, but actually the community was only levying on itself a tax for relief, with most of the burden falling on merchants who honored the scrip for purchases. In effect the CWA and later the WPA took over the program, only substituting specie for scrip. Men still work in the quarry, crushing rock for the roads, and their income (employment peak was thirty men, monthly wage $40.50) is equal to a small factory's payroll. Added to this is a tidy community income from the seventy-five pensions paid to Sigourney's aged, as well as from salaries of various administrative officials.

From a short-range view the importance of this federal assistance is recognized, as when fifty Sigourney businessmen journeyed to Des Moines to protest removal of the CCC camp, but politically Main Street is a dogged opponent of New Deal "spending." Although Sigourney voters, angry and frightened, turned sharply against Herbert Hoover in 1932, they asserted their basic opposition to change four years later by giving Alf Landon a majority over President Roosevelt. Since that time, charges of radicalism leveled at the New Deal have sunk deeper. Main Street merchants definitely believe themselves a part of "business" and follow the lead of their big brothers in demanding a "chance." That it might only furnish them with an opportunity once more to finance public works without the aid of wealthier tax-payers who pay taxes in neither Sigourney nor Iowa they do not consider and probably will not.

But, if Main Street has returned to the standpat political conservatism of Babbitt, it has not been so quick to readopt the rococo characteristics which made him a butt for wits of the 'twenties. The luncheon clubs meet as of old, with "right thinking" still very much the byword; but the tone is subdued. The early Depression years crushed Main Street's pride, of course, reducing its self-assurance, but at least equally important is the fact that in the chastening process the small community developed an ability to look more objectively at itself. For example, Sigourney remembers with embarrassment the signs, BEST LITTLE CITY IN IOWA, which in the 'twenties adorned the roads leading into town. In short, Main Street took on a degree of sophistication during the past decade—a fact which is even more evident in other phases of community life.

III

No Sigourney hostess has yet telephoned the society editors of the *Sigourney Review* and the *Keokuk County News* to announce that a cocktail party will be held on such and such a date or has reported Martinis in the list of refreshments at a bridge afternoon. When she does, it will be an anti-climax, for the Main Street society revolution has been won. A woman may now serve and drink liquor, in moderation of course, without loss of her honor. She may also smoke, though not on the streets or in public places.

The first guns in this battle were fired some years before the 1929 stock market crash—witness the flapper, spiked beer, necking, and the Charleston—but it was not until the old guard had been weakened on the economic front, thereby losing faith in its own general infallibility, that the youthful hordes broke down the barriers of moral righteousness. There were other factors, of course, advertising not being the least. When the first photographs of women smoking cigarettes appeared on billboards ten years ago, they were defaced, but the tobacco companies persevered, spending millions in all advertising fields. Their business judgment, it is now apparent, was good. Movies, too, played an important part in routing old taboos. Women members of the audience identified themselves with the heroine in all other things, and it was only natural that they first accepted, then emulated her cigarette and cocktail.

But not all hostesses serve liquor, and the subject is still a little touchy. Thus this writer does not wish specifically to accuse any of Sigourney's bridge clubs (Idle-A-While, Fortnightly, Matron's Pastime, Sigourney, Pleasant Hour) of these carryings-on. But the extent to which the moral wave has receded is symbolized by the prominently placed punch bowl, with alcoholic content, at the Annual New Year's Eve banquet given by members of the Lion's Club and Junior Chamber of Commerce to their wives, the high point of the social season.

Like most Main Street towns, however, Sigourney is against the sale of hard liquor over the bar and certainly would outlaw the saloon by local option if the State had not already taken the responsibility (but 3.2 beer is available at three of the five cafés). The Sigourney drinker of hard liquor must first pay one dollar for a permit book, then secure his beverage by the bottle at the State-owned liquor store, where the purchase is entered in a book. His advantage is a 25-percent saving over what he would pay in New York, Illinois, or other States licensing private dealers.

Oddly enough, the shift to legal whisky and gin after Repeal was slow. Two factors seem to have been responsible. First, youthful drinkers, having known little or anything else, actually preferred the taste of near beer spiked with alcohol. Second, older men were intimidated by the indignant eyes of the moral element peering through the plate-glass window of the converted bank building, as they waited furtively for their orders to be wrapped. As a result, illegal sale of liquor flourished for some years, until the drinking of liquor became respectable and the younger generation's taste had improved. A few bootleggers still exist, but their living is a poor one, gained from sales to minors and WPA-relief clients, who are barred from the State liquor store. But even this market is cut by the ability of nearly everyone to find an obliging friend or acquaintance who will make his purchase without fee.

No one can say with exactness, of course, whether the total consumption of intoxicants is more or less than during the 'twenties, but it appears that the increase in their use by the ladies is offset by a somewhat greater sobriety in the younger generation. Graver responsibility in an uncertain world, as well as better liquor, has undoubtedly contributed to the decline of drunkenness among youth, but more important is the simple fact that drinking lacks the romance of a decade ago.

In the pre-Prohibition period, a chief topic around high schools was the merit, price, and availability of "donkey," as raw alcohol was affectionately termed. Spines of eighteen-year-olds shivered delightfully as, automobile lights cut off, they drove up dark lanes to half-abandoned farmhouses and waited breathlessly for the bootlegger's mysterious emergence from the shadows. Reports went out of "tins" of the precious liquid buried here and there by the bulk-buying thrifty, and expeditions of the unscrupulous were organized to seek them out. It was high adventure, these young men and their girls sitting in restaurants beneath the inevitable "No Spiking" signs, hands busy under the table pouring alcohol into bottles of near beer; and often, in the excitement, too much was consumed, or the varying potency of the beverage wrought havoc with the drinker's judgment. A general rowdiness resulted, particularly at dances, where it was not uncommon for the young men of Sigourney to engage in mass combat with those of some nearby town—usually What Cheer, which Sigouronians always considered an underhand settlement, its young given to playing dirty in football and its elders not above the outright purchase of referees and umpires.

This is not to say, of course, that Main Street's youth suddenly eschewed all semblance of undecorous behavior. But the jitterbug is less raucous than the flapper, the whisky-and-lime-rickey-drinking young man less rowdy than the "donkey" tippler.

IV

Since to show the effects of repeal it has been necessary to dwell at some length on the drinking habits of Sigourney's population, it would seem well at this point to strike a balance with a report of the community's less frivolous activities.

It is possible to state, for example, that, despite their loss of the cocktail war, Main Street's church societies are still stronger in point of membership than the bridge clubs. Sigourney has its Methodist Guild, St. Mary's Altar Society (Catholic), Presbyterian Kensington Society, Women's Council of the Church of Christ, Evangelical Service Circle, Baptist Sew and So Society, to mention the chief groups, while several of the churches also maintain missionary societies. In these the neighborly helping-hand spirit of an earlier pioneer society is maintained, although it is to be expected that the quiet atmosphere of the quilting circle suffers occasional disruption as members discuss a card party which is known to be going full blast on that very afternoon.

In certain respects, however, the churches have accepted modernization. For one thing, the old-fashioned fire-and-brimstone revival meeting is, in general, a thing of the past; most of the younger ministers are opposed to conversion by this method. The tendency to a calmer spiritual approach has obliterated another familiar institution, the Sunday-school "contest." There was a day when Sigourney's Methodists so agressively competed with those of Delta, seven miles to the west, that other Sunday schools were emptied. It is natural, too, that in an age of economic upheaval the preachers are taking a greater interest in social and political problems.

Not all Main Street churches are so fortunate as to participate in a twenty-thousand dollar legacy willed for the specific purpose of encouraging Sunday-school attendance. Sigourney's are—the donor was a former resident, Sandy Moody, a thrifty bachelor, who spent the major portion of his life as a proofreader for the *St. Louis Post-Dispatch*—but the number of churches is in normal relation to the population, and the standard of living of the ministers is average. Of the seven churches, the Methodist, Presbyterian, Church of Christ, German Evangelical, and Catholic support regular pastors while the Baptist and Adventist do not. Each minister is furnished with a parsonage and is paid $1,500 to $1,800 annually, a few hundred dollars less than his pre-1930 compensation.

But, if Main Street towns are seldom lucky enough to benefit from the philanthropy of a Sandy Moody, the furor which later resulted from his action is typical of those waves of passion which occasionally sweep a small community, dividing it into warring camps.

Sigourney had almost forgotten Sandy Moody when, four years ago, it read in the daily newspapers that he had died, leaving the proceeds of his life's toil to Sigourney. A few items were stipulated: five thousand dollars for a rest room at the cemetery, one thousand directly to each of four churches, five hundred for three stone seats in the courtyard (inscribed on them are the words *Friendship, Sandy Moody*), and two thousand for play equipment to be placed in the community grove at the edge of town. But more than twenty thousand dollars were left

for the use and benefit of children in and about the town of Sigourney for the purpose of encouraging children to attend Sunday school and to acquire Christian ideals and habits necessary for useful citizens.

The difficulty arose in the interpretation of this clause. The church groups were of the conviction that all residue should go directly to the Sunday schools; the fund's board of trustees, made up of local bankers, attorneys, and businessmen, held that it might be distributed for Boy

Scout work and other secular youth activities, on the ground that they, too, encouraged Christian ideals. As a result of the deadlock, no money was distributed at all.

Then the church women acted. First selecting as official orators ten women from each of the four churches named for specific benefits (Methodist, Church of Christ, Presbyterian, Baptist), they called a mass meeting, and the board was bidden for discussion of the issues. Whether the trustees were improperly notified, as was later claimed, or whether fear of the staggering opposition of forty women debaters was too much for it, the board failed to show up. Angered, the women drafted a set of resolutions, which they ordered inserted in the local newspapers, and delivered one final ultimatum to the trustees. This time the trustees came, but all except two resigned before a single speaker could get to her feet. It was a victory for the women, though. A new board, appointed by the court, soon authorized four thousand dollars for the purchase of Sunday-school equipment, the Catholic and German Evangelical churches also benefiting, this time.

Fitting into the older Main Street social pattern, too, are the numerous lodges, patriotic societies, and "study" clubs. Of these only the latter have shown an inclination to change.

V

Succeeding generations of Sigourney's youth have pulled open the heavy plate-glass door of the red-brick Carnegie library, piled their hats and coats on the broad shelf over the radiator at the top of the short flight of stairs, and padded silently across the rubber-matted floor to the bookshelves and magazine tables. On school nights, the heavy oak tables are surrounded by boys and girls of high-school age looking up assignments given them by their teachers; armloads of books are carried home by children of all ages. But somehow the library's presence has not resulted in an appreciation of contemporary literature. Dreiser, Sherwood Anderson, Hemingway are barely present; Wolfe, Caldwell, Fitzgerald, Dos Passos, Faulkner not at all.

The fact is that Main Street's literary affairs are inexorably dominated by that singular figure of American letters, Zane Grey. Of 104 books purchased during the first half of 1939, twelve, mostly replacements of worn-out volumes, were from Mr. Grey's pen. Other popular authors, but trailing at a considerable distance are Gene Stratton Porter, Edna Ferber, Fannie Hurst, Lloyd C. Douglas, James Oliver Curwood, and Peter B. Kyne, while Edgar Rice Burroughs would undoubtedly fare very well if the librarian had not some years ago taken a notion to censor him by the simple process of neglecting to reorder his books. These, with mystery stories, nonfiction works on aviation and exploration (Admiral Byrd's *Alone* and Anne Lindbergh's *Listen! the Wind* were in some demand), and the children's books comprise most of the titles which pass over the librarian's desk at an average rate of fifty a day.

The search for signs of vegetation in this wasteland is not very encouraging, although a few are discoverable. The most important educational force is the radio, and, if the literary tastes of Main Street improve, it will be largely because this institution takes fuller advantage of its opportunities. The possibilities are demonstrated by a sharp increase in demand at the public library for titles discussed by a book commentator on the Iowa State College station at Ames. Meanwhile the women's study groups hear book reviews and occasionally discuss a short story which has been read aloud from one or another of the "quality" magazines. Sigourney has its Stitch and Study Club and Women's Club, both devoting the major portion of each meeting to literary and educational subjects, while the Alpha Delphian Chapter regularly pursues a course of study laid out by its national officers.

Against these encouraging factors is the inability of the library to stock even a fraction of the volumes in which the community should be interested, and here the Depression struck the small-town reader a hard blow. Looking about for a budget item to slash, the eyes of the town council were apt to light first on the library tax levy. For example, the Sigourney library's annual pre-Depression budget for book purchases was two thousand dollars, against four hundred at the present time. After the purchase of replacements, there is naturally little remaining for the acquisition of new books. In querying the Sigourney library to discover the local attitude toward John Steinbeck's social, and from some points of view, slightly salacious novel, *The Grapes of Wrath*, this writer learned that the work created no problem—for the simple reason that, having spent its half-year budget, the library's board was not considering new books.

Thus, since the taste of Main Street's reading public has not developed to a point where it will clamor on its own account for more and better fare and because local councilmen are unlikely to increase taxes for a project they are apt to consider frivolous, any hope of returning the library item in the budget to the old figure seems to lie in a possible crusade by the women's study groups. They would be irresistible in such an action. Undoubtedly some groups have already brought pressure on their local lawmaking bodies; others, probably, have merely failed to think of it or are unaware that budgets are but a shadow of their former substance.

Bearing more directly on Main Street's life than the library is the moving-picture theatre, and here it is possible to present a somewhat more encouraging report. Audiences are demanding a higher quality in plot, direction, and acting.

This is not to say, however, that the moviegoing public has suddenly grown sophisticated. A survey of the Garden Theatre's offerings reveals Sigourney still partial to the he-man-who-doesn't-want-to-fight-but-has-to type of drama; and, despite the undoubted spurring of liquor-drinking and cigarette-puffing by the cinema, Sigourney is for the wholesome maiden against the slinky city gal every time. But the manager has been forced to cease booking the Buck Jones-Ken Maynard type of thriller, and even the so-called "horse operas" of the Gene Autry school command only mild interest. Now, when a *Dodge City*, *Stage Coach* or *Union Pacific*—the old formula more expertly handled—appears on the horizon, he bills it for a four-day run, certain of packed houses. Of course, a picture made from one of Zane Grey's classics is sure-fire, let the producer do his worst.

When no outdoor melodrama is available, the Garden's manager tries to get one of the highly publicized stars in something with plenty of action and not too much sex. Thus Robert Taylor (his producers knew what they were about when he was set to swapping punches on more or less even terms with Wallace Beery) is more popular than the "smoother" Tyrone Power. Sonja Henie, with her skating and wholesome naïveté is popular, and so are Fred Astaire and Ginger Rogers, particularly when they dance. Greta Garbo, Joan Crawford, Katharine Hepburn, and Bette Davis emote too freely, embarrassing onlookers. But the Main Street audience is a young one, and the advancement in its taste, although a high degree has not yet been reached, furnishes a glimmer of hope for better things from Hollywood.

On the radio, Main Street likes the favorites of the rest of the nation, with such variation as might be expected from its taste in movies. A survey of Iowa's preferences made by Kansas State College in the spring of 1939 showed Jack Benny the favorite, with Charlie McCarthy second. A slick little fellow, Charlie lost esteem the further he got from the city, the range of popularity being great even between Iowa's cities and her villages. Other national programs followed at a considerable distance, with those of the Fibber McGee type gaining as they progressed into villages and rural areas. Few rooters were found for the darling of Manhattan's intelligentsia, "Information, Please!"

Besides these, Main Street has hardly any cultural contacts. Few books are purchased, while magazine consumption ranges from pulps up the scale to slicks, with readers of the latter apt to consider themselves somewhat highbrow. Naturally there is little or no access to the legitimate theatre, and that old cultural agent, Chautauqua, has for some time been dead or nearly so. Only slightly more life remains in another summer institution; the tent show, with its red-wigged "Toby," dastardly villain, and heroine of most spotless virtue. But its final doom has been sealed by the improved critical judgment resulting from a diet of movies; increasing numbers view the melodrama as farce. Sigourney's chief interest in the annual approach of Hila Morgan's show is—and in fact has been for twenty years—whether Hila, admitting the encroachments of time, has at last ceased her portrayal of sixteen-year-old innocence.

IV

The major conclusion to be drawn from all this seems to be that, during the decade of 1929-1939, Main Street's domination of America's moral life ended. The small community's hold was broken by a defection in its own ranks as the radio, movie, and automobile brought the ways of the city closer and as the prestige and authority of the older generation were shattered by its inability to cope with the Depression.

Paradoxically, the modernizing process was accompanied by Main Street's readoption, under the pressure of hard times, of some older and simple values. Besides deflating "boosterism," the Depression rained calamities on well-to-do and poor so indiscriminately that women felt no strong necessity for competing in "appearances," which reduced jealousy and its chief product, gossip. It is impossible to state categorically that the size of the electric refrigerator and the make and model of the family automobile have entirely lost their position as arbiters of Main Street's social standings, but their influence has been greatly reduced.

There is danger, of course, that a business boom which may still result from the increased demand of warring nations for U.S. Farm products may upset the rural community's equilibrium, calling back the breast-thumping Babbitt. And since Main Street is notoriously excitable, the United States' entry into the war on the side of the Allies would, despite strong isolationist sentiment, severely test its new-found tolerance. In the last war, the German population of small communities suffered unnecessarily; houses were painted yellow for no good reason, and other forms of persecution were practiced.

Benefit of the doubt should go to Main Street. Babbitry, after all, resulted largely from the businessman's overweening confidence in his own abilities, and there could be little doubt in his mind that a war boom was owing to no stroke of genius on his own part. As for hysteria, it will certainly come if war does, but memory of the stupidities committed during the last conflict should serve as a powerful deterrent to new ones. For two decades Sigourney has recalled with shame the day on which a mob paraded a harmless old German around the square, a sign, I AM A GERMAN SPY, attached to his back. Since officials were hardly interested in espionage agents of that sort (his crime was a Kaiser beard), Sigourney finally placed him on a train going out of town. Moreover, the Germans of Midwestern communities, now mostly second- and third-generation stock, are known to be unsympathetic to Naziism, and therefore unlikely to be charged with undue friendliness to Hitler.

On the other hand, neither is there much chance that Main Street will depart further from its traditionally simple way of life; Mr. Mencken, Mr. Lewis, and their fellow travelers of yesteryear will have to be satisfied with a partial rout of Puritanism and a mere beginning of interest in "cultural" affairs. Yet much of the gap between the small town and the city was closed during the past decade—as much as probably ever will be. Meanwhile, as the urban center improves its civilization, if it does, Main Street will undoubtedly advance proportionately.

. . . Dale Kramer

County Fair

STATE CAPITOL WITH SCOTT'S GRAVE — DES MOINES, IOWA

- FRANK SNYDER PLACE-NEAR DALLAS CENTER. IOWA -

The Farmer's Job

THE "MOUTHFUL" of acronyms—AAA, FSA, FCA, and so on—in
Dale Kramer's Sigourney article, was one indicator that farming on the
former prairies of Iowa was changing. It was no longer the romantic situation of man and wife and family out there in the natural world (as con-
trasted with the urban world of town and city). Farming had become big
business, and like big businesses of other sorts, was affected by the winds of
international economics and international politics.

The next two articles reflect these changing conditions. James Hearst's
1946 "The Farmer's Job" (one of several written for The Nation that
year) is a response to businessmen's criticism of the farmer for asking for
government "handouts." Hearst brought to these articles the insight of a
fourth-generation Iowa farmer and the style and perceptions of a poet.

The Farmer's Job

MY NEIGHBOR, who is a farmer and a very good one, says that city folk seem to think there are two kinds of people in the world—farmers and other people. He professes to be greatly puzzled by this distinction. But he suspects the line is drawn because non-farm people have really no understanding of the nature of farmers or of farming.

The Iowa farmer is sensitive about this lack of understanding. Usually quiet and self-effacing, except with high-pressure salesmen or hogs in the garden, he would like to have his work understood and appreciated—not as a romantic way of life certainly but in terms of its own value. It doesn't take a war to tell him what he is worth to a nation; he knows very well who furnishes the food and fiber for the world and at what cost. He may never have reasoned it out, but he has a stubborn self-respect. The farmer has been the butt of many jokes, the stooge for many a quick turn; he is insulted daily on the radio by hill-billy bands and psalm-singing medicine men. He seldom answers back because he is somewhat inarticulate, as men often are who work by themselves. In his heart he knows that these things are insignificant compared to the forces with which he lives. Yet when he is sorely tried by hecklers, he takes sardonic amusement in the knowledge that if he chose to quit work those vague clouds on the horizon would suddenly materialize into the ruthless legions of famine and starvation.

This loyalty to his vocation is what made possible the farmer's remarkable achievements during the war. In spite of a third less help, worn-out machinery, a losing struggle to obtain seeds and fertilizer, the farmer produced more crops and livestock than ever before. It wasn't easy. You folks who work in offices from nine to five, who have the day off whenever a holiday comes along, who go home on Saturdays at noon, you won't know what I'm talking about. A lot of the boys around here are humping around complaining about lame shoulders or a crick in the back. Some of them say that doctoring doesn't seem to do much good; they think they'll feel better when the warm weather comes. Don't feel sorry for them. Just remember that they didn't get those sore muscles from mowing the yard. You don't turn out three-billion-bushel corn crops or raise a hundred million head of hogs by sitting at a desk and adding up figures.

For a farmer it isn't so much that his job is important as that his job is his life. A farmer wants to make things grow. He wants to put seed in the earth and, come hell or high water, make a crop of it. This desire to grow things burns in his guts not in his head. He tries to keep his head clear for administrative matters. A farmer can no more help wearing himself out trying to raise bigger crops, fatter hogs, or better milk cows than corn can help growing hot in the bins when planting time comes. He is part of nature, too, and we may as well admit it.

He sees a betrayal of values in the "scarcity" programs so indulgently extolled by the National Association of Manufacturers. Once in the early 1930s the locked doors of factories forced the farmer to follow this same pattern. It was the only way out for him at the time, but he has no desire to repeat it.

Consequently strikes make him uneasy. He knows that there is no percentage for anybody in closed factories and idle men. But his attitude toward the cause of strikes has changed profoundly. He is no longer moved by the pleas of big business for "free enterprise" and "free competition." The farmer is a hard man to catch with the same trick a second time. After the First World War, while he was aimlessly scratching himself, he backed into the buzz-saw of free enterprise and lost several fingers. He won't do that again, no matter what his itch. He has discovered the obvious—that industry hasn't been subject to free enterprise since the days of Henry Clay. What the leaders of industry really mean by free enterprise is freedom for them to exploit the people who do the actual work of the world. The farmer is slowly growing deaf to their exhortations. He is equally skeptical of their arguments about the advantages of competition. He has only to price the various makes of tractors or refrigerators to find out that "it ain't so."

His challenge, these days, to industry is this: Come out from behind the protection of your corporate structure and fight like men. If you want free enterprise, then *you* give up all the government privileges and guaranties you have and meet us on our own ground. We will put on a production race with you 365 days in the year. You take what your goods will bring; we will take what ours bring—even on world markets. But for God's sake, let's get going. If you want to discredit representative government and the capitalistic system, just keep on with your stupid acts and statements against the general welfare.

. . . James Hearst, 1946

Hamlin Garland Pioneer Home, Osage

Moravian Church, Grace Hill

Heresy at Cherokee

*RELIGIOUS FREEDOM was the goal of many who left the Old World
for the New; many who came to Iowa came to be free to practice a faith in
which they strongly believed. And Iowa has always been a deeply religious
state, and its churches have represented an important institution in the
state's history.*

*But as we have seen in James Stevens's article, there were problems with
following one's religion in Iowa and other places, especially when strong
adherents of varying faiths were thrown together in small Iowa towns
where everyone knew everyone else.*

*In Hartzell Spence's article following, excerpted from his 1942 biography
of his father, one of the most popular ministers in Iowa history, we also
see another side of the coin. Spence's father may have had One Foot in
Heaven, as Spence's book insists, but his other foot was right in the middle
of earthly church politics.*

*Spence, the author of a baker's dozen of books, was born in Clarion in
1908, and for the same reasons as Ruth Suckow, he grew up in Burlington,
Mason City, Fort Dodge, Sioux City, Lake Mills and other towns. He
took a journalism degree from the University of Iowa in 1930. From 1930
to 1941 he was a correspondent for United Press International. He helped
found Yank, the Army magazine, during World War II.*

Heresy at Cherokee

SOMETIMES AN ISSUE DEVELOPED over a matter that touched collective personal prejudices and proved too fundamental to be handled, as was the Ladies' Aid election, by a quick flank attack. Prejudices caused father his most anxious moments. But if he decided a matter of principle was involved he would defy the entire congregation.

The minister who had preceded father at Fort Dodge was a Southerner. How he had arrived in a Northern church was one of the peculiar mysteries of church politics. During Dr. Caldwell's pastorate a prejudice against Negroes filtered through the congregation until the members would not even employ a Negro sexton.

Father was aware of this, but he knew that a dutiful blast from the pulpit would only intensify the feeling. So he became a personal example of kindliness toward the few Negroes in town. He helped the African M.E. preacher with a revival meeting and called him "Brother" on the street. A few parishioners talked, but not many.

Then one spring day a Negro musician came to town for a recital. "Blind Henry," they called him. A fine pianist, his particular act of showmanship was to invite the town's best music teacher to the platform to play any number she desired. He would play it after her. This gave a local musician a chance to shine and was easy for Blind Henry. Almost every small-town musician, showing off her best work, plays Chopin. Henry knew Chopin by heart.

Blind Henry was to play in our church because it was the town's largest auditorium. My sister at that time was studying the piano. When father told Blind Henry that Eileen would be unable to hear him because of illness, the musician went to the parsonage to play for her. We were so absorbed in listening that we did not notice Eileen's schoolteacher approach to learn why she had not attended school. Miss Millrose, peering through a porch window, saw Eileen not only out of bed but listening respectfully to a Negro being entertained in the pastor's home.

Miss Millrose did not even knock. Back to school she went and, after weeks of petty persecution, failed my sister.

When Eileen brought home her report card, father was so upset he was able to eat only one portion of Swiss steak at dinner. For the first time he, as a preacher, had been attacked through his children, and the unfairness of such tactics enraged him. He walked the floor between his study and the front porch for an hour after dinner, then sought mother.

"All right," he pronounced with the finality of a last judgment, "all right. I'll show them—every mother's son of them!"

Then began an amazing summer. One Sunday morning the congregation found its choir absent; in its place, a traveling troupe from the Piney Woods school was singing spirituals. Another Sunday a Negro bishop from the South was guest preacher. On still other days father exchanged pulpits with Brother Hankins of the African church—all this without a word of explanation.

As the teacher of the men's Bible class remarked one morning, "We come to church to learn right from wrong, but now we can scarcely tell black from white."

A dutiful parishioner repeated the remark to father at the close of service that very day.

"That's fine," father replied quickly. "If Brother Wilson is amused, he can't be very badly upset."

Quietly an argument germinated and spread through the congregation. Those with the dearest memories of Dr. Caldwell, father's predecessor, those who had held church offices under him and now had none, became vocally anti-Negro. Father's friends and church appointees, the farm contingent that is always loyal, and those to whom he had ministered in joy and sorrow lined up behind him.

As the time of school reopening arrived, with the Annual Conference only four weeks away, the fight broke into the open. The first blast came at the fourth Quarterly Conference, which decides whether the preacher shall be invited back for another year. Major Charles Wainwright Cooper, who had fought for the Confederacy and never let anyone forget it, arose at the invitation to new business. The district superintendent was presiding.

"Am I to understand," the major began, challenging father, "that you asked the school superintendent to advance your daughter from the third to fourth grade, although she failed to pass last spring?"

Father's jaw squared.

"I did," he admitted.

"Am I to understand," the major went on, "that you raised the accusation of race prejudice against the teacher who did not pass your child?"

"I did."

"May I inquire the circumstances?"

"You may."

The room was very quiet. This was strictly a private fight. Nobody wanted to get mixed up in it. Members knew from experience that their preacher could not be beaten in face-to-face debate.

"Miss Millrose," father commenced, with the peculiar little sigh that always escaped him when he was fighting to inhibit a show of anger, "told three sisters of this church that my daughter Eileen was as bright as any third-grade child and that Eileen was failed to show the pastor of this church that he could not fraternize with colored people."

"Is it true," the inquisitor pursued, "that you demanded Miss Millrose's resignation?"

"It is not true. I distinctly told Brother Haynes (the school superintendent) that if Miss Millrose would be at all embarrassed I would drop the whole matter and send my daughter to the parochial school."

That was a blast. Father had counted on it to break Major Cooper's attack. He was not disappointed. Half a dozen members leaped up, exclaiming simultaneously, "You did what?" while others looked around apprehensively as if expecting the church to cave in.

Calmly father repeated his remark. The tumult increased, until the district superintendent's voice cut across the babel.

"Silence, brethren!" he shouted. "Give Brother Spence a chance to explain."

Father walked firmly to the front of the room and turned to face everyone.

"In the parochial school," he said, "they do not teach racial intolerance. It is written, 'Love thy neighbor as thyself.' The gospel of Christ is the lesson I want my children to learn, and I will send them where it is taught. It would be a shame if a Methodist child had to learn to be a good Methodist from the Catholics because of bigotry in her own church. Tolerance, brethren, is something we might all learn from the Sisters of Charity."

He left the meeting then, knowing that a terrific debate would follow over the question whether to invite him to return for another year. Anxiously he walked the floor at home. Finally the telephone rang.

"Well, Brother Spence," the district superintendent reported, "you won, but you'd better be careful. The minority faction will take this to Conference."

"I'll be ready," father said, his face ashen.

The next morning, while walking downtown, he met Father Murphy.

"I understand," the priest baited him gently, "that you had need to summon our assistance last night."

"Father Murphy," the Methodist minister said, smiling graciously, "I'd call on the Devil in Hell if he would be of any help. But I figured invoking your assistance would be preferable."

This conversation was overheard by two Methodists and a freethinker who stood outside a bookstore, awaiting delivery of the Chicago papers. By noon the story was all over town, and father's stock began to go up. He might even have warded off the attack at Conference except for an untoward incident that occurred the following week.

A celebrated Negro singer came to town. Father never overlooked the chance to hear a great musician practice and was always discreetly in the background when an artist tested the acoustics of the church auditorium, where important town concerts were always held.

After the practice father walked forward and introduced himself.

"I wish," he remarked, "that I had a voice like yours in my choir."

"Thank you, sir," the singer said respectfully. "Perhaps you can help me. You see—my wife and I can't eat in the restaurant here, and we were turned away at the hotel. I wonder if you have a little room where we may rest until the recital."

Father gasped.

"You come right over to the house," he said. "We have a spare room. And, of course, you'll have dinner with us."

The Negro and his wife remained overnight. By noon next day the anti-Negro group was organizing the parish again.

When father heard that the Negro issue had been revived, he hunted up mother. He found her busy with the morning house-cleaning.

"Do you suppose," he asked, following her into the bathroom, "that those stupid fools really will take this to Conference?"

"I guess they will," mother murmured, picking up the soiled towels and putting them in a hamper.

"But they haven't a leg to stand on," father protested, looking around for a place to put the scrubbing pail she had handed him. "They can't ask me to move just because I want them to be tolerant."

Mother wiped the washbowl with her cloth. "They might make something, though," she said quitely, "of your threat to send Eileen to a Catholic school."

"Ah, bosh," father snorted, setting the pail down where mother would trip over it. "That was just a meeting buster. Nobody took it seriously."

Patiently mother picked up the pail and stood back to put fresh towels on the rack.

"The bishop might," she suggested.

"H-m-m-m," said father, following her into the hall and unconsciously handing her a dust mop from the closet. With hands tucked under his suspenders, he pursued her. "I can fix that. I'll find a precedent for it in the bishop's ministry in China."

He chuckled, took the dust mop, and returned it to the closet.

"What if the men don't apply a specific accusation," mother suggested, "but just ask for your removal?" She walked into Eileen's room and began to make the bed.

"That's a horse of another color," said father, blocking the doorway.

"Yes, it is," mother agreed.

"You don't suppose they'd really do that, do you?" he worried. "They'd want a sure case. Too many people are loyal to me here. I could organize a counter-demonstration that would shiver the bishop's spine."

He trudged down the backstairs behind mother and into the kitchen, where he leaned against the wall while she attacked the morning dishes.

"That," she objected, "would be proof that you needed to fight."

"H-m-m-m," murmured father, "so it would."

He was silent, now, but not for long.

"I wish I hadn't said that about the Catholics."

Mother let him wrestle with that one by himself. She did her housework quickly, without waste motion. Occasionally she handed him a stack of dishes to put away. Dutifully he did so, without being aware of it. Mother got a great deal of work out of him when he was thinking about something else.

"Don't you think what I said to Father Murphy on the street will scotch this Catholic business?"

"No," said mother, giving him a dish towel to hang up, "I think just the opposite."

"Why?"

He had to pursue her into the living room to hear the answer.

"Because you put the church laundry on the front line for the whole town to see. People will resent that."

"But only a few," father argued, busy now slapping a dustcloth over chairs and sofa.

"It only takes one," mother reminded him, improving on the dusting with quick flicks of her own, "especially if that one seeks help."

"From whom?"

Mother pretended to be dusting the piano.

"Oh, from other pastors, perhaps."

Father dropped suddenly into his leather chair.

"That's possible," he said.

"Suppose," mother went on, "that Major Cooper organizes a few of the pastors who were angry last year because you came to Fort Dodge and they accuse you of something specific?"

"Such as—?"

"Well—" mother went to work on the bookcases, sure that father was listening carefully, "in view of your praise of the Catholics, they might ask you to stand trial on charges of heresy."

Father leaped up.

"They'd never dare!"

He watched mother disappear into the library and then went after her.

"What *would* they do?" she asked.

"They'd—" he held out his hand for the dustcloth again, "they'd probably cook up something."

Mother assumed particular industry.

"Suppose," she ventured, "they asked you to preach the Conference sermon and then riddled it with holes? You know any sermon can be challenged if isolated sentences are used for examples."

"H-m-m-m," said father, getting in her way before the folding doors separating library from parlor could come between them.

Mother trudged upstairs to her bedroom and sat down with her darning. Father tagged along.

"You know," he said, "I'd rather have something like that to fight— something I could get my teeth in—than be kicked out without any charges."

"I know you would, dear," mother answered, her needle attacking an enormous hole in her son's stocking.

Father began walking up and down. As his mind took hold of the problem the length of his stride increased. Finally he paused altogether, and a twinkle came into his eye.

"How's this," he beamed. "I will get old George Settles off in a corner and tell him, man to man, that the only thing I'm afraid of is that they'll get help from some other preachers and accuse me of heresy— that I can beat anything else into the ground. I'll tell him I'm only confiding in him because I have to tell somebody or bust wide open, and I know I can trust him. He'll go straight to Cooper as fast as he can hitch a horse, and, mark my words, by sundown Major Cooper will be on his way to Sioux City with as neat a scheme as anybody ever hatched."

Mother nodded proudly. Her strategy had worked. "That's fine, dear," she encouraged him. "But what will you do then?"

"Oh, don't worry about that," father said, and a moment later the front door slammed behind him. Mother, needle idle now, watched him through a window as he strode confidently down the street in the general direction of George Settles's pickle works.

When father returned dinner was nearly ready. Since he had not been home to lunch mother assumed he had been successful. She handed him a bundle of silver with which to set the table.

"Tell me about it," she invited.

"Mr. Settles was easy. After I took him into my confidence, I went over to the bank. Through the window I watched him go over to the courthouse and chat with Major Cooper, who was sitting on his usual bench on the lawn. The major went home immediately. Then I lunched with Dr. Romer, just to be sure that most of our delegates will be on my side. Finally, the major caught the five-thirty train for Sioux City. Undoubtedly he's on his way to see Stillman and a few other preachers.

From the heft of his bag I'd say he was planning to be gone a week."

"He didn't see you!" mother exclaimed.

"He sure did," father chuckled. "I was down at the station, paying a pastoral call on the ticket agent when he showed up. He turned five shades of green when he saw me and mumbled something about going up to the city to sell some cattle."

"What did you say to that?" mother asked, holding her breath.

"I said," father laughed, slapping his knee, "that I hoped he'd get what he wanted."

Two days later father received a telegram from Bishop S–. "Want you preach Conference Sunday sermon," it read, "please reply."

Father found mother in the basement ironing and put the telegram on her board.

"Well," he announced, "here it is."

"They're working fast," mother said, dexterously smoothing a starched collar. Father always had at least fourteen shirts in the weekly wash.

"That's the way Stillman works," father grunted. "You remember how quickly he organized, trying to get Fort Dodge for himself last year. I'll bet a hat he took Major Cooper's bait–hook, line, and sinker."

Mother toyed with the dampened clothes, looking for something easy. She selected a pile of handkerchiefs and went to work.

"What sermon will you preach?"

Father pondered. "How about that one from Daniel: 'O King, I have done no hurt'?"

"No," mother objected quickly, "that would put you on the defensive."

"So it would," father agreed, beginning a tiger pace from the washtubs to the ash pile to the fruit cellar and back again.

"How about that humdinger from Ephesians: 'Put on the whole armor of God'? Maybe by implication they would get the rest of the quotation–"

Mother picked up the verse where father had dropped it. "'That ye may be able to stand against the wiles of the devil. . . .' No, that would only antagonize them."

"How about a missionary sermon? Nobody could find fault with that, especially since benevolences haven't come in very well this year."

Mother selected some table linen from her basket and continued ironing. "No, it must be something special for the occasion."

Father gazed at the labels on a shelf of jelly jars, then wheeled back to the washtub.

"How about building a sermon on Paul's letter to the Corinthians? 'It is a very small thing that I should be judged of you . . . for I know nothing against myself.'"

"That's not subtle."

"No," father admitted, staring into the ashpit, "but it would make a whale of a sermon. Remind me to order some more coal."

Mother put aside her iron.

"Haven't you a book of Bishop S—'s sermons?"

"Yes," said father, *The Cathedral of Pines,* I think it is."

"Why don't you go up and read the bishop's sermons? They might give you an idea."

Father stopped meandering.

"What do you mean?" he asked.

"Well," said mother innocently, "if you are going to be on trial you should be particularly careful not to preach anything which violates the bishop's own theology. You wouldn't want him against you."

Father thought that over.

"All right," he assented, "but I don't see what good it will do."

He stomped upstairs and remained in the library until dinnertime. Then, when we were seated, he emerged and said grace with all the confidence of the redeemed. The sparkle had returned to his eyes.

"Well?" asked mother anxiously, as he began to carve the beef roast.

"I have a plan," he said.

The week before Conference father was a bear. Not only had he to collect all financial arrears and check the annual reports of societies and organizations but he had his Conference sermon to prepare.

He would retire to his study immediately after breakfast. For several hours we would hear him pace up and down, talking to himself. Occasionally a book slammed on his desk. Now and again he kicked the hot-air register with a comforting bang. Then he would emerge, his face tense, and slam out of the house for a long walk in the courthouse grounds. This went on intermittently all week.

Finally the day came for him to leave for Cherokee, where the Conference was to be held. The lay delegates, only two of whom were in league with Major Cooper, had already gone on.

Mother walked with father halfway to the station, talking to him earnestly.

"Now remember, dear," she said in parting, "not a word to anybody. Don't let your habit of talking get hold of you. You don't know who your friends are."

He leaned down and kissed her.

"God bless you," he said. "If the house burns, get the kids and the sermons. Let the rest go. If we have to move I'll send you a wire."

"Oh, send me one anyway," she called after him, with a final show of bravery, "I so seldom get a telegram."

The days passed with aching slowness, the monotony broken only by short letters from Cherokee that increased rather than eased the anxiety.

"Stillman has things well organized," father wrote. "He sees his chance to get into Fort Dodge and is pursuing it with more diligence than ever he chased a sinner. The major is here, of course. Though not a delegate, he explains his presence by saying he came for spiritual guidance. I think he'll get it."

Next day another letter came:

"The bishop took me aside and warned that the brethren will challenge my sermon after the service Sunday. I am sure he is on my side. He told me that once in Hankow, when the bandits came, he took his whole flock for refuge into the Catholic mission because it had a high wall. 'The wall,' he said, 'was really to keep us Methodists out, but I just told the good Jesuit father that we had been battering so long at the walls of Heaven it was no trick at all to break into his cloister.'"

On Friday:

"The report from our parish is the best in the entire Conference. If the good brethren were hunting for a weakness in my armor here, they are very disappointed. Also, I noticed Mrs. Baker and a half dozen other members take the bishop aside. We have some very loyal friends, mother, and they are coming to our rescue, for which God be thanked."

Then Saturday:

"Pray for me tonight and tomorrow, for I shall need you."

When mother read that letter, she summoned my sister and me and bade us bathe in a hurry. Father was in real trouble, and she was going to be with him.

We slipped into Cherokee and went to the Methodist parsonage, where we spent the night. We didn't see father until Sunday morning, when he stepped into the pulpit with the bishop and four district superintendents. We were inconspicuously seated in the balcony and did nothing to attract his attention, but father spotted us during the organ prelude. His eyes brightened, and he started to smile, then quickly rubbed his nose to conceal his curving lips. Then he crossed his knees and began to bob a leg up and down, a sure sign that he was pleased.

As though this were a regular Sunday, the service started. There was nothing unusual about its beginning except that, after the Cherokee pastor had read out the hymns, the choir yelled a little louder and longer than usual for the benefit of the visiting bishop. A district superintendent led the prayer. Another superintendent read from the Psalter. Then the bishop quoted the Scripture and made almost endless announcements. A third superintendent exhorted the congregation to be liberal and started the collection plates on their way. Again the choir sang, as badly as before.

Then father arose, dressed in his best: winged collar and ascot, black vest with white starched piqué facing, Prince Albert coat, and striped trousers. He was an amazing figure, but far more impressive than his habiliments were the angle of his jaw, the glint in his eye, and the softening aura of devoutness contributed by the gentle blue light that came, like a blessing, through a stained-glass window.

Father looked over the congregation serenely, estimating to within ten or a score the number of persons present. Then he took out his watch, detached it from its chain, and set it on the pulpit. Calmly he opened his Bible, read a text, laid the Book down, stepped a little to one side of the pulpit in full view of everyone, particularly the three hundred visiting ministers, and began to preach.

He used no notes, but spoke from memory. His words articulated to the rafters, though they were softly pitched. After the first few sentences he glanced at the bishop, and an impish flash crossed between them. The sermon he preached was a great one. There was no doubt of it in the mind of anyone present.

When it ended there was a hush of respect. The bishop rose and pronounced the benediction. Most of the congregation sauntered out, taking endless time, while the preachers pretended to be talking to one another or perused the notes they had made furtively during the sermon. Finally, when only the pastors and a few interested laymen remained, the Reverend Mr. Stillman rose to his feet to address the chair.

"If it please the bishop," he called out, "I ask that a business meeting be convened at once to deliberate a matter that cannot wait until tomorrow."

The bishop's gavel fell. The preachers tensed in their pews. The dread charge of heresy was about to be levied. A board of trial examiners would be appointed in order to present a damning report on the morrow just before the Conference adjourned. Mother gripped our hands, and her eyes fixed themselves on father with a gaze that did not waver except once, when father deliberately winked at her.

"There has been much talk," Stillman went on, "concerning the ecclesiastical heresy of one of our brethren."

He let that sink in deeply.

"I would be exceedingly reluctant to bring such a charge against a brother without the most careful foundation," he continued, "for, once made, such a charge cannot easily be withdrawn and must of necessity receive right of way until proven true or false."

He paused, as though his task was painful.

"You have a charge," the bishop asked in his routine voice, "to prefer against a brother?"

"I have."

"Will you name it?"

Another preacher intervened.

"May it please the bishop," he asked, "that I be heard?"

The bishop nodded. "If the brother who has the floor will yield."

Stillman sank from the spotlight, and the plan so carefully laid out in corridors and hotel rooms began to unfold, sometimes almost buried in polite words and parliamentary routine.

As the sparring continued, father's leg bobbed up and down, and his lips and eyes threatened to break into a smile. He spotted a few of his parishioners in the church: Major Cooper and Mr. Settles on the attackers' side; Mrs. Baker, who could ill afford the journey, sitting quietly beside Dr. Romer and his wife.

Every time Mrs. Baker's eyes met the major's, the old war horse retired from the field. Many more were there, winking encouragement to the pastor's family up above or guiltily staring at the floor.

For half an hour caution prevailed, then Stillman took the floor again.

"You have heard," he said, preparing now to mention father's name, "how one of our number advocated in open meeting the training of Methodist youth in Catholic schools. This in itself, while worthy of rebuke, is not enough to bring upon his head a serious charge. For that we must look farther afield." Stillman adjusted his glasses and picked up the notes he had made during the sermon. "I would like to make reference to the sermon we have heard this morning."

The bishop appeared to be choking. Father's leg pumped more excitedly.

"The third chapter of Mark, from which our text this morning was taken, truly says: 'For whosoever shall do the will of God, the same is my brother.' That is a noble text. But there is another admonition in that chapter which Brother Spence seemingly has forgotten. Let us refresh in his memory: 'Whosoever shall blaspheme against the Holy Spirit hath never forgiveness, but is guilty of an eternal sin.'

"Now let you one and all be judge whether an eternal sin has been committed here this morning. Our brother told an anecdote which happened to our church in China. With gripping reality he described how the coolie, starving during the great famine, went into the church and, from the altar of God, stole the rice which had been laid there as an offering and took it home to his family. With copious tears our brother says—I read his very words: 'Was that a sin? To steal from the altar of God to feed his children? I think not.'"

Stillman pointed around the auditorium. "Mark that well, brethren," he cried. "He said: 'I think not.' He set himself up as judge of what, in the eyes of the Lord, shall be called a sin. The Bible says: 'Judge not that ye be not judged.' The Bible also says: 'Thou shalt not steal.'

The crime depicted was a double one: stealing from the very font of God, the church. By what right does our brother cloak himself in the mantle of the Holy Spirit and judge his fellow men? Has he taken unto himself the power of judgment reserved for the Holy Trinity? I shudder at the implications which must be in the minds of all of you. I could say more, but this is enough."

The cudgel passed quickly to another and yet another. Several quotations from the sermon were dissected, drawn, quartered, and damned. Then father's defenders sprang up, the church rang with oratory, and all the while the bishop's complexion grew redder and redder.

Finally father could stand it no longer. Rising deliberately, he stepped to the pulpit, picked up a little gray book, opened it conspicuously at a center page, and handed it to the nearest district superintendent.

That brother looked at the title, read a few lines, opened his mouth in amazement, and quickly passed the book along. Father and the bishop tried hard not to watch. But the assembled ministers saw and grew curious.

Dr. Benesh, the district superintendent who had led the offertory prayer, hurriedly descended from the pulpit and placed the volume in the hands of a conspirator.

That brother read, reread, and almost strangled. Then he hastened to Mr. Stillman, who was rising to his feet to make the fatal charge. Stillman frowned with annoyance at the interruption and waved the book away. But his friend insisted, whispering audibly. Impatiently Stillman took the book and gestured to throw it aside until his eye caught the title. He turned to the appointed page and read, then weakly sat down.

The stillness of a sacrament now hushed the church.

Ponderously the bishop rose to his feet.

"If there is a charge to be made against a brother," he said solemnly, "let it be made now. There has been debate enough."

Not a word was uttered anywhere in the great church.

"None appearing," the bishop continued, "I will proceed to close. But before I do, I would like to add one remark to what has been said. In the third chapter of Mark there is still another useful text. You will find it in the twenty-fourth and twenty-fifth verses. 'And if a kingdom be divided against itself, that kingdom shall not be able to stand. And if a house be divided against itself, that house will not be able to stand.'"

The bishop's bushy eyebrows turned down into a pontifical frown.

"I charge every man here," he roared, "as the first duty of his new pastoral year, to go home from this Conference and write a sermon on that text. Let it be preached in every church in this Conference on Sunday morning next."

The preachers departed quietly. Mr. Stillman remained, head bowed over the little gray book, reading the bishop's sermon that father had delivered to the Conference word for word.

. . . Hartzell Spence, *One Foot in Heaven* (1940)

Tulip Festival, Pella

The Dutch in Iowa

OF ALL THE ETHNIC GROUPS which came to Iowa, three have tried to maintain some of the Old World culture—the Bohemians in southside Cedar Rapids, the Germans in the Amana villages, and the Dutch in Marion and Sioux counties.

In Marion County's Pella and in Sioux County's Orange City, the cultural effort comes full bloom in Spring with the well-known and longingly-looked-for Tulip Festivals. Pella's comes first—the tulips bloom earlier in southern Iowa—followed a week or so later by Orange City's.

Every Iowan knows about Pella and Orange City, but for all that, and for all of Iowa's writing traditions, it remained for an easterner to catch the Old World quaintness of Pella in words. Berton Roueché's essay was originally written as a "profile" for the New Yorker—*it appeared there, not in a spring issue but in an issue dated at Christmas time! A bit later, it was reprinted in the old but new* Saturday Evening Post—*whose editor just happened to have grown up on a farm outside of Pella, and to have been educated in Pella's Central College. Needless to say, Cory Servaas is also Dutch, and although she presently resides in Indianapolis, she has many close relatives in and around Pella.*

Pella: Oasis in the 20th Century

PELLA (POP. 7,800) SITS ISLANDED in the gently rolling corn-fields and pastures of Marion County, in south-central Iowa, some 40 miles southeast of Des Moines. As one approaches it (as I did) on the backwater highway from the south, it has the look of any prairie town— a cloud of leafy green billowing up across the open farmlands, a sudden thrust of grain elevators, of power-plant chimneys, of a water tower. The familiar continues—a Hy-Vee Food Store, an A & W fast-food drive-in, the Dutch Mill Motel, Don's Skelly Service, a Budweiser tavern with a window sign: "Mixed Drinks." There is a right-angle turn. Highway 163 becomes Main Street—becomes every other small-town Main Street: a long, long street of small clapboard houses, most of them white, with sidewalks and shade trees and porch swings and a letter carrier trudging along with his bag. But then the scene abruptly changes. A vista appears on the left. It opens, widens, becomes a park-like square: a good four acres of spreading maples and formal planta-tions of ornamental crabapple trees and flower beds and wagon-spoke walks and slatted green benches and a lily pond with a sculptured foun-tain.

I slowed my car and looked. At one end of the square, lifting up from a spacious stylobate reached by two broad flights of shallow steps, were two great white columns surmounted by an elaboration of bells and rearing heraldic lions and a glittering golden crown. I followed the creep of traffic around the square. The business buildings that faced the square were narrow and brick-built, most of them two floors, with stores on the street and apartments above. Many of them had stair-stepped gable roofs or balustraded roofs or mansard roofs or steeply pitched roofs finished with curved red tiles, and the facades of all but two or three of them were bright with intricate designs—painted, sculp-tured masonry or glazed ceramic tile. I found a parking slot near the soaring columns and got out. The sound of a carillon filled the air. I recognized the stately lilt of Offenbach's "Barcarolle." It seemed to come from the top of the columns. I stood and listened and stared. "I know what you mean," Dennis Friend, the former news editor of the Pella weekly *Chronicle*, told me later that day. "I know exactly. I was a newcomer here myself—from Omaha. I remember the day I arrived to take that job. My wife and I drove around the square. We looked at each other, and drove around again. And Konni shook her head and said, "This isn't Iowa. This is Europe.'"

Pella is not Europe, but it is, in certain conspicuous respects, Euro-pean. It had its origin in the religious ferment that troubled mid-19th-century Holland, and it still strongly reflects its roots. It was founded by a young dissenting minister of the authoritarian Dutch Reformed Church named Henry Peter Scholte and some 100 like-minded followers in 1847, and until well within living memory it was almost entirely Dutch. It is now merely predominantly (about 90 percent) Dutch. All the leading families of Pella are of Dutch ancestry, and many of them bear the names of the earliest settlers—Kuyper, Vande Voort, Vermeer, Gaass, De Vries, Van Gorp, Dingeman, Lautenbach, Leydens, Roorda, Van Zee, Bogaards. The Pella telephone directory lists several Smiths and four Joneses. There are, in contrast, 51 Vermeers (or Ver-Meers), 49 Van Zees and 45 Van Wyks.

The Dutchness of Pella is the natural legacy of its several vigorous founding families. The town itself, however, was (and to a large extent remains) the almost single-handed achievement of Henry Peter Scholte. Dominie (as he seems always to have been called) Scholte—born in Amsterdam in 1805, a graduate of Leyden and the recipient of a comfortable mercantile fortune—created Pella. It was he who chose Iowa as its site and it was Scholte who bought, for cash, the land upon which Pella was built, parceling it out at reasonable prices to his followers. It was he who plotted Pella and (recalling the ancient Palestinian city of Christian refuge) gave it its name. It was he who designed the central square as Garden Square and contributed the land for another square of similar size, West Market (now a park with a picnic shelter). It was he who named the streets of Pella. The original east-and-west streets honored the republican ideals of the time (Liberty, Independence, Union) and the standard American heroes (Columbus, Washington, Franklin). The principal north-and-south streets were less conventionally named. They designated what he conceived to be the ten stages through which a Christian must pass to redemption: Entrance, Inquiry, Perseverance, Reformation, Gratitude, Experience, Patience, Confidence, Expectation and Accomplishment. (These names were changed by a self-conscious city council shortly before the First World War to conform to a more American tradition: Reformation Avenue, for example, became Main Street, and Gratitude became Broadway. Nevertheless, the old names have not completely vanished from the scene. They are perpetuated at the Pella Country club, where they serve, not inappropriately, as the names of the holes of its nine-hole golf course—all of them but Accomplishment.) It was Scholte who brought a post office to Pella, and he served as its first postmaster. He was a founder and the first editor of the town's first newspaper, the *Gazette*. He was, of course, the first pastor of the first church in Pella. It was he whose gift of land (a city block for a campus, and two farms to provide endowment) established, in 1853, the still functioning and flourishing Central

College of the Reformed Church in America. And on September 17, 1847, less than a month after he and his followers arrived in Pella, Scholte gathered his flock together on the site of the projected Garden Square, where (as he recalled some years later in his memoirs) "we made our first declaration to become citizens [of the United States], so as to identify ourselves as soon as possible with the land of our adopt-tion." It was a declaration and an identification (proclaimed in Dutch by a company of men in wooden shoes, red shirts and black velvet jackets) that would seem to have forecast the future of Pella: a rejection of Holland and ardent retention of everything Dutch.

Pella, in the first year or two of its settlement, was a straggle of log shanties and cave-like huts roofed over with prairie-grass sod. Its Yankee Iowan neighbors called it Strawtown. The first permanent dwelling to be built in Pella was built for Scholte and his wife and three children, and it was built for permanency. Today, it occupies much of the block just north of the square. It is a handsome house, a freehand copy of a plantation house that Scholte had seen and admired in Missouri—a long, rambling white clapboard affair with galleries and bow windows and fanlights and much jigsaw ornamentation—and it is still by far the most imposing place in Pella.

Scholte's house is now the home of his great-granddaughter. Her name is Leonora Gaass Hettinga. Mrs. Hettinga is around 60, a tall, attractive woman of disciplined poise and posture. I had tea with her one afternoon in her sunny Victorian parlor. "Oh, no," she told me. "I was born in the old Gaass house, but I've lived here most of my life. And, of course, I'm the last person who will ever live here. We've given the house to Pella—to the Historical Society. They plan to preserve it as a museum, and in many ways it *is* a museum. Almost everything you see here goes back to Dominie Scholte's time. You may have no-ticed that big iron chest near the window. Dominie Scholte brought his fortune to America in that chest, and it later served as the safe of the old Pella National Bank. The work of renovation has already started here. Martha Lautenbach, of the Society, and a couple of work-men are busy in the east wing right now. And Martha plans to furnish part of it from her family's collection of antiques. The arrangement is that I have this wing for the rest of my life. I couldn't ask for anything more. I love this house. It's such a beautiful house. An architect once told me that it could only have been built by a poet. I'm not sure I know what he meant, but Dominie Scholte did have taste, and he certainly built his house to last. The foundations are stone and four feet thick. We made some changes in the plumbing a few years ago, and the work-men broke three jackhammers trying to get through to the cellar. And the clapboard siding is walnut—solid black walnut. It's probably worth a fortune just as lumber. But there is a sadness here, too. Dominie Scholte's young wife—lovely little Mareah Krantz—was never happy here. She was so young—only 26 when they left Holland—and she had been raised very gently and very elegantly in France. She was never cut out to be a pioneer. She may have traveled in a covered wagon, but she was wearing a blue silk dress that had been made for her in Paris and a bonnet trimmed with flowers and lace. And she was attended by her personal maid, little Dirkie. There's a family story about their arrival here. They had all been traveling for days from the Mississippi River port at Keokuk. The wagon train came up from the Skunk River ford and stopped in this empty prairie. Dominie Scholte helped Mareah down from her seat. She looked around. 'But, Dominie,' she said, 'where is Pella?' 'My dear,' he told her, 'we are in the center of it.' I'm sure she tried to make the best of her lot. She had her children and her servants and her square piano and her beautiful Paris clothes and her 23-room house. I've always admired her reaction when they opened the barrels of lovely old delft ware they had brought from Holland—and found almost everything smashed to smithereens. She simply gathered up the broken pieces and used them to pave a little garden walk. It's sunken away and vanished now, but I found a pretty little blue-and-white piece in the lawn one day when I was a young girl. Mareah lived here for 44 years. She died in 1892, at the age of 72, and she is buried beside Dominie Scholte in the family plot at Oakwood Cemetery. But her last words were, 'I'm dying a stranger in a strange land.'"

The immediate past president of the Pella Historical Society is a recently retired teacher of theater arts and communications at Central College named Maurice Birdsall. Birdsall is a plump little man, and he lives alone with a little Boston bull named Doonie in a cluttered little house (circa 1853) on what was once Reformation Avenue, about four blocks from the square. I called on him one morning. "Well," he said, settling down in a throne-like chair in front of a smoldering fireplace fire. "I'll put it this way. I'm not a native, and with a name like mine—I mean, what could be more *English* than Birdsall!—I'm not even Dutch. But I am a Pellan: I've lived in Pella for more than 40 years—since 1938—and I love it. I came here as a teacher, of course. Which was a most fortunate thing. I mean, I could never have made it as a businessman. This is a Dutch town, and in those days, before the Second World War, it was even Dutchier. I knew a couple—I won't mention their names, except to say they weren't Dutch—who came here from somewhere and opened a little business on the square. And the second day they were open a man came in—he was Dutch, of course—and advised them to sell out before they went broke. It was good advice, and they took it and left. Those were the days when if a Dutch boy or girl had a date with a boy or girl who wasn't Dutch it was a disgrace. It's different now. But there are still a lot of families who would feel real shame at a mixed marriage. Especially to a Catholic. Catholics—because of all those years of Spanish domination of Holland—are beyond the pale. As for the Dutch churches—the Reformed and the Christian Reformed—they seem to build a new one every year. I think there must be 16 churches in town now. The congregations are constantly outgrowing the capacity of the buildings. I was raised a Methodist. but I like the Dutch. They're a very fine people. Take that saying 'Dutch treat.' People think that that means the Dutch are stingy. Actually, they are extremely generous. They're just not showoffs. They frown on check-grabbing. I love Dutch culture—Dutch antiques especially. As you can see, I'm a collector.

"Let me tell you about some of my nice things. I won't go into the furniture; it speaks for itself. But this little silver box. It's not a lady's compact, although I'll understand if you think it is. Actually, it's a Sunday peppermint box. In the old days here, all the way into the 1940s, the Sunday services were very long—an hour of prayer and a two-hour sermon. The ladies carried those little boxes of peppermint drops for the children if they began to get restless. I have another little box—. Oh dear. Now, where did I put it? Well, no matter. It's a lovely little box the ladies carried for themselves. It held cotton soaked in cologne that they could sniff to revive themselves if they began to feel faint. Of course, the ladies were expected to sit quietly in their pews all through the service. The men had a masculine privilege. They could stand up and stretch."

Birdsall heaved on the arms of his chair and stood up. But it wasn't to stretch. He stepped to the fireplace. "My real collection," he said, "is my delft. This mantel, for example—it's faced in delft tile. Ah, I see you're surprised. You didn't know that delft could be *brown* and white. It can be many colors, although blue and white is, perhaps, the classic combination. Brown and white may have been the original delft. I know it was very popular circa 1660. They also made a beautiful polychrome. I'm afraid the best of my collection is on loan to the Historical Society Museum. That's just east of the square on Franklin Street—next door to the Wyatt Earp House. Oh yes—we claim Wyatt Earp. He spent his boyhood here. But no matter. I'll put it this way. Delft is my passion. I wonder if you know that it wasn't even called delft until around the 1890s. It began, of course, simply as chinoiserie—an imitation of Chinese porcelain. That would have been in the early 17th century. Delft was merely the name of the town where the best of it was made. This is interesting: Delft was originally a brewing center, but something happened and the breweries went broke, and to save themselves the owners turned to making this heavy glazed ware. There were 17 factories there by the end of the 17th century. Then there was a shift in taste, and Meissen ware, or some call it Dresden, came into fashion. The Delft factories were out of business for many years. My delft is all old delft. Modern delft is entirely different. The color is no longer cooked into the clay. Some of it is very pretty. But I prefer my early delft. I wish I could tell you the value of my collection, but I dare not. I wouldn't want to tempt some vandal. Although of course, there isn't much of that here in Pella. This isn't Des Moines. My only hope is that I can keep my collection intact and leave it to our museum. But you know about pensions in these days of inflation. And Doonie and I have to eat."

Birdsall is not the only Pellan with a passion for delft. Delft of every kind—old delft, new delft, even imitation delft—is everywhere in Pella, and it appears in every form. Every home has its plates or pots or cups or bowls or trays or vases or pitchers or salt and pepper shakers or flower holders or figurines, or at least a decorative tile or two. The fronts of many of the buildings around the square are decorated with delft-tile panels, and so are many stores and offices and professional waiting rooms, and delft of every quality is sold in a dozen shops and stores.

I lodged in Pella at the Dutch Mill Motel on the southern outskirts of town. I was comfortable there in a second-floor room (whose furnishings included both the usual Gideon Bible and a copy of "Reach Out: An Illustrated Edition of the Living New Testament, paraphrased by Ken Taylor, additional text by Harold Myra") with a view across the highway of one of Pella's many large and pleasant parks. But the Dutch Mill Motel has no cafe or coffee shop, and I took all my meals in town. I always had breakfast, and usually lunch, at the Central Park Cafe. The Central Park Cafe is agreeably Dutch in appearance (delft-blue façade, shuttered casement windows, much decorative delft tiling inside and out, and delft-blue booths and chairs) and also in much of its cuisine ("Our Speciality, Dutchman's Delight: Imported Holland Cheese Drizzled Over Hot Pella Bologna"), and its staff includes some of the prettiest, smilingest, most scatterbrained waitresses I have ever known: "Oh, gee, I'm sorry, I thought you said scrambled."

The Central Park Cafe opens at five o'clock in the morning and closes at ten at night, and Loren Vande Lune, the owner, seems himself to work that 17-hour day. I often saw him there in the late afternoon; he was usually there at lunch; he was always around in the morning. I see him in memory—a vaguely troubled-looking man of around 40, thickly sideburned, heavily mustached—standing thoughtfully at the kitchen door, pacing the aisles between the booths and the tables, sitting with a group of coffee drinkers at a big, round table in the rear of the room. He sometimes sat down in my booth and sipped a cup of black coffee. One morning he joined me for breakfast.

"I don't know how much you know about Pella. Some towns have their high-class people and their low-class people, and the two don't ever get together. Pella is different. The well-to-do people here are humble people. The Bible group I belong to meets at the home of a millionaire. He and his wife are just plain people, and they have a nice, plain home. They like nice things. I mean, they like good food, and they have their cars and their private plane. But they don't show off. You wouldn't know he had a dime, to look at him, and his wife does all her own housework. And their kids work. I've had a lot of rich kids in here working waitress, even cooking. This is a democratic town—real Dutch democracy. Take that big table back there—those men sitting there drinking coffee. They're all kinds. They're businessmen and professional men and farmers and clerks and guys that work with their hands. Everybody here knows everybody else. And nobody tries to grab the check. They toss a coin to see who pays. The Bible says thou shall not gamble. I suppose you could call what they do gambling. But I look at it another way." He took a sip of his coffee. "I consider it a scientific method of determining who will commit an act of charity." Vande Lune looked at me, a smile formed, he broke into a throaty rumble. It was the only time I ever heard him laugh.

"No, I'm sorry," Leonard Gosselink told me. Gosselink, another of Pella's many fourth-generation Pellans, owns and operates Gosselink's Book Store, a few doors down from In't Veld Bologna, on the Main Street side of the square. "We don't carry secular books anymore. You might try Ken's Photo and Hobbycraft on Union Street. And, of course, there's the Carnegie-Viersen Public Library just across the square. Our book business now is all in the Christian category—Christian living, marriage and family, personal testimonials, devotional and inspirational and Bible study. It's the same with records. We specialize in Christian contemporary music—what they call Christian rock and roll. 'Let's Just Praise the Lord,' by Bill and Gloria Gaither, is very big. And so is B. J. Thomas's 'Happy Man.' Oh, you're welcome. Drop in any time. And God bless you."

I dined my first night in Pella (on the recommendation of Dennis Friend of the *Chronicle*) at a restaurant called the Strawtown Inn, and I ate there every night thereafter. Its name recalls the sod-roofed shanties of pioneer Pella, but the name is only a name. Strawtown is a thoroughly urban restaurant, and a good one. It is situated on the western edge of town, three or four blocks from the square, and is housed in a tall, narrow, red brick building (circa 1855) built in the attractively functional mid-19th-century row-house style—an English basement, two full upper floors, and a dormer-windowed attic. The attic at Strawtown is the bar. The two floors below, reached by a ladder-steep stairway, constitute the restaurant proper, and the basement is a tavern (stone walls, exposed beams) called De Kelder (or cellar), which offers a chophouse menu of steak, ribs and fried chicken, with a salad bar. Drinks are available, but most De Kelder customers drink the house (jug) wine or beer. As everywhere else in Pella, Coors and Budweiser are as popular as Heineken. The Strawtown is a formal restaurant (14-foot ceilings, white tablecloths and napkins, candlelight, fresh flowers, reservations required), and its three rooms together seat only a little more than a hundred persons. I had my first dinner at Strawtown at a front window table on the second floor in a delft-blue-and-white room, and I ordered from a delft-blue-and-white menu of heavy glazed stock. The listings were all in Dutch, but with English translations. There were 15 entrées, among them *bevulde karbonade* (stuffed pork chop), *ossenhaas* (Cornish hen stuffed with mushrooms), *Hollandse rollade* (Dutch spiced beef) and *Hollandse gebakken kip* (Dutch baked chicken with paprika). I had the chicken. My meal began with an appetizer of tiny meatballs in a spicy Indonesian sauce. Then came a cream-of-cauliflower soup. Then the chicken, served with a dressing of rice cooked with mushrooms and onions. With the chicken I had a half-bottle of a non-vintage red Burgundy. There was a choice of apple bread or hard rolls. Then a salad of Bibb lettuce and tomatoes, with an oil-and-vinegar dressing. My dessert was *Hollandse kus:* vanilla ice cream with Dutch Advokaat liqueur. The coffee brought me back to earth. It was the standard watery cafe coffee of motel America.

"Well, the proper name—the Dutch name—is Tulpen Toren," Lloyd Vander Streek, the president of the Pella Park Commission, told me. We were standing at the foot of the double-columned monument that dominates the south end of the square. The carillon cleared its lofty throat. The melting opening chords of Schumann's "Traumerei" chimed gently down around us. Vander Street raised his voice. "But everybody just calls it the Tulip Tower. It was designed by an architect named John Lautenbach. He did the original design in 1940, and this is a reconstruction built in 1968. It was a gift to Pella from Mr. and Mrs. Peter H. Kuyper, Stu's parents. You may have heard of Lautenbach. he was born and raised here, but he moved out East and made quite a reputation in New York. He came back here in the early '50s and built himself a home out in the country. He died a few years ago. I suppose the Tulip Tower does look a little strange to a newcomer. There's an inscription on the garden wall—well, I copied it down one day, and I brought it along to show you. Here's what it says: 'Erected to the Glory of God and Country with Prayers for the Ultimate Victory Over Malice, Scorn, Hatred, Envy, Criticism, Judgment, Bigotry, Prejudice, Intolerance and Apartheid the Anti-Christ Found Lurking in the Church.' I'm not sure I really understand it. Lautenbach used to say he got the inspiration for the tower from the Bible – he likened the columns to the columns in the Temple of Solomon. What the tower is, of course, is the center of our annual Tulip Festival. That's held the second weekend in May – Thursday, Friday, and Saturday up to midnight. As you may know, we observe the Sabbath here. So the festival closes at midnight sharp. We don't even clean up until Monday morning. The festival includes parades, dancing in the streets, costume entertainments and the crowning of a Tulip Queen. We can usually count on an attendance of around 100,000. I own the Pella Bootery across the street, you know, and I stock wooden shoes for the festival. You wouldn't believe how many pairs I sell. But the focus of the Tulip Festival is tulips. That's a large part of my job on the Park Commission. All the flower beds you see in all our parks are tulip beds. And our main streets are bordered with tulip beds. We estimate that we have in excess of 100,000 tulips in bloom at festival time. Oh, it's a wonderful, beautiful sight. Our bulbs are all imported from Holland. We plant about 30,000 new bulbs every fall. You have to keep renewing the stock, weeding out the old, if you want to get big blooms. But the Dutch are thrifty, you know. We don't throw our old bulbs away. We give them away for home gardens. They do well enough there. Our colors are bright and cheerful: reds, yellows, pinks, whites. We avoid dark colors in the parks: the blacks, like Queen of the Night, and the purples – all those new inventions. But these and all other kinds are grown for private displays. Our tulips bloom for about a month. But, as I say, we Dutch are thrifty. Our flower beds don't sit empty. When the tulips are over, petunias go in. I think they're very beautiful, too. We have what you might call a petunia festival all summer long and into the fall. Now let's go back to the store. I want to fit you for a pair of wooden shoes. You'll be surprised how comfortable they are with a little piece of foam rubber at the instep."

Sunday in Pella is a difficult day for a visitor. The town observes the Sabbath with an almost Puritan rigidity. I arrived in Pella on a Tuesday, and just about everyone I talked with through the rest of the week told me – warned me – of its Sabbatarianism, but, even so, the reality took me by surprise. With certain humanitarian exceptions, no places of business – not even chain stores – are open on Sunday. It is generally considered reprehensible to wash one's car or mow one's lawn on Sunday. Pella has (by my count) ten service stations, but only one or two

("They're owned by out-of-towners," an attendant at Braafhart's Standard Service told me) are open on Sunday, largely to serve the traveler. The only eating place I found open for breakfast on Sunday was the Burger Barn. The Strawtown restaurant—but not De Kelder—opens for a couple of hours on Sunday for lunch (or noon dinner), but reservations are required two or three days in advance. The bar, however, is closed. The only place I could find to eat on Sunday night was George's Pizza, just off the square, on East Franklin Street. Most—perhaps almost all—Pellans observe the Sabbath in church, and many of these churchgoers attend both morning and evening services. The only Sunday morning sound in Pella is the sound of church bells, and the only stir in life is the bumper-to-bumper crawl of church-bound traffic. I spent the morning walking in the park across the way from the Dutch Mill Motel, and I had its eight or ten acres entirely to myself. In the afternoon, I drove down to the square. I strolled and sat on a bench and read the Des Moines Sunday *Register* for an hour or two. I found my way to George's Pizza around 7:30 that evening, and I dined (soup, pizza, the usual transparent coffee) as leisurely as I could, along with a scattering of other Sunday strangers in town. It was almost 8:30 when I gave up dawdling and finished, and as I stood at the cashier's counter paying my bill I saw a gathering surge of cars moving around the square. I walked up to the corner, to Paardekooper's darkened drugstore, and stopped and looked at the cars going by. There were sedans and pickup trucks and decorated vans and four-wheel-drive Scouts and Broncos, and the occupants were all young—a teen-age boy and his girl. I marked a red Dodge pickup and watched it turn right off Main Street, move past the Solomonic Tulpen Toren, turn right again onto Broadway. A couple of minutes later, I saw it coming south on Main Street. I watched it turn and move past the tower again. I stood there alone on the corner and watched the endless circling and recircling for 15 or 20 minutes. I guessed there were at least a hundred cars involved in that obsessional parade. Once a boy in a gray Impala gave me a monkey smirk, and once a couple smiled and waved. I walked back down the block to my car. A couple were coming across the street, heading for George's, and I stopped them. I nodded toward the square. "What's going on up there?"

They turned and looked. They exchanged a glance. The woman laughed.

"You mean those kids?" the man said.

"Yes," I said. "What's it all about?"

"It doesn't mean anything," the man said. "It's just what the kids do during Sunday evening church and afterwards. It's like a custom."

"It's just something to do with your date," the woman said. "It's a way of showing off your girl. They call it 'Tooling the Square.'"

Bob Van Hemert, the manager of the Pella Chamber of Commerce, tilted back in his chair in his big corner office in the yellow brick Wyatt Earp House. He is a big, comfortable man, with a big, smiling face. "Oh, the Dutch," he told me. "My grandmother was born in Holland, and Dutch was her only language. My parents both talked a lot of Dutch. I speak a little. I'm all Dutch, and I'm proud of it. I'm proud that this is a Dutch town. I'm proud of our Tulip Festival. I'm proud of our good Dutch cooking and the Dutch look of the square. And Dutch pride keeps this town as clean as any in the nation. But there's more to be said for Pella than just being Dutch—a whole lot more. I'm happy to be here to say it. Pella is a prosperous town. Our unemployment is practically nil. We have eight manufacturing plants here, and they employ almost half of our population—3,300 men and women. Our pay rate compares favorably with any comparable community in this area. Clerks average $3.10 an hour. Machinists average $6.20. Secretaries average $4.30. Truck drivers average $5.10. Our biggest employer, of course, is Rolscreen. But we've also got Vermeer Manuvacturing and Van Gorp. Business is good all over town. There's a waiting list for space on the square. You've seen our swimming pools and parks and our hospital. Our industrialists are municipal benefactors. We needed a three-million-dollar addition to the hospital. The community raised the money in a matter of weeks. And I'll tell you something else not many towns can match: 40 of our people—at least 40—are millionaires."

"My father was a house painter," John Hoogenakker told me. "So were his father and his grandfather. So am I. That makes me a fourth-generation painter here in Pella. I started work back in 1937. That was the Depression, don't forget. But from that first day I went out to work I've never had a slow time. I've never had a day off that I didn't take myself."

"I'd say John is 100 percent correct," Edgar Roorda told me. "I started my Pella Building & Supply Company right after I got back from World War II, and I've never had to lay a man off for lack of work. I've known a few who lacked the desire to work. But that's different. There's money in this town, and just about everybody has some of it. The average cost of a new home now in Iowa is $45,000. The average here in Pella is at least $55,000—maybe close to $60,000. And there's this: I've never had one of my houses lost by the owner because he couldn't keep up the payments. The people here in Pella know what they can afford. They don't jump in over their heads trying to impress the neighbors."

"I guess I've worked for Rolscreen most of my working life," Henry

Roozeboom told me. "I get four weeks' paid vacation every year. I get 11 holidays a year with pay—all the regular ones plus Good Friday and my birthday. Everybody at Rolscreen gets his birthday off. They give us life insurance, dental insurance, Blue Cross and Blue Shield and a Christmas bonus. They also have a profit-sharing program. Everybody gets about 15 percent of his gross earnings every year. The average share is around $2,000 per person. But there's more to it than that. Rolscreen is a non-union shop. Three times in the last 15 years, the union has tried to organize the plant. The first election went lopsided against it. The second was a little closer. The third was more against the union than the second. Why did we turn the union down? Well, we listened to the organizers, and we thought a little bit, and we did a little figuring, and it turned out that if we got the union pay rate we'd all take a big cut in pay."

I talked with Dr. Kenneth Weller, the president of Central College, in his bright, book-filled office on the second floor of Central Hall, the administration building, overlooking a quadrangle campus with a long pond and a humpbacked Japanese bridge. In the distance, I could see an avenue of flags stretching in the breeze—the flags of Britain, France, Austria, Spain, Mexico and the United States. Students were standing in groups or moving along the walks. Downstairs in the lobby I had seen a wall plaque with a Zen-like truism: "Anyone can count the number of seeds which come from an apple, but only God knows the number of apples which can come from a seed." Dr. Weller gave me a look of gleaming satisfaction. "No," he said. "No, indeed. We are not a Bible college. We're much too old and established for that. We're not even exactly a provincial college. Half our students spend part of their academic life studying abroad, in one of the several countries where we have an arrangement. Those flags represent our foreign connections. The fact is, we require only one course in religion. No, what we are is a Christian college in the philosophical or ethical sense. We're not interested in doctrine. Our basic tone is a concern for values. We're weak on piety and strong on life in its wholeness. We're concerned with how things work, but also with what ought to be. We remember here that Watergate was not the work of uneducated people. It was the work of highly educated people deficient in morality and ethical sense. We attempt to teach that ethical sense—to reestablish it, I should say. To that extent, we're concerned with the total lives of our students. Pella has always been an appropriate setting for our work."

A bell rang. A couple ran hand in hand across the bridge. Dr. Weller had his back to the window. He straightened a file of papers on his desk. "Last Monday," he said, "we had a young male student killed in an auto accident. His friends organized a memorial service. It was spontaneous. There were Scripture readings and readings of secular poetry. Four hundred people attended. Our enrollment is 1,500. We have a sense of community here, and I think that that turnout is a good demonstration of it. We think of it as a Christian sense of community. And it isn't just here at Central College. It embraces the whole of Pella—the college, the churches, the business community, everybody. It *is* the whole of Pella. Even newcomers here seem to feel it. I know I did. I'm Dutch myself, but I'm from Michigan, and I've been here only since 1969. There is a pervading community sense of heritage— an almost mystic feeling of roots. And roots are a source of community. Responsibility equates with community. You see this responsibility, this morality, this ethic in the personal frugality here and the public generosity. I'm sure you've heard about the generosity of our industries. But they aren't the only givers. Everyone gives to his capacity. It's something that goes much deeper than the more conspicuous pieties— deeper than the Sabbath and all that. It's the real thing." He touched the file of papers again. "Now, don't misunderstand me. I'm not saying that we're unique—that we're an oasis here in the middle of the 20th century." He stopped. He sat smiling at me across his desk. His smile faded. "No," he said. "I'll amend that. We *are* a little oasis here. I'm afraid that's exactly what we are."

... Berton Roueché, 1979

Pella Tulip Festival Street Scene

Iowa Stubborn

POPULISM HAS BEEN DEFINED as a "political philosophy directed to the needs of the common people, and advocating a more equitable distribution of wealth and power."

In Iowa, populism has most often been a medium of agrarian protest, beginning with the elections of 1892 and 1896, and the nomination of General James B. Weaver of Bloomfield as the Presidential candidate for the People's Party. Among Iowa authors, the leading populist spokespersons were Hamlin Garland and Herbert Quick, both of whom were influenced by the "single tax" philosophy of Henry George, and, later on, Dale Kramer, whose The Wild Jackasses: The American Farmer in Revolt *(1956) was a popular history of the populist movement. Kramer had succeeded H. R. Gross as editor of Milo Reno's* Farm Holiday News *in the mid-thirties.*

Populism has continued to influence the Iowa political scene, both in collectivist movements such as the National Farmer's Organization, and in less organized protests such as the one which non-Iowan Stanley High wrote about for The Freeman *in 1950. (The article also appeared later in* The Reader's Digest.*) As a footnote to the story, the McKinley protest results can now be reported. The "bad news" is that the McKinleys lost their battle and had to spread their rotting potatoes over their rich fields as fertilizer. The "good news" is that Agricultural department officials were convicted of fraud in the referendum referred to in the following story.*

Rebellion in Mitchell County

LAST FEBRUARY 15 a special agent of the U.S. Department of Agriculture went to St. Ansgar, Iowa, under orders to get the evidence which would brand four of the area's most successful farmers as "lawbreakers." The ensuing inquisition lasted 23 days. The special agent left with a dossier of 40 alleged law violations—involving possible fines of $12,000. The Department of Agriculture immediately moved to make a painful and public example of these farmers.

Harold L. McKinley and his three sons own and operate four large farms. By deliberately violating the Department of Agriculture's directives, these farmers had invited this action. They hoped thereby to challenge the tactics by which the Department was moving to governmentalize U.S. farming.

The resulting exposures have aroused Midwest opinion and forced the nation's most powerful bureaucracy into a major retreat. In a resolution unprecedented in the history of the state, the Iowa legislature by an overwhelming vote of both parties in both houses condemned the Department and backed the McKinleys. "The outcome," said the Mason City, Iowa, *Globe-Gazette*, "will go a long way toward telling us just where we stand today in the march down the pathway that leads to socialism." The resistance of the McKinleys, says the Omaha *World-Herald*, "epitomizes the age-old battle against tyranny of men who mean to be free."

The immediate issue is a 1950 decree of the Secretary of Agriculture extending to the potato growers of 12 northern Iowa and 20 northern Indiana counties the restrictions of Marketing Order 60. What is more significantly at stake is the Department's overall governmentalizing program. In challenging Order 60, the McKinleys, said the Waterloo, Iowa, *Courier*, struck a blow on behalf of all the nation's farmers against bureaucracy's expanding system of "unreasonable and unfair interference in the farmer's business."

Under Order 60, potato growers were directed to market their crops only as prescribed by the Department of Agriculture. On threat of court action and fines, only potatoes of specified sizes and grades could be sold or given away; the size and grade were fixed by the Government. Both could be arbitrarily changed on one day's notice. Government inspectors were required to examine every shipment. To finance this policing, every farmer had to pay the Government a fee on every lot he sold.

While the farmer who was subject to Order 60 could sell potatoes of only certain sizes and grades, growers elsewhere in the country, not subject to the order, could sell potatoes of any size and grade. Such orders, officially called "marketing agreements," have been applied in numerous areas to producers of vegetables, fruits and milk. They are designed to reduce the amount of surplus produce which the Government, under its price-support program, is obliged to purchase. This price-support program itself invites overproduction.

But the McKinley case has revealed, said the Iowa legislature, that these "agreements," "by methods reminiscent of dictatorship governments," have become part of an expanding system of "government by directives which, if unchecked, can result in loss of the basic freedoms on which this country was founded."

With what looked like democratic procedure, the administration of Order 60 was vested in a farmers' committee picked by the farmers themselves. In practice, growers found they were allowed only to make nominations. Actual selections for this committee—with its power of economic life or death over every potato farmer—were made by the Secretary of Agriculture. He could select growers or nongrowers. Without giving notice or reasons, he could discharge any committee member. Unless financially able to fight in the courts, the average farmer had no appeal from the decisions of this bureaucracy-picked body.

The Department's plan to fasten Order 60 on the farmers of northern Iowa and Indiana was announced in the spring of 1950. Like other "marketing agreements," extension of this order required the favorable vote in each district of a two-thirds majority of the producers of the crop involved. Potato growers in the Iowa district voted overwhelmingly against it. Indiana growers also voted negatively: 198 to 2.

Faced with its inability to get a separate "yes" vote from the growers of Iowa and Indiana, the Department ordered a new referendum, this time to include Wisconsin and Minnesota as well. Thus it ruled that the votes of the dissenting districts in Iowa and Indiana be lumped with districts in Minnesota and Michigan which in 1949 had voted favorably. The Department of Agriculture had turned loose its vast propaganda and pressure machine in this gerrymandered area.

The referendum was held September 25-30, 1950. For the 18,000 growers involved, 30,000 ballots were printed. On the face of each, the potato grower, with most of his current crop still unmarketed, was warned that if Order 60 were voted down there would be an immediate "termination of price support for the balance of the 1950 season."

Balloting was conducted without proper safeguards against multiple voting or other fraud. Farmers had to vote without the protection of secrecy; their ballots had to be signed and mailed to the Department's regional office in Chicago, where Department officials had complete charge of the counting. Organized growers of Iowa, Indiana and Wisconsin formally petitioned the Secretary for permission to have farmer-representatives present, but the request was not even acknowledged.

A sample investigation subsequently made in a Wisconsin area by lawyers for the McKinleys revealed that the Department had counted the votes of that area as *for* Order 60, but affidavits secured by the McKinleys from the potato growers showed that every voting grower in that district had voted *against* it.

"A clerical error," said the Department. Order 60 was promptly extended to the growers of northern Iowa and Indiana, and the Department's inspectors were sent out to insure its enforcement.

Forebears of the McKinleys migrated from New York State to Iowa in 1855. For the dependable quality of their crop shipments, the McKinleys have a four-star rating—the highest obtainable. They have consistently refused to take Government farm benefits. Like most Iowa farmers, they have kept their potato acreage each year well below the Government allotment.

Faced with what the journal of the Wisconsin potato growers called the "undemocratic compulsion" of Order 60, the McKinleys decided that open resistance was their only recourse. They sent their potatoes to market as they had been doing for more than a quarter of a century—without submitting them for Government inspection. When they had more potatoes than they could sell, they gave some to a local orphanage, which is also a violation.

Confronted with this open defiance, the Government asked for a temporary injunction against the McKinleys. This was granted. While the remaining bulk of their 1950 crop rotted, unsold, the McKinleys prepared to carry their fight to the Supreme Court if necessary. Said Harold McKinley: "It would be less expensive to submit to this unconstitutional abuse of power, but I couldn't do it and look my sons in the face."

Potato growers of the entire region rallied to support them. Wisconsin growers raised a fund to contest the Order and offered aid to the McKinleys. Similar action was taken by the Vegetable Growers Associations of Iowa and southern Minnesota. Indiana growers formally resolved that "all possible support be given to H. L. McKinley and Sons"; North Dakota growers sent a contribution to aid the McKinleys in their fight against the "dictator methods of the Department."

"The wrath of potato growers is getting so keen," said the St. Ansgar *Enterprise,* "that Government officials who started proceedings will wish they were well rid of them."

This prediction has been confirmed. Last August another diretive of the Department of Agriculture terminated Order 60. "Lack of interest," the Department explained. James Kennedy, Iowa's representative on the North Central Marketing Committee, gave another reason: "Fear of letting the McKinley case come to trial." With the agreement ended, said Mr. Kennedy, there will be "no need to bring the matter to trial. The federal court could dissolve the injunction, and evidence collected by the McKinleys would gather dust."

To prevent a trial—and the consequent baring of the Department's tactics—the Government has attempted to get the McKinleys to withdraw from the suit. The McKinleys have refused to do this unless the Department, conceding the truth of the accusations against it, recommends in federal court that the temporary injunction be dismissed with prejudice in favor of the McKinleys.

"My sons, overseas veterans of World War II," said Mr. McKinley, "represent an aggregate of ten years of service. We all feel that this dictatorial use of power represents what they spent ten years of their lives fighting against."

... Stanley High, 1950

Harold McKinley, St. Ansgar, Iowa

Iowa Stubborn

Townspeople: Oh, there's nothing halfway about the Iowa way to treat you   When we treat you   Which we may not do at all. There's an Iowa kind of special chip-on-the-shoulder attitude   We've never been without That we recall. We can be as cold as our falling thermometers in December   If you ask about our weather in July. And we're so by-God stubborn we can stand touchin' noses   For a week at a time and never see eye-to-eye. But what the heck, you're welcome   Join us at the picnic,   You can eat your fill of all the food you bring yourself.   You really ought to give Iowa a try   Provided you are contrary. We can be as cold as our falling thermometers in December   If you ask about our weather in July And we're so by-God stubborn we can stand touchin' noses   For a week at a time and never see eye-to-eye   But we'll give you our shirt   And a back to go with it   If your crops should happen to die

Farmer: So what the heck, you're welcome   Glad to have you with us

Farmer & Wife: Even though we may not ever mention it again.

Townspeople: You really ought to give Iowa   Hawkeye Iowa Dubuque, Des Moines, Davenport, Marshalltown, Mason City, Keokuk, Ames, Clear Lake   Ought to give Iowa a try.

... Meredith Willson, *The Music Man,* 1957

State Fair

THE IOWA STATE FAIR was born in Fairfield, Iowa, in 1854.

Phil[lip Duffield] Stong was born in Van Buren County, Iowa, just fifteen as-a-crow-flies miles south by southwest of the Fairfield fair site in the Fair's forty-sixth year.

The Fair, later moved to Des Moines, was just seventy-eight years old and Phil Stong was thirty-three years old when their past, present, and futures were linked by Stong's first novel, State Fair. *In that Depression year of 1932, the jam-packed grandstand and infield roared with astonishment as two hard-driving, smoke belching steam locomotives, one labeled "Hoover," the other "Roosevelt," smashed into each other, head-on, at a hundred miles per hour. But Stong's novel created an even greater "Bang" and attracted a far, far larger audience, not all of whom approved. "It's a dirrrty book," said one Iowa businessman after reading this sentence: "There was nothing under the lovely kimono but the lovelier Emily."*

Since 1932, the Fair has continued to draw national media attention. Stong's novel was filmed in 1933 with Will Rogers as Pa Frake; it was made into a bright, lively musical comedy in 1945 and used as a basis for one later film featuring the (pardon the expression) Texas State Fair. And Holiday *magazine has carried three stories about the Fair: two by Paul Engle (1956 and 1975) and one by Stong, in 1948. It was not easy to choose among these three; any one might have served equally well, although the 1956 Engle story is the better of his two.*

In 1956, Stong wrote a sequel, Return in August, *to his novel, attempting to repeat the success of the earlier book. But this novel, which brought Marjorie Frake and the Des Moines newspaper man together again, did not draw the crowd the first book had.*

A historical note: an Egyptian belly-dancer, "Little Egypt," was the sensation of the 1893 Chicago Columbian Exposition. The thousands of Iowans who attended that fair probably forgot there was an Iowa Building on the grounds before their home-bound train reached Oak Park; but they carried the image of Little Egypt with them to their graves. Forty years later, in 1933, at the Chicago Century of Progress, it was Sally Rand, a young lady who was said to dance entirely in the buff, whose name became an Iowa and American household word. Whatever the degree of Sally's exposure, she concealed herself so well behind two lavish rainbow-hued feather fans that only an eagle-eyed Iowan who could spot the difference between a boat-tailed grackle and a red-winged blackbird across the back forty could tell for sure.

State Fair

THERE WAS A TIME when "going to the Fair" meant a night journey in a truck with all the family, and with a hog or a blue-blooded bull or a few show-worthy, bad-tempered fowls crated up beside the baskets of quince jelly and angel-food cake which made up the womenfolk's stake in the rivalry of the Fair. That night you had to keep feeling in your pocket to make sure your pickle money or the extra dollar grandpa had given you for dissipation on the roller coaster had not slipped through a hole; and you had to pretend to be asleep in spite of the jolting, when all the time you were wide-awake and had your eyes fixed on the sky ahead where the first light from the fairgrounds would appear.

There wasn't much talk after the first hour or two, and of course you did fall asleep at last; and when you woke up, there was the the Fair, and the campground waiting for you.

That is one way – and perhaps the best way to go. But there are other good ways: by train, for instance, or by bus and by big sedans (76,000 cars were parked at the Fair last year), and even by planes flashing along from all the spokes of the compass toward the fairgrounds. For one week in August each year since 1854 (except for the interruption of war) the State Fair is the capital of America's Corn Belt, the site of the greatest food festival in the world. Last year it was celebrated by more than half a million people, through whose efforts most of America – and a good deal of Europe – eats.

The glow from the Fair warms the returning native long before it can be seen. He can feel it in the club car running westward just out of the grimy suburbs of Chicago. He has had an evening on the New York Central, or perhaps the Pennsylvania, surrounded by stately gentlemen absorbed in the *New York Times* and the *Wall Street Journal* and by cold, correct and lonely women dressed by Sophie Gimbel and Nettie Rosenstein. The radio on the train last night gave stock-market reports, a little soft music, and nothing more.

This morning, on the Rocket, he is already in the Midwest, and the club car is full of other pilgrims to the Iowa State Fair. Not the farmers, who have created the Fair and to whom it belongs, but visitors and acolytes from outside who assist at the ceremonies in every way, from setting up radio stations or selling cotton candy or guessing people's weight or presenting a much-expurgated fan dance to looking over the stock exhibits for the Department of Agriculture or making a survey of the Four-H Clubs for the Farm Bureau. There will be a sprinkling, too, of research men from the eastern agricultural colleges, and probably a breezy young man from *Variety*. If the young woman across the aisle happens to be the fan dancer, she will be just as correct as the ladies of last night, but friendlier – and a lot better-looking.

A poker game will start up soon and a gin-rummy game or two; and as the train nears the Mississippi, drinks will be ordered in a hurry. In Iowa, spirits may be sold only by the bottle on a state liquor license, though beer is plentiful, even on the fairgrounds.

The porter, who has been traveling this road for years with State Fair passengers, knows when to turn the radio on, and at the first words that boom from the loud-speaker, the card players pause and every head in the car goes up.

"Temperature 102. Tomorrow and Wednesday, fair and warmer."

A sigh of relief goes round the car and everybody grins. "Good Fair weather."

Nobody knows why the Fair does its best business in a temperature just under boiling. But a comfortably cool gray day cuts the box office receipts in half. Without the sun, Iowans just won't make merry. There are a few air-conditioned hotel rooms in Des Moines, but you have to reserve one months ahead, and then you wonder why you bothered, for the descent to Avernus is twice as awful. The streets shimmer, your collar melts, your shoes stick to the pavements; but out at the end of the long trolley line will be white pavilions and lemonade and iced beer and bands playing in the shade. The mighty race of Iowans will be eating fried chicken, hot roast beef, and hickory-smoked Hampshire hams when the foreigner from the East can face only a sliced tomato or a bit of ice cream.

The Iowans are right, of course; for seeing the Fair burns up as much energy per hour as plowing the roughest field. There are 378 acres of grounds – full of stock pavilions, exhibitions and industrial buildings, small concessions, the grandstand, and the Midway – something over four million dollars worth of permanent installations. The judging of livestock begins at eight A.M.; there are harness and running races and rodeos all afternoon, and at night there is a big show in the grandstand with fireworks till eleven. Since there are only eight of these fifteen-hour days, one has to keep moving not to miss anything; and one has to eat every two or three hours, to combat exhaustion.

Probably a European observer in the present state of the world would consider all this eating excessive – if not callous. But he would be forgetting that the tribe of Midwest farmers, reduced one-third in numbers by the draft, worked double-time, plowed at night by floodlights, had their twelve-year-old children driving tractors to produce the food that set new records for this country and broke Hitler's grip on the continent of Europe.

An English photographer sent by a New York magazine to cover the Fair in 1946 spent Fair Week in a daze. So much food, and none of it boiled. So many acres of shiny parked automobiles. Farmers buying Piper Cubs and helicopters. "But where are the wagons and bicycles?" he asked. "And why are all these city people here?"

They were not city people, but plain dirt farmers, solid, prosperous, well-dressed. If Will Rogers were to play in *State Fair* today, he'd have to spruce up a bit more than he did in 1932 — much more than he ever did in private life. His beloved seersucker pants might do around the Fox lot in Hollywood, but they'd look pretty dowdy at the Iowa State Fair.

Though the Fair is strictly a family outing, the visiting family separates after breakfast, each member in a hurry to reach the building representing his special interest. The men and the Four-H youngsters flock to the livestock barns — except for those who already are installed there for the duration, sleeping in the upstairs dormitories or on a cot alongside Blue Boy or Lord Lard, or ox-eyed Jersey Juno, who won the blue ribbon last year for milk production. If a family member is showing any of these lordly creatures, he will be busy all day and every day till his class comes up for judging.

Swine and sheep and cattle and horses have to be curried, fed, watered, cheered up, and above all, kept cool. The stock pavilions are the most carefully designed and solidly built of all the Fair buildings, and the best ventilated. After all, they house for a whole week tenants whose value runs into so many millions that even the State Fair publicity office hesitates to estimate it. "Nobody would believe us," they say. These pedigreed animals are delicate and nervous and when you are showing them you are as worried as the manager of a new soprano before her debut at the Metropolitan. It is not unusual in the cattle barn to see a pretty girl squatting in the straw and sponging the face of a mean-looking bull, while her own face streams sweat that she doesn't bother to wipe away.

The stock people will not soon forget that $5000 Berkshire boar that in 1947 minced daintily around the judging ring, acquired his blue ribbon, cakewalked back to his stall and lay down dead.

On the other hand, hogs are such ornery animals that they are likely to catch cold in the middle of summer and die of pneumonia, a fact that so impressed Henry King, director of the 1933 movie version of *State Fair,* that, after paying $5000 for Hampshire Blue Boy at the Iowa Fair, and three thousand for Esmeralda, its Duroc girl friend, he spent several thousand dollars more for understudies. For the same amount of money he could have hired several of the highest-salaried human stars to do the fifteen minutes worth of acting required of the hogs.

Stong 219

To take care of Blue Boy and Esmeralda and the understudies, the motion-picture company employed for forty-five dollars a week a young man out of the stock pavilion, one Martin Fabricius, who held the degree of Bachelor of Science in Animal Husbandry from the State College at Ames.

Martin was unimpressed by Hollywood, spent all his waking hours beside Blue Boy's mahogany-railed pen, declined to meet Janet Gaynor or any other stars—"Girls are all alike," he said—and after three weeks got homesick. Not for a cent under fifty dollars a week would he stay any longer. It took several conferences and some hot words between executives, but finally even movie officials had to admit that it was a poor gamble to risk $10,000 worth of high-strung hog for five dollars a week for six weeks. Martin stayed. After the picture was finished, the bachelor of science went back to his farm in Iowa and Blue Boy was sent to a model farm in Sacramento, where he died, as *Time* magazine put it, "of overtraining and overeating."

Fabricius was a typical example of the serious-minded, educated younger generation of farmers who come in such numbers to the Fair. You seldom see them in the grandstand or on the Midway, for they congregate in the stock-show buildings and stand in crowds before the industrial exhibits, absorbed in the newest farm inventions. A new machine shown at the Fair may affect the working hours and the production of millions of farmers throughout the whole Missouri Valley.

Scientific mastodons like the combine and the hay baler have revolutionized farm life. But even a minor gadget like the posthole digger has saved untold man-hours in the few years since it was invented and introduced at the Iowa State Fair.

Interior fences in Iowa have to be changed frequently. You may graze cattle on a plot one year, grow wheat the next, raise clover the next and turn the cattle on it. This requires two changes of fencing and perhaps a hundred fence posts, for the light brush and barbed-wire fencing that will keep cattle in pasture will not keep them out of growing grain, which they can ruin in a night (at ninety dollars an acre on the current market).

Ten years ago, a man could set about twenty posts a day by hand. Today he takes out his tractor with a squizerroo that looks like a Buck Rogers gimmick for going to the center of the earth. He pulls a lever and his gimlet yanks out a posthole in less time than it would take even the best dentist to drill to one's forebrain.

Then there is the corn-picker. A farmer does not drive his wagon slowly while his children and neighbors heave corn into it. He drives a truck lightly up and down while a machine tosses corn into it as gaily as a pickpocket looting at Mardi Gras.

These machines are what the young men look at, at the Fair, and what they buy with the money they made by nearly killing themselves with work through the war years. And these are the beneficient robots that may save the world by feeding it.

The women at the Fair are also bent on feeding the world, or their section of it. There is no temptation now for them to linger at a bingo game for nylons between the gates and the Women's Building or the Educational Building, where canned goods and other culinary entries are judged, for the Fair has outlawed games of chance. The one ingenious circumvention of this rule – a wheel of fortune with a live mouse, which, by popping into one hole or another, picks the winning number – does not attract the women. Half of them are sorry for the mouse and the other half are afraid of it.

The mouse wheel presumably gets its license by "teaching animal behavior." Another educational exhibit which might conceivably interest women is patronized almost exclusively by men: the display of embryos in bottles, which is called *Life Begins.*

Bingo and mice and embryos notwithstanding, the women find ample excitement in the Women's and Children's Building.

It houses the home economics and hobby exhibits, a recreational center, the baby-health contests, and a day nursery, to say nothing of a peaceful dining room where the infant Iowan can have his formula prepared by dieticians trained at Ames, and a mother can recharge her energy with an appetizing meal or a glass of iced tea served in the Iowa manner with plenty of sugar and lemon juice.

In the Women's and Children's Building one may learn the newest magic of pressure cookery and home freezing and vitamin juggling. But if, as Ruskin said, "cookery means the knowledge of Medea and of Circe and of Helen . . ." (if Helen needed to know about the cookstove) "and of the Queen of Sheba," there are other sorceries that the women practice in that sacred building at the Iowa State Fair. A male intruder at these rites is not in actual danger of being torn limb from limb by matronly priestesses, but he may wish he had been before he makes his getaway from their shrine.

Escaping the hissing pressure cookers, he may blunder into a room full of gargantuan, hostile infants competing for the Baby Health prizes. Fleeing from these, he can hardly avoid a fashion show, or a concert of P.T.A. musicians who call themselves the Mother Singers. If he dashes through a doorway across the hall, he is likely to step into a rapt circle of females waving palm fans and staring at a woman on the platform who is making a Flower Arrangement out of two Golden Glows and a stalk of Jimson weed. If he runs from their indignant eyes, he may burst into the auditorium just in time to see the Linn County Pageant or a herd of tunicked ladies doing a determined folk dance.

Outside the temple of Ceres and P.T.A., all is normal and reassuring. The bands play, the midget railroad train careens around the park, the psychological mouse jumps in and out of holes, winning hams for Iowans; and now that the judging of livestock and jams and pickles is over for the day, everybody is heading for the grandstand, to see the bland vaudeville, with nothing more ribald than some Scotch and Irish jokes and some pratfalls, the horse and auto races, which are one hundred per cent moral because betting is not allowed.

By half past five, if the fiery sun is not lower, one at least believes that soon it will be (in spite of daylight time); and with nothing to stick to one's ribs since lunch but seven hot dogs, four hamburgers, a cubic foot of cotton candy, three sacks of popcorn and assorted pops, colas and ades, one is beginning to look forward to the big plate of baked ham or fried chicken, mashed potatoes, and the pie à la mode that even now are being served in the dining halls and tents dotted about the fairgrounds.

There won't be time for more than two pieces of pie, because the Midway must be covered before the big State Fair Revue at the grandstand, which starts at half past seven.

By half past six, with supper over, the sun really has dropped a little; the girls from the Four-H dormitories are coming out in pink and yellow dresses, after a long day in jeans, washing the faces of discontented cows; the Four-H boys and some of their Des Moines cousins are sauntering down the boardwalks in clean white flannels, looking sidewise at the girls; and even the women who have Flower-arranged and Mother-sung and pressure-cooked all day are wearing thin, pale dresses and silly hats over their pink plump faces, and showing a tendency to giggle.

The Midway is always the same, and always new. The dwarfs, the giants, the tattooed men, the hairy apes are here, visible in glory for seven days, like a comet lighting up the dark and quiet night of the sober Midwest.

Old Fair-goers would be grieved and disappointed if any of the traditional shows were missing. The sudden death in Pittsburgh of the Fat Man en route to the Fair in 1946 drew a two-column front-page headline in the Des Moines *Register*. People could have gone to see his Fat Wife and Fat Daughter, who had bravely come ahead when Papa was taken to the hospital; but it hardly seemed decent, when always, time out of mind, they had been the Fat Family of the Fair.

If the prizes at the rifle galleries and the hoop-la stands were anything but hideous and useless, that would be unfitting too. The Iowan who is a crack shot or hoop-thrower expects to go home from the Fair with kewpie dolls and plush pigs and table lamps encrusted with polychrome and dripping tassels—and a ham or two, also by way of coals to Newcastle.

The barkers have changed somewhat, it is true. The words and the sleek good looks are the same, but the music is different. Their voices are lower now, and smoother. They have listened to and learned from Frank Sinatra. Either you come in and see Zotz, the What-is-it, or you feel you have broken a nice boy's heart.

The girl shows are right and proper too, a traditional part of the Fair, though grass skirts and bras and sequined panties may be scantier than ever, and the motions of the dance less inhibited. Still, five inches of ankle in 1902 must have had as startling an effect on the libido as five feet of girl in 1948.

But a new girl show appeared on the Midway in 1947—just one girl. The hot and weary people emerging from the freak show, too languid for hoop-la contests, bored with embryos in bottles, saw and stopped before the pitch of Sally Rand. At a rate of 10,000 every evening, they bought tickets and went in to see her.

The dance is beautiful, and Sally herself, only a lovely clean-cut face above the slowly moving, swathing ostrich plumes, is a new kind of State Fair enchantress. Even the women like her. "She looks like such a *nice* girl," they said.

Sally is an expert showman and press agent for Sally Rand. On the grounds, she lives in her own circus van, air-conditioned, decorated by W. & J. Sloane of New York, fitted with its private telephone. It must be the most un-private private telephone number in the world, for Sally gives it to everybody she meets, with the least flicker of a leer in her blue eyes. "If it gets too hot for you, my wagon is cooled, you know." But she gives it to women and children too.

When she is dancing on the Midway many of the matrons who expected to have to drag father away from her in time for the fireworks have to be dragged themselves.

It was thanks to Miss Rand that the grandstand filled up slowly on those August nights of 1947. Her admirers missed part of the State Fair Revue, the first riotous ensemble, "Tally Ho," with "the entire Ballet, dressed in dashing red-flecked riding costumes," depicting "in a rollicking spirit, a Ride to the Hounds."

When the red-flecked riders gave way to *Treasure Island,* a wonderful and awful mélange of Robert Louis Stevenson, Gilbert and Sullivan's *Pirates,* and the Arabian Nights, the audience was larger.

And of course nobody wanted to miss the grand finale, when Miss

Victory was shot from the mouth of a cannon *three hundred feet*, or fifty in all, not including the arc, across the race track.

The fireworks that concluded the show in 1947 seemed slightly tame compared to those of the year before, which displayed Bikini under the atom bomb. The fireworks people cannot do without war and disaster. When the Four Horsemen do not ride, rockets and Roman candles and set pieces of F.D.R. or Lincoln or George Washington blossom and fade in the sky, to no quickening of the heartbeat.

An old Fair-goer remembers better spectacles; the Battle of Manila Bay, with Spanish men-of-war sinking fast and furiously and the Stars and Stripes flashing out above the burning sea; between wars, a sortie back into ancient history, with all the colonnades of Pompeii sinking under red lava from a sky-high Mount Vesuvius; then the fresh sensation from a brand-new war, the Battle of the Argonne Forest.

The atom bomb which has staggered the world delighted rather than dismayed the pyrotechnicians of the Iowa State Fair. The tiny Pacific island outlined in lights rocked, quivered, exploded and burned under its carefully designed mushroom of colored smoke.

The fireworks end at last, and the crowd begins to pick up handbags, gather extra jackets (it might just possibly have turned cool toward midnight) and slip tired feet back into castoff shoes. But the pygmy man on the stage there, under the floodlights, is speaking again into his amplifier.

"Folks, friends, please—a moment. Before we disperse from this glorious celebration, one small request. Will you all, each of you, fish in your pockets and your purses for a match, a cigarette lighter. Wait. When the band blows one big resounding note, light up. Send forth a little candle in a naughty world."

The response is universal. Men dig match books from their pockets, hand some of them to the women beside them who do not smoke. On the lighted stage facing the grandstand the Music Department of the Women's Club, Cedar Rapids, takes a deep breath and a firm grip on its instruments, lets out a tremendous squawk of various sound, and from one end of the long grandstand to the other, tiny lights spring out, pinpointed like a quilt of luminous stitches. Under the long roof, people jerk upright, visible as in daylight. And they sigh, from 30,000 throats.

The Fair, breaking up for the night, flows in two directions at once, like an addled river. The larger current (between 70,000 and 100,000 people) moves toward the outside gates, the parking field, the East Des Moines streetcar lines, or the faint hope of empty taxicabs. At the other end of that long avenue stretching due west toward the river and the city, are the crowded hotel lobbies, the airless boardinghouses, the tumbled suitcases and borrowed electric fans and yesterday's wilted clothes. It is going to be another hot night in town.

For 5000 Iowans, however, there is a shorter, happier path to bed. If you are one of these, you turn left when you leave the grandstand and walk past the Midway and the Old Mill and the roller coaster, past the shuttered dining halls and the lemonade stands; past the little man folding up his scales and grinning at you because for nine hours now he will not have to guess the weight of anyone who scowls because he does not miss, or rattle off any more of his old jokes in his hoarsely gentle voice. You will meet members of the bands, lugging their big brass pretzels toward home and rest.

Far across the park there is the rumble of heavy wheels around the stock pavilions. The real monarchs of the Fair, hog, bull, and stallion, are taken home as soon as their classes are judged, and the young men—and some of the women—who have shown them ride with them. All night they will trundle over the roads toward the home farms before the hot sun rises.

Your path begins to climb a dark hillside, past the glimmer of 19th century white gingerbread outlining the old Exposition Building. That is the building you always see in your mind's eye when you think of the Fair. It has always been there since you saw if first from your father's shoulder. You hope it always will be.

The sleepy guard at the entrance to the campground nods at you and turns his stile, and you are almost home. This is the unchanged and the unchanging Fair. The Tama Indian who always has sat there before his tepee, like Buddha, smiling at the passers-by, is there now, rolled up in a thin blanket on the ground. The people ahead of you turn in at their tents, calling soft good nights. The flaps and sides of the tents are fastened up, and some of the cots have been pulled out on the platform before the entrances. Maybe you will pull yours out too, this hot night; but probably you won't have to.

That was a good tent site that grandfather staked out in 1892, near the top of the hill where the breeze could reach it under fine shade trees, and near the spring. The spring has not been so important these forty years since they built the bathhouses and put in faucets everywhere. But it still flows and its water will make the best boiled coffee in the world tomorrow morning.

... Phil Stong, 1948

Dubuque from Kelly's Bluff

The Cities of Iowa – Dubuque

YOU WON'T HAVE TO READ too carefully to discern some resemblances between Bissell's 1954 Holiday *essay about his home town and Marquis Child's 1932 essay about the imaginary "Winslow." As Childs says, and as Bissell's essay demonstrates, "a river town is a special kind of town." But Childs stands away from his subject, while Bissell, even when he is writing about the past, is a part of his. Childs is neutral about "Winslow"; Bissell is anything but neutral about Dubuque. Childs observes and reports the life of the very rich; Bissell reports from within the world of the very rich, a world of which he was a part and Childs was not. Finally, Childs is serious, and Bissell is – well, Bissell!*

Bissell was the great-grandson of a pioneer Dubuque garment manufacturer. The great-grandson was born in 1913 in "the old house on Fenelon Place," a mansion paid for by the continuing success of the business. Like his father, Bissell graduated from Harvard; but the family business was not for him. He became a seaman and tugboat crewman, then, with his wife's encouragement, a writer. He is best known for his 7½ Cents, *which became the Broadway musical* Pajama Game, *then a musical film with the same title. He died in 1977.*

Good Old Dubuque

SMITTY AND HIS WIFE and three kids live in a houseboat on the Mississippi on the south side of Dubuque harbor, right across from the shipyard. Every time the shipyard launches another barge or a towboat the wave it kicks up nearly puts him up on the tracks, houseboat and all, even including the double-drainboard sink (the "zinc") and the new overstuffed parlor suite and all that new linoleum tile and the wedding pictures in color.

"I got a notion to take it to law," Smitty says. "It stands right there in the law books somplace that nobody got a right to launching these here barges and like to ruin everybody else's property.

"Last time they launch a barge over there, one of them hunnerd-ninety-five-foot jumbos for North River Transit it was, why, they send such a wave over here the refrigerator like to fell over onto Lorraine Lou. If it would of, by God, they would have one of the sweetest lawsuits on their hands. But do they care? Oh no! Do they think of my wife and kids? Oh no! All them big operators cares about is to just get another barge contract so's to raise more misery for me. You know what I'm agonna do next time? I'm agonna get me a good rifle and shoot somebody over there and don't get no idea in your head I'm akiddin' 'cause I ain't. This here has gone far enough and if the Coast Guard can't give a man no protection, then it's about time for a man to take matters into his own hands. Lorraine Lou! How many times I got to tell you to stay out of that flatboat? Now leave them sparkplugs alone. Get into this houseboat before I work you over with a broom handle. If that foolish child lives to be ten years old it will be some miracle."

"Well if she is crazy she comes by it natural," says Lorraine, his wife (just plain Lorraine). "If anybody would of told me ten years ago when I was on the farm that I'd end up with a crazy man living on a houseboat why I would of worked 'em over with an ax."

Somebody in the Smith family is always about to work somebody over.

When I was fifteen, I left Iowa and went away to school down in New Hampshire, and the conversation used to go like this:

"Where do you come from?"

"Dubuque, Iowa."

"Ha-ha, that's good. But seriously, where *do* you come from?"

Then I would have to explain that I really did, that my father and my grandfather and my great-grandfather also came from Dubuque, and that it was a real place with streetcars and movies and electric lights and a golf course and kids even had to go to dancing school there. But nobody really believed it. They thought Dubuque and Peoria and Kalamazoo and Chillicothe were places made up by Carl Sandburg or Sherwood Anderson, because nobody with any sense would give towns such funny names, especially Dubuque, the mention of which was always good for a laugh on the B. F. Keith vaudeville circuit.

Well, that was twenty-five years ago and the streetcars are gone now, although some of the tracks remain, wandering around town, appearing and disappearing here and there, and on dark foggy nights in November some of us old relics who were in high school in 1928 can hear the ghost of the West Dubuque car squealing her heels as she grinds around the bend at West Third and Alpine by the old Langworthy house. As for dancing school, that's gone too, along with Red Grange and changing to winter underwear. But Dubuque, the old and lovable, goes on forever despite parking meters, the Cadillacs jamming Main Street, and the mink coats in summer storage down at Rhomberg's. Yes, even old Dubuque now has mink coats, plain, blue, white and pink.

Every year the Mormon flies invade the downtown section on two or three June nights and expire in piles a foot high around the street lamps just as they always have. Every night the beer bottles fly across the room and the fist fights go on until closing time in the taverns along Central Avenue. Every hour the big mikado engines of the Illinois Central blow their lovely steam whistles for the grade crossings. And every minute that ticks by out here by the river is a genuine gold-plated Dubuque minute, medium rare, and with plenty of fried onions and a stein of Star beer on the side.

Yes, they try to kill her with their glass-front stores and supermarkets and tearing down the old post office and selling the old steamboats and all such foolishness, but Dubuque she don't go down so easy as all that. Senator Allison is gone, and Major Day and Frank Stout and Judge Bonson and Captain Killeen and George Meyers and Diamond Jo and Tim Kelly, all of them are gone, and so are the lead miners and the Indians, and the new crowd are doing their best to modernize the old town, to get her to have a new hairdo and try a sidecar cocktail. But she just wants to sit on the side porch of a summer afternoon with a palm-leaf fan and plenty of Star or Potosi in the ice chest. You can't change Dubuque any more than you can change Dublin or Duluth or Dubrovnik or any of those other crazy old places.

There's one thing *everybody* is interested in, and that's drinking. Boy how they pour it down, everything from dandelion wine to the Tim Kelly specials (six ounces of warm gin in a barrel tumbler) with plenty of high-proof Bourbon in the middle. Those rough tough lead miners that started this town in 1830 are all marked by limestone slabs now, but their drinking habits live on in Dubuque, where the sweetest young matrons, crusty bankers and humble potato-chip vendors give their all daily in glorious co-operation with the larger distilleries and breweries.

Dubuque was founded by a man named Julien Dubuque. All anybody really knows about him is that he picked a pretty spot here beside the Mississippi for a town and that he worked the lead mines and married an Indian girl named Potosa. Nobody knows for sure that the Indians were fond of him or that Potosa was a "beautiful Indian maiden." Anybody who has spent much time among surviving Indians of the Central West will probably come to the conclusion that she was not only unbeautiful but no doubt had a few teeth missing. As for the great white father, Julien Dubuque, he was a smart Canuck who found out how to make money off the lead mines. He came right in and took over—a promoter, all right. At this writing there is not much evidence in the files about the man Dubuque, but we do know he was a lively boy who liked to dance and play the fiddle. Although he was very fast at making deals and built up a local empire and a "fortune," he went off the track in the end and died with everything mortgaged to the great Chouteau family of St. Louis. We dug up his bones a while back and reburied him under a limestone turret on the beautiful bluff where Catfish Creek joins the Mississippi, a wonderful spot on a summer day, where you can sit alone in the waving grass and watch a towboat coming up the long straight stretch of river from Massey Slough, listen to the drowsy hums of bees, and watch the clouds drifting down toward Pilot Knob.

(Traveling Salesman: Ain't there nothing to do in this burg on a Sunday? Room Clerk: Well, it's a nice pretty walk to Dubuque's grave.

Traveling S.: I always knew this town was dead but I never realized she was buried too.

CURTAIN)

It was back in 1785 that Dubuque came to town, and by 1835 things were beginning to hum here. The Langworthy brother crossed the river and took up where Julien left off. Loud noise reverberated off the bluffs as whisky, women and gunpowder became more abundant. They began to build a town on the flats under the bluffs, and the steamboats began to arrive from St. Louis; the steamboats weren't so beautiful in those early times, but they seemed to be, and they brought kegs of cut nails and a printing press and handsaws and Monongahela rye and news from back east.

I often lie awake at night here by the Mississippi, listening to the crickets and to the towboats blowing for the East Dubuque drawbridge, and wonder what it was like in those early times. Oh, I know how they made bread, where they got their boots and tobacco and what kind of clothes they wore and how they made a living and how much it cost for a jug of vinegar; but I mean how did it *feel* to be here a hundred and twenty years ago, and what did it *really* look like when there was a log cabin where the dime store is now, and an Indian camp by Ragatz's drugstore? Those are the things that by the accident of birth I can never know, no matter how much history I read.

One thing I know, the Mississippi looked and smelt and acted the same as it does now. It goes on past town pretty much the same as it always did, in spite of the dams, with a few dead fish floating belly-up, and a lot of mud and silt from up in Minnesota. A sand bar probably looked the same a hundred years ago, and the carp or buffalo or gar smelled the same after lying dead in the July sun for a few days. Spring came as it always does, and the willow trees feathered, and the mallards, teal, canvasbacks and wood ducks settled down into the sloughs to feed, on their way to Canada, and the big wide sheet of water kept on moving down the valley the same as it will a thousand years from now. Only it was clearer, then, and deer and timber wolves came down to drink, and Indian blood stained the oak leaves back up in the draws.

So Dubuque and his beautiful Indian maiden frolicked and drank French brandy in the Happy Hunting Grounds. Great-grandfather Bissell left New York State and came west and lit in the raw, rough and noisy mining town by the river, and he decided they needed him here to teach school, practice law, and help out at the Universalist church.

Steamboat whistles blew louder and oftener, and steamboats grew longer and prettier and faster, and the bartenders wore diamond rings on their big fingers. There was the *Grey Eagle,* Capt. Daniel Smith Harris. After she hit the Rock Island bridge and sank, her pilot, Capt. William Kelly, took off his cap, blew his nose, and said: "The *Grey Eagle* was the sweetest thing in the way of a steamboat that a man ever looked upon. Long, lean, as graceful as a greyhound, white as snow. . . . If the *Grey Eagle* had a soul—and who knows but what she had—she will be reconstructed at the resurrection day, and will ply in celestial waters, carrying angels on their daily visits with their harps, and golden vials filled with the fragrance of flowers which are the prayers of saints.

Captain Harris will be her commander and I his pilot."

That's pretty high-powered stuff for an old steamboat pilot.

Smitty came through here a few times driving a transcontinental tractor truck. Then one time after he delivered his load in Seattle he quit and came back to Dubuque and began to build his houseboat.

"But listen, Smitty, you been all over, coast to coast—all the towns you seen, how come you decide to settle down here?"

"My mother dropped me on my head when I was a baby, I guess. Oh, I dunno, it just struck me somehow. The river, and then the bluffs over in East Dubuque, and the towboats. And then there's a lot of trees around town. It's nice and shady. And that silly old courthouse. And that there cable railway up to the top of the hill. Then there is plenty of jobs here most always. And nobody bothers you too much."

Smitty spits in the river and looks out toward the channel where one of the big steam towboats of the Mississippi Valley Barge Line is creeping up on the drawbridge, with ten barges of Illinois coal in front of her. A plume of steam goes up, and the sweet sad old music of her whistle spreads over the valley from bluff to bluff.

"I must admit they's plenty goof balls in this here town. Almost a record, I do believe. But that's the same everyplace nowadays."

From over at Molo's boat yard across the harbor comes the ping of a live-oak caulking hammer. They've got another wood barge hauled out and Fred Geiser is driving oakum. Fred's the last of the old wooden-barge men around; everything is steel now. Fred's moving pretty slow these days, but he's still good for thirty or forty years more around those barges, I'll bet.

"I guess the river kinda appealed to me more than anything. Mighty pretty, ain't it?"

When they tear down old houses in Dubuque the joists and beams lots of times will have a hole bored in the middle near each end. This is the kind of thing that archaeologists puzzle over. In a thousand years some bright boy at North Pole University is likely to write a paper on "Hole-Bored Joists of the 19th-Century Eastern Iowa Strata." Well, friends, the reason the joists have a hole bored in each end is that they were sawed up in Wisconsin and were the grub planks that held raft cribs of lumber together for the trip out of the Chippewa and down the Mississippi to Dubuque, Clinton and points on south to St. Louis.

Those were the rip-snorting days of the terrible Black River rafts-men who lived on straight whisky and wildcat steaks, the golden age of the Upper Mississippi, when the sawmill owners built their palaces and Dubuque was the Key City to the state of Iowa and the Great

West, if not the Universe. Knapp-Stout and Co. alone brought out over two billion—let's have that again—two billion feet of pine in rafts up until 1896. So no wonder Frank Stout had not one but two palaces: one with a private race track; the other, the town house, a magnificent affair of red sandstone with tower, arches, columns, stained glass and a porte-cochère heavy with bronze ornamentation, arabesques and five cartouches with the Stout monogram. The 19th Century was in full bloom and never did it flourish with more of a wallop than in Dubuque. They laid the old streets, built a bridge across the Mississippi (Andrew Carnegie himself was the salesman for the iron), the sawmills screamed, and there was a steam train that crept up Eighth Avenue to the hill district. There was the Diamond Jo Line of packets and the extravagant bar of the Lorimer House and on New Year's Day the sports made their calls in varnished cutters.

Great-grandfather died and left an orphan child aged eleven, but grandfather went to work in an office and played the game according to Horatio Alger's rules. By the end of the century he was ready to build his own palace, with a ballroom and bandstand on the third floor, and the Saturday-night bath in a washtub on Burch Street was a thing of the past. There was a Persian corner, and a fireplace with Delft tiles around it, and the girls fixed up the parlor with cattails and shawls, and everybody played lawn tennis and billiards, and they used to actually read books in that far-off day, and they used to sit around and talk; and instead of gawking at Twenty Questions on TV they played it themselves.

So Dubuque drifted along and the Standard Lumber Company burned up and the last log raft came down and then there were no more rafts. And the steamboats disappeared one by one. Mr. Boldt, who owned the first confectionery store and soda fountain, or if not the first, the most famous, bought a one-cylinder Cadillac. Father, in white flannels, won the Golf Club tennis championship. In a sweltering upstairs bedroom in the old house on Fenelon Place I was born, to the music of the seven-year locusts, in time to hear the factory whistles blow for the Armistice, five years later. I had a new tricycle by then, which was far more important. The only effect the war had on Dubuque was to cause a lot of feuds as to who was "pro-German," and there were plenty who were, in this German town. So they quit teaching German in the public schools and then it was 1920 and we had Prohibition.

Things got rougher during Prohibition and a guy could get full of holes over in East Dubuque, the way Bon Bon Allegretti got it one night. Even now in some old saloons across the river, you can find some old boy with a twitch in his cheek who wears a neat suit and white shirt and gaudy tie, and he can tell you about the Prohibition days in

East Dubuque, and the time he met Al or Ralph Capone on business. It's not too bad an idea to buy this fellow some drinks, because he can tell you All About It.

"I remember the night Allegretti got killed real well," he will say. "I was tending bar at a bum little dump called Paradise Garden then and I didn't get off until late that night because—"

Well, it goes on from there and if Hollywood could get ahold of some of this stuff there would be no television problem.

Up on Eighth Avenue there's a tavern operator who plays the piano with his back to it and then turns around and plays the bass notes with his feet. Down in jungletown by the Illinois Central Railroad yards the bums from Butte and Conneaut and El Paso stir their mulligan with a spring knife and prepare for bed wrapped in newspapers.

"I seen Denver Smoky last week in K.C."

"I ain't seen Smoky sence we met in Oregon three years ago."

"He got a lot thinner sence I seen him last."

They squat by the river and wash out their socks and hang them on a willow to dry while they take a nap. When they wake up they sit on a log and watch somebody go by in his cruiser brandishing a Tom Collins. That gives them an idea and they go uptown and get a gallon of wine and bring it back and drink it. The redwing blackbirds flutter in the willows and when evening comes the nighthawks begin their booming dives as the sun goes down in the direction of Nebraska.

"Dubuque," says Smitty. "Two sash-and-door mills and five hundred gin mills. Boy, this here town just kills me."

There is no past, present and future time here in Dubuque, there is just Dubuque time. People try to live up to the modern age but it is a losing game because Dubuque wins out every time. There is an old guy around here who says that one of these days the price of lead is a-going to go sky high and then the miners will come back—and the girls from Cincinnati; and there are farmers who have a shaft sunk in the south pasture, and they grub around in it between plowing, harvesting and doing the chores. But mostly the amateur geologists sit around down at the Page Hotel eating and drinking, and then grabbing a cab to East Dubuque, across that big new steel bridge, to see the floor show. After a hundred years we are about used to the idea that we won't have another lead boom. But the lead mines are still with us—nearly everybody's house is on top of an old lead mine and every pasture has its old open pits, now overgrown. "No city in the Union," said an editor in 1880, "is surrounded by larger and more magnificent mines and caves than Dubuque." Well, they're still here if you want to hunt around for them.

"Did you say you came from Idaho? That's where the baked potatoes come from, isn't it?" some bright character from Back Bay used to ask me.

"No, no, *Iowa*. Not Idaho and not Ohio. *Iowa*."

"Oh. Well, those flat plains must be an awful bore."

Flat plains! Dubuque is so steep that if we happen to have a little sleet storm the night of one of the Christmas dances half the customers can't get home up the hill afterward and have to sleep on couches downtown after a lot of telephone calls to Mother. No, it's not flat. It's beautiful and steep like Pittsburgh and in fact there are streets so steep nobody ever uses them. The Sports Car Club of Milwaukee comes all the way over here every year to have its Hill Climb, and the Fourth Street Elevator is the only cable railway left in the Middle West since Duluth foolishly scrapped hers. (Cincinnati doesn't count; that's way down east.) I have a friend who used to chain his Model-T Ford to a tree in front of his house every night, not so it wouldn't be stolen but so it wouldn't roll down the hill. One Halloween the boys from St. Columbkille's soaped the streetcar tracks on Bryant Street, the steep part where it goes down into South Dodge, and the old four-wheel trolley shot down the hill, jumped the tracks and lit over in the woods where Merly Appel's store is now. The only way you can get to some of the houses in Dubuque is to walk up a flight of stairs from the street, down on the level below. So there are the flat plains of Iowa.

No, Dubuque isn't in Idaho, nor Ohio either. Dubuque is in Iowa. You buy a copy of *A Slow Train Through Arkansas*, the Chicago *Daily News* and a package of Wrigley's genuine Chicago gum and get aboard America's fastest and most thrilling railroad train, the Twin Cities Zephyr, out of the Chicago Union Station. Spend the time dozing in the Vista Dome or rioting in the club car with the Minneapolis wheat kings and cattle buyers from Fargo, and only two and one-half hours out of Chicago, behold—East Dubuque, Illinois; change cars for Dubuque, land of charm and sawdust and the Shot Tower.

Well, at last we come around to the Shot Tower. In Dubuque the Shot Tower is like the pyramids in Egypt, a completely useless relic of the past, and just as colorful. There she stands right down beside the Illinois Central Railroad bridge, tall, haunted by a thousand ghosts of ancient times, visible from everywhere, empty, immense, unforgettable, impervious to time, a never-ending subject for the highschool poets and a perpetual reminder of the ephemeral nature of man.

But if the Shot Tower is only a hollow monument, its neighboring pile of brick and limestone is mighty solid and alive—that's the Star Brewery. Dubuque must have its beer if not its shot. In a hot summer day when the horse mint and mullein and elderberry flowers sizzle in the cinder ballast beside the railroad tracks, approach the Star Brewery boldly and enter, and you will be taken into the cooling room and given a copper mug of the genuine brew.

Then you can stand by the big reciprocating steam engines and watch the flywheels spin and enjoy life free of charge and wonder why they need steam engines to make beer and look at the river flowing right by the front door bound for Hannibal and St. Louis.

That's Dubuque, that's the Upper Mississippi, that's where the West begins, that's my home, girls and boys, in the richest state in the Republic, where the farm hands shoot the crows with gold buckshot.

Architecturally speaking, we have everything in Dubuque except a full-scale replica of the Taj Mahal, and the Egelhof Funeral Home is even a step in that direction. Starting up in Eagle Point Park with the earliest house remaining in our city, a saddle-bag log cabin built before 1830, we run the gamut of architectural curiosities right up to John Roshek's new house, which has mobiles, raw-silk dish towels and a Toulouse-Lautrec poster in the furnace room.

One of the prize exhibits is the old Langworthy house, which is even worth driving over winding Highway No. 20 from Chicago to see. It's a mammoth octagonal house with a pilothouse on top. The Brussels carpet in the grand parlor was brought up from New Orleans on the steamboat about a hundred years ago. To add a confusing note, Ed Chalmers, last of the Langworthy tribe, who now inhabits this famous and beautiful old home, keeps a 1926 Silver Ghost Rolls Royce town car parked in front of the house on Alpine Street. Across the street is the old Scribe Harris home (brother of Daniel Smith Harris who captained the *Grey Eagle*) and in the carriage house, carrying on the idea of living simultaneously in the past and present, is my brother Fred's collection of antique automobiles, including such delectable numbers as Sears, Stevens-Duryea, Metz, Stanley Steamer and International, and a comprehensive assortment of high-wheel bicycles, ancient marine engines, license plates dating back to the Flood, five thousand queer spark plugs, a 1908 Marsh and Metz motorcycle, a lot of kids' overshoes, tricycles, scooters, thirty-three empty Coke bottles and two Edison phonographs.

Then there's the Villa Baloney, the old Hamm house, Ziepprecht's Haven, the Bell House, the Connolly Carriage Co., Cooper Castle, the pilothouse off the steamer *Aquila* set up in brother Fred's back yard, the Diamond House, the Huss House, an Egyptian jail, the Sink, the Block House, Schmidt's Wall, Cod's Skyline Retreat on the summit of majestic Ben Kiene—well, there's virtually no end to the list of examples of the builder's art and the mental aberrations of architects. Marine architecture is also important in this old river town, some representative examples being Duncan's Folly, the Floating Cave, Pampoo, the Cork, the Treatment, and Slim Duccini's island home, with although on dry land qualifies as marine property as it is under water every year in the spring rise.

My friend Tom, who has just picked up a 1953 Ford with a Cadillac engine and a special rear end made by the Space Cadets (Mfg. Division), took me for a little day trip up to the Waukon Centennial not long ago. We went up to see what was going on, have a beer with the local merchants, and see the Indian powwow ("in their genuine old-time tribal dances, folks"). I was in the back seat of the Ford-Cadillac keeping in touch with the outer world reading Major as we headed out for Gutenberg and Garnavillo, when by chance I looked over Tom's shoulder at the speedometer. The reading was 101.

And yet, not so long ago there was a golden, happy time before Cadillacs, when out on the side porch was an open box of Page & Shaw's chocolates on the wicker table and the "help" brought in a pitcher of lemonade and some sliced pound cake, macaroons and a pile of devil's food. Those were the days of easy living, when for months on end the only crisis that faced the family was when the chauffeur surrendered to nature and environment and went to East Dubuque on a big toot and was not available the next day to drive grandfather to the office in the big gray Hudson. I never heard the word "taxes" mentioned in all my youth. The problem was whether to go to Lake Louise or Duluth for Margie's hay fever and whether Fritz was handling the rose garden properly.

But we still have winter, a great big one with city and county schools closed after the blizzards, and ice skating on the harbor. And we have spring in the Upper Mississippi, a spring to make poets jump up and down, lovers swoon, and old men feel young again. In autumn the air is so clear that from Sherrill's Mound, a few miles north of town, you can see nearly to Greenland; that is the time when we pile in our flatboats and take the kids upriver and cook large steaks on some narrow island with the leaves falling all around, and listen to the cannonading of the duck hunters in the sloughs. Already the water is as cold as Lake Superior, but young Nat insists on "one last swim," while Tom and Stasia go exploring up the island and little Sam is given a clamshell to inspect.

These things don't change, and Dubuque doesn't change, in spite of television and speedy motorcars—and that's why we like Dubuque. She is a funny old girl in some ways, but a lot more honest and lovely than those skinny dolls in the fashion magazines, and we all love her. If we go away we always come back sometime. And while we're away, we're thinking back to that goofy old town by the river.

"There's something different about this here town. I don't know what it is or how to tell it," Smitty says. "I ain't too normal myself. Maybe that's why I feel right at home here."

... Richard Bissell, 1954

Shot Tower, Dubuque

Industrial Iowa

AMERICANS WHO DO NOT KNOW *this prairie land, except by hearsay, or who view it only from a jet plane at 35,000 feet as they fly over it on their way to either coast, usually think of Iowa as a flat rural land, planted river to river, border to border with corn, with breaks in the corn fields for islands of buildings housing farmers in bib overalls and wide-brimmed straw hats.*

"Ding" Darling helped plant that notion with his cartoons of fat, straw-chewing farmers, and Iowans away from home nourished it with that song ending,   *"And that's where the tall corn grows."*

What these outlanders (and perhaps even some Iowans) don't know is that, beginning in 1880 or thereabouts, Iowa's rural population has been on a steady decline in numbers; the State's slight population growth through the succeeding decades has been in its towns and cities. What has brought rural people to the urban areas has been jobs—jobs in stores, in offices and in factories.

As long ago as 1856, a far-seeing writer prophesied that Iowa's future would lie in "manufacturies" in its major river valleys—the Mississippi, the Iowa-Cedar, the Des Moines and the Missouri. And, although there are small manufacturing plants in or near many an Iowa town, it is in Davenport, Burlington, Keokuk, Muscatine, Bettendorf, Clinton, Dubuque, Waterloo-Cedar Falls, Cedar Rapids, Marshalltown, Des Moines, Fort Dodge, Ottumwa, Council Bluffs and Sioux City that Iowa's major industrial plants are to be found.

And although there is a furniture factory in Dubuque, a writing-instrument factory in Fort Madison, an office furniture factory in Muscatine, an electronics factory in Cedar Rapids, appliance factories in Newton and Amana, and a toothpaste factory in Iowa City, the majority of Iowa factories produce goods that are related to the harvesting of crops (corn, soybeans, hogs, cattle) on Iowa's still-numerous farms—oatmeal, popcorn, honey, hams, beer, farm tractors and other farm implements.

But, as Michael Walker's essay on the following pages demonstrates, even the handling of Iowa's golden crops is an industry, and one of the state's biggest at that.

Although Michael Walker is not a native Iowan, he grew up in Wayne, Illinois, in that State's farm country. He did his college work at Drake University in Des Moines, taking an English-Journalism degree in 1979. For a year he was a staff writer for the Des Moines Planet. *With the demise of that paper, he became a copy editor for the Meredith Corporation (an Iowa manufacturer that is one of the nation's largest producers of magazines) and then was assigned to Meredith's newest magazine,* Metropolitan Home.

As a free-lance writer, his work is seen frequently in The Iowan, *published in Des Moines and Shenandoah. The following article originally appeared in the Summer, 1982, issue of that magazine.*

AGRI: *Getting Iowa's "Gold" to Market*

THEY RISE, TOTEM-LIKE, from the seemingly endless savannas of corn, soybean and wheat that blanket Iowa, Wisconsin, Illinois, Minnesota, and Kansas, in places where lunch is called dinner and dinner is supper. In the midday sun, their flanks are like flint; gray, stolid, imperturbable; at twilight and at dawn, they cast stark silhouettes against the horizon.

Three hundred and thirty-four strong, owned by 135,000 farm families in nine states, these are the co-op elevators that comprise the backbone of AGRI Industries, a seventy-eight-year-old grain cooperative based in West Des Moines, Iowa, whose unprecedented growth in the past ten years has seen its influence range as far afield as Moscow, as close to home as its titanic grain-handling facility in Avon, Iowa. Its ancillary businesses now include an equipment-leasing company, a commodities futures trading company, a travel agency, a brewery, a stevedoring concern, a farm management division, fertilizer division, and insurance division.

But above all, AGRI is in the grain business. In 1981 the company moved more than any other co-op. And, in most cases, AGRI moved this vast harvest in its own hopper cars (the company and its members together operate some 6,500 cars) to its own terminals on the Mississippi (four in all), where it is conveyed in barges wholly or jointly owned by AGRI to company-operated export facilities in Louisiana (125 million bushels exported to twenty-five nations around the world). The company also ships grain by rail to another export facility in Houston. Further, AGRI is one of the few companies, let alone co-ops, making direct sales of wheat and corn to the Soviet Union. At the center of this activity is the West Des Moines headquarters, where more than 300 employees work in a sleek, almost self-consciously modern building garnished on the outside with a chocolate-brown AGRI logo.

For all its complexities, though, AGRI is still technically run by its far-flung pride of local elevators, a fact which the company's president, B. J. "Jerry" O'Dowd, says he never forgets. "There isn't a day that goes by that I don't talk to them," he insists, a sentiment echoed by AGRI public relations director Maurice Van Nostrand, who is downright partisan when it comes to the local co-ops. "The whole system is dedicated to the furtherance of those farmers' interests," he declares. "It's more democratically controlled than the government."

As Van Nostrand is fond of pointing out, AGRI itself is more or less a superextension of the local co-ops it represents. Each of the company's member co-ops is watched over by a board of directors elected by the farmers the co-op represents. In true democratic fashion, every farmer receives one vote regardless of the size or output of his operation. AGRI, in turn, is supervised by a twelve-member board of directors chosen from the ranks of these local concerns. Nine of the directors must be actively farming land while they serve; the other three are active managers of local AGRI co-ops. And it is this twelve-member board that votes to pass ultimate judgment on the business recommendations emanating from AGRI's key management, which includes O'Dowd and Van Nostrand, vice-president Pat Kevelin, controller Gene Peters, and director of finance John Long.

What do the local co-ops get in exchange for their grain and elevator space? For one, a portion of after-tax profits (or "savings," in cooperative parlance), in cash and stock, which is passed on to the individual farmers in proportion to their grain contribution. "The bottom line turns them on," says AGRI board chairman Russell Frascht, in reference to the co-op members. "They share in profits through patronage. But if you do something they dislike, they sure let you know about it."

Frascht knows whereof he speaks; his Greene, Iowa, farm is part of the same system. "My grain goes to the local elevator at Greene," he explains, "and is marketed 100 percent through AGRI. From there, depending on the type of grain, it is usually trucked to the AGRI facility at McGregor and loaded onto barges bound for AGRI's Louisiana export terminals near New Orleans."

Until recently, the bottom line that Frascht speaks of was impressive indeed. In 1980, AGRI profits totaled $21 million on revenues of $3 billion, up from $2.7 million in 1977. In 1981, however, profits plummeted to $3.3 million, due in part to high interest rates and sluggish grain sales. This downswing was compounded by financial mishaps at the part-AGRI-owned Farmer's Export Company (which cut into profits to the tune of $8.5 million), losses at the recently acquired Pickett's Brewery in Dubuque (a $700,000 loss), and red ink ($2 million) at the soybean-processing division.

In 1982, the company continues to be bedeviled by the economy, not to mention last spring's tragedy at the AGRI-owned Bluffs Elevator Company in Council Bluffs, Iowa. On April 20, an explosion of as-yet-undetermined cause (though grain dust is suspected) rocked the facility, killing five employees and injuring twenty-some other persons. The resultant loss of property and grain was estimated at $10 million. Nevertheless, the company continues to expand, if at a less vigorous clip than in the past few years. In May, 1982, it leased, with an option to buy, five Texas-based grain elevators from a financially ailing cooperative there. The move, says Van Nostrand, was made in part to stimulate AGRI wheat-milo trade through its Houston export terminal.

The AGRI of today is a direct descendant of the nation's first-ever cooperative, which opened in Rockwell, near Mason City, in the 1880s. Its success spawned thirty to forty counterparts across the state, which, in 1904, banded together to form the Farmer's Grain Dealers Association. The need for such an arrangement, says Van Nostrand, stemmed from the changing role of the farmer at the turn of the century.

With this group, the farmers found a collective voice that could speak out, through legislative lobbying and the like, for their special interests. When Iowa began producing enough grain to seek out-of-state markets, says Van Nostrand, the cooperative concept went regional.

This happened in 1943 when the Farmer's Grain Dealers Association opened an office in Fort Dodge, Iowa, and began stalking the grain trade outside the state in earnest. From these beginnings came a steady expansion: the massive Avon, Iowa, elevator began operation in the mid-1950s; in the next decade barge-loading stations were completed along the Mississippi at McGregor, Muscatine, and Meeker's Landing; and in 1965 the company's first soybean processing plant opened. Then came rail-car fleets and unit trains.

"It was a solid company with great strength," recalls Van Nostrand, "and that strength came from the loyalty of its members and the increasing ability of Iowa farmers to produce grain. There's a lot of tenure to it. We're very lucky. We're sitting in the middle of the most productive agricultural area in the world."

In 1978 Jerry O'Dowd arrived on the scene as president, fresh from the eastern regional vice-president's slot at Continental Grain Company, one of the privately owned grain-merchandising giants. It is under O'Dowd's flamboyant arms-and-elbows management that AGRI's growth really began to take off.

"In my style of management, I like to delegate a lot of responsibility," says the fifty-five-year-old O'Dowd. "At Continental, I had the longest rope and the shortest knife. I insist on no surprises. I like people who rock the boat, but I don't like superstars; I like the guy who goes up to bat."

O'Dowd is seated behind the desk in the designer-furniture splendor of his office at AGRI's West Des Moines headquarters. Behind him a videoscreen glows with rows of grain figures. Jacket off, attired in a blue dress shirt and yellow tie, he gulps from a can of Welch's grape juice and recounts the course that led him to the helm of AGRI: father and uncles in the grain business; at thirteen, a runner in the Kansas City Board of Trade; high school years spent working in the grain elevators; two-year stint in the air force; subsequent B.A. in business administration from the University of Missouri at Kansas City; then into the grain business full throttle.

In 1950, he worked at the Mid-States Grain Company in Fort Dodge; in 1963, he accepted Continental Grain's offer to come to Des Moines and "open up Iowa," where, he boasts, in under ten years he increased his merchandizing from 10 million bushels of grain his first year to 100 million bushels upon his departure. In 1975, he moved to Columbus, Ohio, and a new position with Continental: eastern regional manager. Three years later, he accepted an executive search firm's invitation to come to Des Moines and head what became, soon after his arrival, AGRI Industries.

O'Dowd's handling of AGRI has reaped much comment from his business associates. "Under Chuck Hanson [O'Dowd's predecessor] we had McGregor, Muscatine, Meeker's Landing, Farmer's Export, and smaller offices," muses board chairman Frascht. "Now we've got four river sites, the leasing company, Farmer's Commodities, Pickett's Brewery, plus larger offices. . . . We have grown." Says Van Nostrand, "O'Dowd's a very flamboyant leader with lots of ideas and his own management style. He doesn't like negativism; he wants lots of ideas. The board grants him broad authority, which they recognize and live with."

O'Dowd's energetic brand of management ("I'd go to hell to sell grain if I thought the devil would buy it") has no doubt figured hugely in AGRI's remarkable growth since his signing on. Still, the company has eaten a few slices of extremely humble pie recently, the worst of which was the Farmer's Export affair.

A huge Kansas City-based grain-marketing co-op, Farmer's Export—owned by AGRI and other co-ops—was created to compete with the private grain companies for a share of the international grain-export trade. (AGRI has since gone after foreign business directly via its Houston terminal.) In the winter of 1979, Farmer's Export, through over-trading in soybean and corn, lost $40 million, of which AGRI was obliged to absorb $8.5 million from its profit margin. Farmer's Export has since been reorganized, and O'Dowd feels that its assets (a portside Ama, Louisiana, elevator, to name one) make up for its losses.

Another miscue, at least initially, has been the acquisition of the Pickett's Brewery, bought primarily, says O'Dowd, for its proximity to the Mississippi River banks in Dubuque, where barge-loading sites are scarce. Losses for the brewery operation hit $700,000 in 1980, its first year with AGRI, and O'Dowd says an unprofitable beer distributorship that went along with the sale has since been closed. Although Pickett's sales in Iowa, according to AGRI's 1981 annual report, were 156 percent higher for the last month of fiscal 1981 compared to the same period in 1980, O'Dowd concedes it's been a hard sell. "It's a tough racket," he says. "The beer costs us two cents, and the can costs ten cents."

But there have been successes, of course. The subsidiary leasing company, now in its third year of operation, has expanded to include an excavating equipment and leasing concern in Houston, both of which are expected to help shield the company against the caprices of the grain-selling business. And O'Dowd says the leasing venture has thus far made $1.5 million on an investment of less than $500,000.

The Des Moines-based travel agency, purchased, at least in theory, to provide travel arrangements for the co-op members, has also done well (though its original *raison d'être*, as O'Dowd points out, is a bit far-fetched). The stevedoring operation, which provides manpower for both its Jacintoport, Texas, facility and AGRI's nearby Houston exporting terminal, has paid off as well. "We wouldn't have turned a black figure in January [1982]," declares O'Dowd, "if it hadn't been for the stevedoring company."

It is late in the afternoon, and O'Dowd is in his office, preparing for an upcoming trip to Russia to negotiate a grain deal. As he and his secretary work out the logistics (carried out as if he were flying to Fort Dodge rather than Moscow), he fields the inevitable questions about AGRI's future. Does he anticipate AGRI growing large enough to battle openly with the Cargills and Continentals of the grain business (which still dwarf AGRI and other co-ops)? In response, he recites a litany of his company's well-known fellow travelers. "Sunkist is a co-op," he offers, "and it's a hell-raiser. Sioux Bee is a co-op." He gestures at the now-empty juice can. "Welch's is a co-op." In the final analysis, he concludes, he would just as soon see AGRI become more effective, "return more to the owners," than to grow larger.

Behind him, beyond the smoked-glass windows, the sun is setting, casting long shadows across West Des Moines. Meanwhile, as O'Dowd prepares to leave for the day, 334 stark silhouettes across the Midwest are beginning to take shape, long and black, on the western horizon.

. . . Michael Walker

AGRI soybean processing plant, Mason City

Once More to the Land

FOR ALL OF IOWA'S industrial assets, for all of its tourist attractions, the mainstay of Iowa economy is still the Iowa farm, with its resident farm family producing annually an important share of the food needed to feed a hungry world.

"Land That They Love" is Iowan Merle Miller's 1956 paean to a Hardin County farm family that might have been, as Miller says, any farm family in Iowa.

Miller was born in Montour, Iowa, in 1919 and graduated from high school in nearby Marshalltown. From 1935 to 1938 he was a staffer for the University of Iowa's Daily Iowan, *a position which Dale Kramer and Hartzell Spence had held just five years earlier. Like Kramer and Spence, he also served on the staff of the United States Army's World War II magazine,* Yank.

He is the author of numerous magazine articles and books.

Land That They Love

ALMOST EVERY COUNTY AGENT in Iowa could suggest at least one farm family that would welcome a visitor who had spent his first 12 years on an Iowa farm and wanted to find out what had or had not changed in the nearly 25 years since. I liked Dick Pulse's letter best; he is the extension director of Hardin County in central Iowa. "The Maurice Cook family is not average or typical—but who interesting is?" Pulse wrote. "They have a 235-acre farm near New Providence; there are three sons, Kenneth, Frank, Lisle, all of whom want to be farmers themselves. There have been Cooks on their land for four generations now, and it looks to me as if they've settled down for quite a stay— "farm problem" or no farm problem.

"The Cooks are modest and value their family relationship above everything else. They really know how to plan and work together. They are highly respected by just about everybody in the county . . . Besides, you'd have a good time with them."

The Cook place turned out to be the first on the right on the graveled road leading east out of New Providence, population 250. In the 27-mile drive from my home town, Marshalltown, I had counted only two farmhouses that didn't have television antennas. The new barns I saw were smaller than I remembered and the farmhouses were larger. Professor Herb Howell of Iowa State College at Ames later explained, "Twenty-five years ago a farmer's standing in the community was measured by the size of his barn; now his house is more important. Now he'd rather send his kids to college and make do with the old silo, and he might even get a quick freeze before he buys a new tractor."

Most new Iowa farmhouses are ranch types, with a picture window which often seems to overlook the pigpen. The two-story Cook house has 11 good-sized rooms; it is brick, which is rare in Iowa, and contains what Mrs. Cook, Fern, described as "something I've dreamed about ever since I heard about it, radiant heating." It is the first radiant heating in Hardin County, and people still drive all the way from Marshalltown to take a look at it. The house was completed in 1948, which was a good year for the Cooks and for most of their neighbors; there has not been such a good year since.

Fern explained the practicality of her heating system by pointing out that the menfolk invariably stretch out on the living-room floor for a half-hour nap after their noon meal. "They used to catch colds," she said.

Fern's picture window overlooks a seemingly endless series of pleasantly half-rolling fields. Fern is a slight woman, her once black hair now gently gray. She used to put Kenneth in a baby basket on the edge of the oat field as she helped Maurice sow the crop.

"I was born just across the field there," said Maurice. "I always knew I wanted to own this land, never had any doubts about it, never wanted to be anything but a farmer, never wanted to live anyplace else."

Except for four years at William Penn, a Quaker college in Oskaloosa, Iowa, where he met Fern, and a quarter at Iowa State, Maurice never has lived anyplace else.

But at fifty-one, erect and muscular, with deep, unshadowed blue eyes and cheeks burned russet by the sun and the wind, he is not a provincial man. On their annual vacations during the slack days after the oats are harvested and before it's time to pick the corn, he and his family have traveled by car from Niagara Falls to Mexico. Two summers ago he and Fern flew over to Germany with 34 other Iowa farm families; their son Frank was stationed at an air base near Frankfurt. Fern took along a homemade angelfood cake as well as some of Frank's favorite butterscotch frosting; she stopped off in Wiesbaden for 22 birthday candles.

"Saw a lot of pretty sights over there," said Maurice, "but I never saw anything I'd say came even close to that—" and he pointed to a pale-green meadow where his white-faced Herefords were grazing.

Maurice's father would have been shocked at the idea of flying to Europe; he was not much for travel anyway. "Wherever you go, you just see more people," he used to say, "and we've got plenty of people right here."

Of course, Maurice added, there are probably a good many other things he does that his father would not have understood. The elder Mr. Cook died of a heart attack at the age of seventy-one, a few minutes after he had bought three truckloads of cattle and had helped load them for the trip home from Des Moines. The Cooks do not retire. For that reason, among others, they are strongly opposed to Social Security for farmers. Maurice believes that the law of supply and demand should and will someday again determine a farmer's income; he believes that industrious and competent farmers survive and prosper and that the incompetent and lazy will, tragically but inevitably, be pushed to the wall. Nevertheless, neither he nor any of his neighbors has ever turned down any checks for taking part in whatever program Congress in any given year has decided is the best vote-getting solution to the agricultural problem.

The Cooks are in the upper-third income group in Hardin County. Their 235 acres, on the other hand, have to support two families. Maurice's father was born in the same house as his son; Maurice's seventy-six-year-old stepmother lives there now. The sturdy white frame house is only half a mile south of the equally sturdy white frame house to which Maurice's eldest son, Kenneth, recently brought his bride, Evelyn.

Frank, the middle son, used to talk some about moving to town to become a mechanic. But when he got back from overseas, he and his young wife came straight to the farm, and after his graduation from Iowa State next spring, he hopes to rent a place nearby. The youngest son, Lisle, was one of two Iowa farm boys sent to a national Four-H Club congress in Washington this summer. He will finish at Iowa State in June, 1959, after which he intends to come back to a farm near New Providence. Lisle doesn't know which one, and he doesn't know which of several girls he will marry. But should the girl he decides on not like farm life, Lisle would not change his plans. He would change girls.

The Cooks had never been separated until Kenneth went into the Army in 1951; they want to spend the rest of their lives as near neighbors, but achieving what they refer to as "the Cook dream" will not be easy; they are living through what the professors at Ames call "a revolution."

"The machine age has finally caught up with the farmer," Rex Conn, the knowing farm editor of *The Cedar Rapids Gazette*, told me. "With machines, a farmer can do five times the work he did twenty-five years ago—but people aren't eating five times as much. All the farm programs, every one of them, have been just patched at and mended. The fact is we need fewer farmers in this country. That's a tough thing to say, but it's true."

"Money," said Professor Howell. "That is one of the things that has happened to the farmer in the past twenty-five years—maybe the most important thing. A farmer used to be an artisan—and he still has to be, but now he's got to be a capitalist, too. Tractors, trucks and cultivators—all these things make for more efficiency, but they also cost hard cash."

About half the agricultural students at Iowa State will be forced to become county agents or agricultural scientists or combine farming with factory jobs in Des Moines or Cedar Rapids. One out of every three students educated in agriculture at Ames will go to another state for his job.

Very few of the 13 male members of Kenneth's high-school graduating class in New Providence were able to become farmers, although almost all of them wanted to be.

"They mostly just couldn't get together the wherewithal," Kenneth explained.

Kenneth, who once dreamed of becoming a big-league shortstop but decided he wasn't good enough, has been making and saving money almost ever since he can remember.

"When I was ten I bought a baby beef; it was with Dad on a partnership basis. He cost $35.93, which made $17.96 I had to pay. This money I had earned the year before; I had raised chickens and mowed some lawns. We got this first calf on December 16th and sold him on August 9th, making a net profit of $45.68, of which half was mine. I called him White Sox because he had two hind feet that were white. Each evening after the chores were done, I led him up and down the road to train him. Then I showed him at the county fair. He got a red ribbon. I decided to work harder the next year to get a blue ribbon."

Some Iowa farmers give calves to their children; Maurice believes that ten is not too early to learn about profit and loss. When he was twelve, Kenneth one night forgot to feed his calf; the next year it did not even place at the county fair; he was convinced that his negligence was the reason, and he never forgot again.

"If you're a farmer," said Maurice, "you can't ever forget anything, and you have to realize there's a time for everything, too—just like it says in Ecclesiastes. The man who's repairing his manure spreader on the day he ought to be cultivating his corn is in for real trouble.

"And you've got to keep putting it away for a rainy day—or for the summer it doesn't rain at all."

Maurice is conservative where money is concerned, particularly for something personal. The Cooks waited 11 years before they bought a brand-new car, a four-door Ford sedan, to replace a secondhand Model T; they paid cash for it.

On the other hand, Maurice has no objection to borrowing from a bank—usually at 5 per cent—for a new piece of equipment or for feed for his livestock.

He and Fern had $800 between them when they started farming in June, 1928. Maurice bought three elderly plug horses, and at a farm sale he picked up a seeder, a plow, a cultivator and a disk and harrow. The machinery cost a dollar apiece. Those first few years he farmed on a share basis with his farmer, much the same kind of arrangement he has with Kenneth today.

Kenneth had three times that much cash on hand when he started last year. Even so he might not have been able to make it if he had had to rent a farm from a neighbor. His house is rent-free because his parents believe that the work he and Evelyn do on the house will increase its value.

"You can say that these are difficult times for us," Maurice told me, "but I wouldn't exactly call what we're going through now a depression."

He remembers, as I do, the times in the early thirties when Iowa farmers would take hanging ropes to mortgage foreclosure sales and bid anywhere from a penny to a quarter for a 160-acre farm and all its equipment. After the sale, everything was returned to its original owner.

Maurice is not likely to forget the fall and winter of 1932; on September 19th, after Fern had started the week's washing, Frank was born, prematurely and assisted into the world by Maurice's stepmother. At ten that morning, after things had quieted down in the house, Maurice went out and burned the 90 of his hundred head of hogs which had died of cholera. He had not had the money that year to have them vaccinated.

Maurice could not afford coal that winter either. Corn was bringing 10 cents a bushel; so the Cooks burned it in the kitchen stove. It made a noisy, popping fire, and the flame was bright blue, the heat intense, temporary and very localized. Watching it burn, Fern said, a person didn't know what to do. A person didn't know whether to laugh or cry.

They ate a lot of oatmeal that winter, rolled from their own oats, and for dinner they often had hominy, made from their own corn. Both were cheap and filling, "and we got mighty tired of them," said Fern, "but we were never hungry. We were never ever hungry."

"You can see what I mean about this not being a *real* depression," Maurice added.

This year Maurice and Kenneth planted 100 acres of corn, 60 of oats and 60 of alfalfa. They plant their crops on a four-year rotation basis—corn, corn, oats, alfalfa. Their land is just as black and just as rich and fertile as when the sod was first broken. Somebody once said that the Iowa farmer has a gift from four gods—the god of rain, the god of sun, the god of ice, and the god of geology. Farmers like Maurice and his sons have added a fifth, the god of science.

Maurice plants hybrid corn—as do about 99 per cent of the farmers of Iowa—because he now gets as many as 80 to 100 bushels of corn an acre as against 30 to 50 with nonhybrid corn. Six years ago he changed over to hybrid hogs because they have larger litters and, before that, he and Fern decided on hybrid chickens because they lay more eggs.

They feed their crops to their livestock (500 hogs, 125 cattle, 24 sheep) and last year they bought as much corn as they grew. They buy cattle weighing about 400 to 500 pounds; they feed them and sell them when they weigh 1,000 to 1,100 pounds. When the cattle are ready for the market, they are loaded into trucks rented from a firm in New Providence, and the next morning the cattle are sold in the Chicago stockyards. Maurice and Kenneth usually ride right along with them; a broker does the actual selling, but the Cooks like to watch. They market their pigs locally—on a day when the market is rising, if there is such a day.

In a good year, the Cooks get back as much as $1.50 for every dollar's worth of feed they put into their livestock. In a bad year, they get less than a dollar; last year they got 91 cents.

The difference between a good and bad year depends "on about a thousand things," Kenneth says, "but you notice we always get back to the weather." Corn, which dominates nearly all conversation in Iowa from about the first of June until it is picked in late October or early November, needs rain in June or July, hot weather in August. The Cooks listen to weather reports on the radio at least three times a day.

And there is sickness and death, of course. Despite penicillin and cobalt and copper pills and farrowing stalks and commercial feed that is filled with proteins and minerals, and despite the veterinarian, hogs die, and cattle, for seemingly no explainable reason, get runny noses, lose weight and have fevers, and a crop of oats sometimes develops smut and the corn gets worms.

Maurice believes that to be a good farmer a man ought to be something of a philosopher; he ought also nowadays to be a soil expert and a mechanic and an economist and a veterinarian. Like a good doctor, he should also keep up with what science is doing to help him. And even so, forces over which he has no control may overwhelm and destroy him.

Most of all, he must be an optimist. When I asked Maurice how he thought it would be possible for him and all three of his sons to continue farming at a time when prices for everything they would buy are rising and everything they might sell are falling, Maurice said, "Lisle won't be home until 1959, and you see," and he smiled, "I have faith."

Today's businessman-farmer, however, is vulnerable in a way the old-fashioned farmer could never have imagined. To be on what he calls "the safe side," Maurice would like to keep an operating bank balance of $30,000, which, according to the bankers I talked to in nearby Eldora and in Marshalltown, is not unusually high for a man farming 235 acres. Last year Maurice paid out $12,000 for cattle; he bought $12,000 worth of high-protein feed, and another $1,200 for commercial fertilizer. He ended the year with less money than he had when he began, and the pattern is likely to be repeated this year. He has already sold some of his hogs on a falling market; he needed the money to pay his taxes.

"If things keep up the way they are," Dick Pulse said, "Maurice and a lot of other farmers are going to have to cut way down on their expenses. That doesn't mean most farmers around here are going out of business; it just means they'll have to get along with old buildings and beat-up equipment; and they won't be buying any more wall-to-wall carpeting."

Maurice keeps meticulous records of every penny spent or earned, of every pound lost or gained by his animals. He is a member of the Farm Business Association, one of the services offered by the extension of the state college; it is headed by Professor Howell. Two or three times a year a supervisor comes around to check over Maurice's books, correcting mistakes, advising him on tax problems, reporting on successful new experiments at the college, and comparing Maurice's record with that made on farms of similar size.

Pulse said, "Maurice Cook didn't stop learning after that quarter at Ames, and his sons won't either."

By now Maurice has almost every possible kind of mechanized equipment—from a manure spreader to a hay chopper—about $18,000 worth, all told. He got his first mechanical corn picker in 1939, a one-row job; now he has a two-row picker. When he husked his corn by hand, he managed to strip an acre during a backbreaking 10-hour stint. Now he can get through 10 to 15 acres a day.

"I guess I used to work harder," Maurice said. "Not longer; I always got up four-thirty or five in the morning and still do, and in the summer it's sometimes eight-thirty, nine before Kenneth and I are through. Physically harder, I mean; it's one thing to walk behind a team of horses all day and another to sit on the foam-rubber seat of a tractor.

"Maybe I worry more now, though," he added.

Farm life has changed in other ways, too. In the old days, meaning up to, perhaps, 10 years ago, when Maurice bought his first combine, a threshing ring of anywhere from six to nine neighbors went the rounds during the harvest season. In those days, Maurice said, a man had a chance to get together with neighbors he hadn't seen since the last harvest. A week or so after the rounds were completed, accounts were settled at an ice-cream social. Maurice misses both the ice cream and the sociability. Now the job is done in a couple of days, with Maurice and the boys helped by a neighbor, who brings along his tractor. In turn, the Cooks help the neighbor.

Fern likes the new way better. It used to be that for two or three days in August—a time when the temperature in Iowa often gets up toward a hundred in the shade—she cooked the noon dinner for the members of the ring. Not only were the men hungry, there was considerable competition among the wives to serve the most talked-about meal. Fern usually had scalloped potatoes one day and mashed the next; she either fried chickens or prepared three or four rib roasts; then she'd serve creamed peas and sliced tomatoes, both from her own garden. There'd be cabbage slaw with marshmallows and pineapple, homemade rolls, coffee, lemonade, milk and dessert. The dessert was usually pretty much the same—cherry pie, homemade canned peaches and angelfood cake. Most threshers had some of all three, and by midafternoon they were ready for a cold ade of some kind and homemade cookies which Fern and one of the boys took out to the field in a pony cart.

Fern did her cooking on one of those old-fashioned ranges, which in August heated up the whole house before it started cooking the food. Nowadays she cooks on an electric stove, and she also has an electric blender and a grill. Cooking really isn't half the work it used to be; the other afternoon she got home from a visit to Ames at four; some of her supper guests had already arrived; they were friends of Evelyn and Kenneth, all of them members of the Baptist Roger Williams club at the college. In the next hour and a half Fern baked 10 cherry pies, and fried chicken for 28 people.

She still cans a lot of vegetables and fruit, but she used to put up as much as 500 quarts of beef and pork and chicken, too. Now she sometimes buys canned or frozen vegetables at the grocery store in New Providence.

Home butchering is only a memory in the Cook household—and, for Fern, an unpleasant one. "The people who think you ought to do your own have either forgotten or never knew what it's like to stand and render lard," she said. "Personally, I am very much in favor of progress."

Progress means that twice a year a commercial freezer concern in Eldora picks up a live animal, butchers it, and a few days later returns the meat, wrapped in neat packages, each stamped with the date of the butchering and the cut of meat contained therein. Fern now freezes all the chickens the family can eat. Her mother would probably have been shocked by it, but the Cooks buy part of their milk, too. They keep only one milk cow. The chickens, which are mainly Fern's responsibility, pay for the groceries. She sells about 60 dozen eggs a week to an Eldora produce company.

Fern also does most of the work in a quarter-acre kitchen garden, besides cultivating her roses, many of which tumble over trellises she built herself. Fern's favorite is a hybrid tea, the Peace rose, partly because she likes its name. Fern often broods about wars. "If only everybody had a family," she will say, "if only everybody belonged someplace, the way we belong to New Providence."

Fern, like Maurice, sometimes looks back on the past with longing. When she and Maurice returned from their honeymoon—most of which was spent in Des Moines, buying furniture—practically the entire town of New Providence turned out and gave them a "shivari." Dishpans were banged, cowbells rung and raucous songs were sung outside their darkened windows. At first, Maurice and Fern pretended they weren't there; they were expected to. Then everybody was invited in for ice cream and cake.

The shivari is a thing of a past, however, and last year when Frank brought his new wife Phyllis home from Germany, where she had been a civilian employee of the Air Force, Fern gave a reception for them.

"It was nice enough, but the shivari was more fun. Anybody can have a reception," said Fern.

A retired professor at Ames, a man of many and independent opinions, had this to say: "The farm family is just about like the city family these days; they watch the same television programs; they never get around to reading the same books; they get the same pap in their newspapers, and they drive the same cars. Only thing, in the country you do have neighbors. In the city you meet somebody lives next door to you, and you try to pretend you're invisible."

Phyllis had not only never lived on a farm before; she had never even visited one. When Frank told her that his father's corn grew as high as a telephone pole, she saw no reason to distrust him. On the other hand, most of her knowledge of farm life had come from reading novelists like Erskine Caldwell and Sinclair Lewis.

She has since found that Iowa corn seldom gets more than eight feet tall, and that Iowa has the highest literacy rate of any state in the Union. True, there is more talk about hog prices than Marcel Proust, but, Phyl told me, "I never had to beat my way through any crowds to get into the Boston Public Library."

The Cooks occasionally watch a network television program; they speak of Hal March as if he were a member of the family, but their set is usually tuned to the extension station in Ames. They are not much for reading—the farm journals, yes, the local newspaper and *The Des Moines Register*. Once in a while Kenneth will look through a bulletin from Ames, but a book from one of the digest book clubs had been in the house about 10 days when I arrived and was still wrapped when I left.

"There don't seem to be many novels written about people I know anything about," Fern told me.

New Providence has neither a state liquor store nor a beer parlor, and in 51 years Maurice has never felt the need for an alcoholic drink or a cigarette. None of the Cooks drink. Frank started smoking in the Army and still does, but the painful subject is never mentioned between him and his mother. It never will be. When he is home, he smokes only in his room or out of doors. There is no movie theater in New Providence; the Cooks see a movie maybe once, at most twice a year.

Religion is just as important in their lives as it was in the lives of their grandparents. The Iowa farmer is usually a devout man; his welfare depends on more than hard work and skill, more even than on the unpredictable ways of Congress; rainmakers to the contrary, it still depends mainly on the weather, and that in itself is likely, in the words of Maurice, "to cause a man to give some thought to his relations with his God."

The Cooks are Quakers, as are most of the citizens of New Providence. On a Sunday morning as many as 160 of the total population of 250 usually attend Sunday school in the meetinghouse. About 200 turn up for the morning service and about half that many on Sunday evening. Prayer meeting is every other Thursday at seven-thirty, and the church supper is on alternate Thursdays.

The Cooks almost never miss an event at the meetinghouse. Fern is painfully aware that the top half of the wall to the right of the pulpit is darker than the lower half right now because Fern's energy gave out when she was halfway through washing down the wall. In addition, Maurice has been superintendent of the Sunday school, and Kenneth teaches the class for young married couples. It is called the "As You Like It" class because, according to Kenneth, "we discuss just about every subject under the sun." Fern has had a class of her own most of the time since she first came to New Providence.

"City people are always asking what in the world we do in the evening. I often wonder the same thing about *them*."

She handed me the community calendar for the week. On Monday, the school board met; so did the town council, the Boy Scouts, and the Bible Club. There was a father-and-son banquet at the school on Tuesday, a school game on Wednesday, for which, as usual, nearly the whole town turned out, and on Thursday the Child Study Club got together at Evelyn Faust's house. Members were asked to bring cookies. In addition, the church choir practiced at seven-thirty that evening, and at the same time the governing council of the church met. On Friday afternoon, the Literature, History and Travel section of the Women's Club gathered at the home of Mrs. Ross Reece. Light refreshments were served. One or more members of the Cook family took part in each of these events.

Saturday was free, although there were 11 at the Cooks' for dinner that noon. Very often there are more on a weekend. In addition to the writer, Evelyn and Kenneth were there; Frank, Phyl, and their year-old son Robbie, the Cooks' only grandchild so far, were home, and

Lisle brought along a couple of college friends. There were two meat-and-potato meals that day. There always are at the Cook house, except in the dead of winter, when supper sometimes consists of no more than frankfurters and baked beans and sauerkraut and apple pie.

"We're big eaters around here," Fern told me, "but we don't gain much weight." Maurice weighs just five pounds more than he did in 1928.

That Saturday afternoon everybody except Kenneth and Maurice, who had their own work, went over to Evelyn and Kenneth's house, which is part of the family farm. Paper was stripped from some walls and paint applied to others. Fern made a pot of cocoa, and the cooky jar was brought over and emptied. Lisle, who claims he learned how to cook just by watching his mother, made another batch of cookies the next morning.

Very often in the summer and early fall there is a game of croquet or of softball after dinner. The Saturday evening I was there everybody was pretty tired, and we stayed inside and talked for a while. Then Frank made fudge, Phyllis popped corn, and Fern, using a projector borrowed from a neighbor, showed the movies taken last November at Uncle Wilmer's place. Wilmer was a patient at the Mayo Clinic in Rochester, Minnesota, at corn-picking time; so 39 of his relatives and neighbors pitched in and picked and cribbed his corn.

After we had looked at the pictures there was some talk about turning on the television set, but everybody was really exhausted. By ten, the house was dark, and so was all of New Providence. The only light anywhere was the 60-watt bulb in the chicken house.

The last evening I was with the Cooks we played rook, a game using special cards and requiring more skill than cunning. It is as close to gambling—and it is not very close—as any of the Cooks has ever come. "Even in the Army?" I asked, having been an Army man once myself. Frank and Kenneth said yes, even in the Army.

Afterward, before we went to bed, we were talking about the story I was going to write. I told them it would not be easy. Yes, things had changed. When I lived on a farm near Montour, Iowa, our toilet was outdoors, and I used to take my baths in a washtub in the kitchen on Saturday nights, and instead of radiant heating we had a stove that warmed an area of a foot on each side and no more.

"Us, too," said Lisle.

And, of course, I said, Kenneth is going to put a radio on one of the tractors, and in my youth we'd just had this one headphone set in the sitting room, and I'd never seen a tractor, only a picture of one, in, I thought, the mail-order catalogue. My grandfather had denounced Herbert Hoover's Federal Farm Bureau as "damn' socialistic interference with the laws of nature," and Heaven knows what my grandfather would have said about the farm proposals of both parties in the year 1956. And we went to the Methodist Church, not quite so often as the Cooks go to the meetinghouse, but two or three times a week, and I once had four desserts at a church supper and didn't get sick, and the telephone switchboard in Montour then was just about the same as the one in New Providence now; it closed at nine in the evening and except for emergency calls didn't reopen until five the next morning.

The trouble with the story I was going to write, I said, was that while farm life had changed, it seemed to me fundamentally the same and, what's more, probably always would be, and how could that fact be easily put into a magazine article?

Lisle, who is what the neighbors call a natural-born farmer, said, "There is an old French saying, and in English it is, 'The more things change, the more they remain the same.'

"You think about that a while," he told me, "and you'll see what I mean." Lisle is nineteen.

Well, I have thought about it, and I see what he means.

... Merle Miller, 1956

Village of Eldorado

Lord's Portion Day

Clear Lake

The Lakes of Iowa

R. VERLIN CASSILL'S ARTICLE on "Iowa's Great Lakes"—Spirit, the Okobojis, Clear—omits any reference to Iowa's other lakes—Storm, Wall, Black Hawk, Lost Island, and a baker's dozen of others—that are Iowa's legacy from the great glacier that long ago thrust its icy tongue down into the warm heart of Iowa. But those other lakes are there, and people know them, boat on them, fish and swim in them. And there are also the vast manmade lakes which Cassill does not even hint at—Red Rock, Saylorville, Macbride, Coralville, Wapello, Beeds, Darling, Rathbun—which are now bringing the folk of southern Iowa the advantages that northern Iowans have had ever since the white man discovered the clear cool waters of the north.

Although Cassill's roots are in south-central Iowa, he was born in Cedar Falls in 1919 and grew up in several Iowa towns—his parents were school teachers. He hiself has taught at several colleges and universities, including the University of Iowa Writers' Workshop and, currently, at Brown University.

He is the author of numerous short stories and novels. His wife, Kay, a native of Des Moines, is also a writer and teacher.

Iowa's Great Lakes

ACROSS THE NORTHERN COUNTIES OF IOWA the roads lie straight as the boundary tapes on a green tennis court. In summer, the growing corn raises the levels of most horizons like an incoming tide, and these flat horizons are calibrated monotonously by farmyard elms and the little groves of trees that shade our evenly spaced small towns.

Farther east and south in Iowa, hills and gorges support a few pockets of stubborn wilderness amid the flat prosperity of a state determinedly given to cultivation. This land along the Minnesota border has a regular and tidy beauty. But no drama. The streams are hardly decisive enough to separate one farm from another. The only real landmarks are the town water towers—silhouetted against sunrise and sunset; incandescent red-topped pendants in the noon sunlight.

This is a genial, workaday countryside—not, in any ordinary sense, seductive to the tourist. A stranger might drive 200 miles across the state without spotting terrain that invited him to more than a casual roadside picnic. Yet if he chose the right roads, the same 200 miles would provide him with a choice of natural pleasures and resorts worth a longer stop, for the glaciers that rubbed out Iowa's hills and valleys left here a scattering of lakes as compensation.

It is true that these lakes of ours, dwindling in size from 5,700-acre Spirit Lake to nameless ponds and kettle holes, are merely the fringe of the lake region that spreads across Wisconsin and Minnesota. Our lakes show where the glacier ran into Iowa conservatism and stopped. Maybe they are ours only by the grace of a political boundary, but when the weather settles warm in May, something in Iowans looks as far as Clear Lake or the Okoboji region without caring what goes on beyond them. In the good months we respond to a distinctly native mixture of the memory and desire that turn other people in *their* states toward *their* north and *their* blue water.

It is not only Iowans who come to fish, boat, swim and lie about at our lakeshore resorts. Clear Lake, Spirit Lake and West Okoboji draw summer residents and visitors from all over the Midwest. Clear Lake lies due north of Des Moines—3,600 acres of water elevated like a low mesa a hundred feet above the surrounding prairie. A teeming population of sailboats tacks about all summer long. Bauhaus and Le Corbusier's ideas are steering cottage architecture away from the dear old up-lunging monstrosities sheathed in buffalo-colored shingles that used to be the standard. Clear Lake Jaycees even talk about building a ski run nearby to round out a winter-sports program that already includes an annual snowmobile rally, iceboating and fishing through the ice.

Four counties west, in the Iowa Great Lakes area, the resort business is moving with a similar flourish. Among these "Great Lakes"—fifteen of them laid out like a skeletal footprint on a map—only Spirit Lake may not be quite so popular as it once was. An early writer described Spirit Lake as "obese," probably meaning only that its shoreline was as smoothly rounded as a corn-fed grandmother's waist. Obese it is, however—a very bland, shallow lake, now rather out of competition with its bustling neighbor, West Okoboji.

West Okoboji can and does boast of being one of the three "blue-water" lakes in the world—lakes where a rare form of algae produces a color deeper and more intense than the reflection of the sky. Arnold's Park amusement center rocks and rolls on its southeast shore; on its bays and promontories most of the expensive new building in the region has gone up. Minneapolis, Des Moines, and Omaha money puts its boats on West Okoboji, and the Midwest's jet-set youngsters drink in its hotel bars. Buying liquor by the drink became legal in Iowa in 1963, forty-four years after Prohibition began. Thereafter conventioners and fishermen could indulge with grace in what had for so long been something between a sport and a crime in the state. West Okoboji resort operators have made renovations with this in mind; like all good Iowans, they would hate to think they weren't squarely abreast of the times.

Nevertheless, one of the chief pleasures of visiting the Iowa lakes is to find in these waters reflecting images of the past and, if you can, to sense the qualities that have made them inordinately precious to Iowa for just about as long as there have been Iowans. From the time the railroads closed in on them in the 1870s and 1880s, Clear Lake, Spirit, and West Okoboji have been Iowa's summer resorts. Before Iowa became a state, discriminating Indians used to pitch their wigwams on the lake shores in hot weather.

For an insight into our possessive pride in these lakes, leave your car and walk a hundred yards into Cayler Prairie. The prairie is now a State Monument a few miles from Okoboji water. It was not set aside as a natural rarity, but rather to preserve a bit of the commonplace of another age from the plows that have changed the rest of the state. Within this preserve there is nothing but native grasses, some tall, some short. The tallest whiten at their tips, tracing lacy patterns, like frost on a window pane. The shorter grasses suggest the underbrush of a miniature jungle. Even now, with farms at your back (toward which you can turn if you need reassurance), to stare up at those wave-slanted prairie slopes is to have a direct, sensuous experience of vastness and an intimation of terror. Not the big panic; just an echo of the vastness that broods over the South Pacific and other lonely surfaces of our planet. On the prairie you begin to *need* the lake over the hills as a soldier on a tedious sea journey needs an island.

In the days when Okoboji, Spirit, and Clear Lakes were becoming resorts, a lot of Iowa still looked like Cayler Prairie. Now it's all farms and towns. Good towns, but *inland* towns; inland towns par excellence. Provincial, too, if you wish, and I think there may be some inarticulate frustration in everyone who lives this far inland, an unappeased racial memory of the water voyage that brought us to this continent. You can hear that memory grumbling if you park your car on the main street of a town like Humboldt on a shadowless afternoon in July.

It's hot there, first of all, and the obvious relief from such heat is a dip in cool water. But as my Iowa relatives would say, "If that's all you need, you can jump in the tub and turn on the electric fan." The Iowan needs more than that. However busy the afternoon traffic may be in Humboldt, the wide, straight street, open to the sky, seems to sleep. In this midcontinental doze, there's a kid coming down the sidewalk with the heat striking through the soles of his sneakers. He stops at the window of a hardware store, blinks, and stares at some gold, scarlet and steel-colored fishing lures on a display card. He reads the advertising as though it were an enchantment. Behind the window display, toward the back of the store, there are green and blue shadows like those the boy has seen when he opened his eyes underwater. He fingers the money in his pocket. His lips gape and close, gape and close, like the mouth of a resting bass. He wants one of those lures as no wide-awake fish will ever want it. He knows that Humboldt and the street behind him are all a dream. He will wake up when he gets to Clear Lake among his peers and puts that lure down where it belongs.

To wake from the slumber of their little towns, Iowans have always needed the lakes, with their cosmopolitan coming and going of strangers. The resort people have always done their Iowa best to respond to the call for glamour. A year after the railroad came to Spirit Lake, in 1882, the Orleans Hotel opened for business at the water's edge. According to its own publicity, the Orleans had "nine handsome towers and three thousand feet of veranda, all sixteen feet in width." Within its ornate ballroom "a fine band discoursed sweet music; hops were held twice a week."

A $7,000 steamboat, the *Ben Lennox*, was built and launched at Arnolds Park. It made its first trip up through East Okoboji Lake to the Orleans in 1884. Within the decade *Ben* and the older *Favorite* and *Alpha* were joined by other little white steamers: the *Hiawatha*, *Lelia*, and *Queen*. The boats ran excursions from the hotel down through the narrows into West Okoboji and "did a fair stroke of business," while halfway across the state at Clear Lake a steamer called *Lady of the Lake* carried guests to and from a towered wooden hotel on an island called The Island.

In these bright years fishing was better in the Okoboji area than it used to be, for a fish hatchery had begun to replace the losses from the uncontrolled fish-harvesting of the 1870s. The roller-skating craze of 1880 hadn't yet lost momentum. The mixture of urban and rustic pleasures at the Orleans spread the resort's reputation throughout the Midwest.

Unfortunately, the Orleans and the hatchery had been planned at a time when the lake waters were high. Within a few years the water level fell, and the lake shore crept yearly farther away from the hotel. Because the bottom of Spirit Lake slopes gently, each one-foot fall in the water level caused a very considerable shrinkage of shoreline. The tanks at the fish hatchery were fouled and dried up. Steamers could no longer pass through the narrows between East Okoboji and Spirit Lake. Squeezed by the nature and the local prohibitionists, the owners of the Orleans gave up. The nine towers were razed in 1896. The roller-skating rink was turned into a storage warehouse. Over at Clear Lake, fire swept the fabulous hotel from The Island. But Iowans kept coming to their lakes as loyally as before. Chautauqua programs featuring lecturers and musicians pulled them in. Religious camps on the lake shores led them up from the drier, hotter counties. The Spirit Lake Cornet Band played for them in the cool evenings. The Mason City-Clear Lake interurban railroad brought such crowds over for Clear Lake's three-day Fourth of July celebrations that old-timers remember how the young bucks and boys hung like clusters of bees on the outside of cars.

The hull of the *Ben Lennox* was split up for firewood, but the *Queen* was moved from Spirit Lake to West Okoboji, and went on carrying tourists. After the failure of the hatchery, a "fish car" stocked the lakes with full-grown game fish freighted over from the Mississippi's backwaters.*

New generations of luxury hotels succeeded each other as quickly as fire, termites, and hard times demolished their predecessors. A Manhattan Project at the turn of the century put up an airy, porch-girdled Manhattan Hotel, a bathhouse, and a tall toboggan slide on the West Okoboji shore. At Clear Lake a grand hotel, The Oaks, swirled its wide verandas on a knoll at the end of a formal esplanade that tied it to the lake.

Fire took these glories too. Indeed, in the history of Iowa's lake resorts, fire seems a kindly nemesis, foreshortening epochs of pleasure

---

* The *Queen* is now at Adventureland in Des Moines.

before their charms were tarnished—whisking off casinos, Chautauqua halls, amusement piers and luxury hotels to a Midwestern Elysium where gingerbread woodwork, "hops twice a week," and cornet music in the evening will never look quaint or sound flat.

Of those good times not much is left but the photographs. Only the Lakeshore Hotel at Clear Lake lasted into this decade as a modestly elegant survivor of more gracious seasons. The Lakeshore, alas, had no panoply of wooden towers, but it was nonetheless an extraordinarily handsome white frame building, a child's stone-throw from the water's edge. In its breezy and spacious dining room iced-tea spoons tinkled in tall glasses, as they had when guests watched *The Lady of the Lake* on her way to The Island. Until recently the annual tournament to decide the world's court-whist championship was played in its lounge. A screened porch extended the length of the building on the side facing the water, and the rooms that faced onto the porch had such a cool austerity of proportion and overwater daylight that one thought of cabins on a side-wheel steamer making the North Atlantic run.

Besides the image of good times vanished, the lakes still prompt in sober Iowans an awe of nature beyond mundane calculations about how the land can be squeezed to produce more corn and hogs. Lady poets who were given to celebrating the Legend of Spirit Lake in anapestic verse have vanished with the towers of the Orleans Hotel. But the people who maintain lakeshore religious camps to this day know what they're about when they bring the young folks here, and if you expose a natural scientist to touristic nonchalance toward nature, you're likely to tap a romantic passion that is fundamentally nonsocial.

Richard Bovbjerg is a University of Iowa faculty member who teaches in the summer at West Okoboji's Lakeside Laboratory. The laboratory has been maintained on Miller's Bay since 1909 by the co-operative efforts of state universities and colleges. Bovbjerg's specialty is aquatic ecology; his passion is the benign harmony of organic and inorganic forces. Bait him by telling about the nostalgic trance that came on you in the beer, popcorn and capgun-smoke smell of Arnolds Park, and you'll get the passion in full voice and great detail.

To hear him tell it, the great natural design is broken chiefly by such things as the pollution from the religious camp across the bay and the human indifference to nature manifested by the commercial amusement park. He is happy to report that his students are above the social temptations of Arnolds Park. Throughout the summer they live in "rustic" barracks built of native stone. Around the barracks and labs the grounds are left purposely untended—just about the only place in Iowa where a weed has an established right to grow in peace.

By day, afloat and ashore, young entomologists, taxonomists, and biologists hunt rotifers, oligochaetes, and parasitic nematodes where you and I might expect to find only bait. They bring their collections home to laboratories as rich in smells as a stone-walled Iowa fruit cellar. If they break off their studies before bedtime, they may go down the road to drink a little beer in the back room of a grocery store, and if they go all the way around to Arnolds Park to ride the roller-coaster or date the sunburned kids from Des Moines, Primghar, or Sioux City — well, that's their *rare* escape from the realities of the dissection knife and the plankton trap. Their Beauty and Truth crawl, hop, swim, sprout and ooze on the rocky bottom of Okoboji or in dusty thickets.

You may interrupt Bovbjerg's good-natured rant to observe that healthy Christians and moon-calf jitterbugs are part of a larger ecology, not self-evidently worse than those of sub-vertebral species. On this he can be coaxed into sighing agreement. But he will go on worrying. He mentions that twenty-two species of snails that lived on the laboratory grounds fifty years ago aren't there now. Perhaps no one cares about snails. They certainly aren't on Iowa menus. Perhaps no one *should* regret their disappearance, Richard Bovbjerg would admit. But their disappearance raises questions: What else is gone? What fullness, ripeness, and harmony that we don't know how to miss because we can no longer name it?

Not to admit such questions, not to linger with the conjectural answers that rise from one's own yearning for satisfactions that present time won't give, is to leave all present pleasures at the Lakes shallower than they are meant to be. One of the nice things about sipping a legal Martini and brooding through plate glass at the stony color of Clear Lake is to be reminded how, once upon a time, the voices of WCTU campers sounded their temperance songs on the open air nearby, in moonlight, under the elms and oaks. Nostalgia comes with the price of a visit. If you forego it altogether in favor of water-skiing or fishing through the ice, you'll never grasp what makes these lakes different from those elsewhere. Perhaps the best way to take nostalgia neat is to take an evening ride on the *Queen* at Okoboji. Down on the pier in front of the Roof Garden and Fun House at Arnolds Park there is a sign advertising the old, iron-hulled *Queen* as a "turbo-jet" boat. That nonsense is perhaps meant to persuade the small fry to go along with their romantic elders. Though a modern diesel has at last replaced the grunting old steam engine that used to power it, the wedding-cake lines of the superstructure never came from any contemporary drawing board. The *Queen* has a draft so shallow she can pull up at almost any private dock on the lake, but she looks as high as she is long. On the top deck at seven o'clock in the evening you're still up in the sunlight, while on the shadowed deck below, crew-cut boys in red vests usher the last passenger aboard.

The trees over the amusement park are burnished to a metallic smolder of green, and like the roller-coaster, the deck of the *Queen* seems to be up among them. Past the dock there is a merry-go-round so dense with horses and uprights that its center is in colorful gloom, like a flower bed at ground level. Only behind you, to the north and west, the lake lies cool and already misty against the thin blue edge of the prairie.

On its circuit of the lake, the *Queen* runs past Des Moines Beach, Fort Dodge Point, and Omaha Beach. Omaha Beach does not commemorate the landing in Normandy. It is so named because Omaha people bought adjacent lots here, wishing, as Des Moines and Fort Dodge people did, to stick with home-town friendships in vacation times.

While the light fades, the *Queen* passes Dixon's Bay, where the original inn was built to meet the modern tastes and requirements of 1896. Its replacement—called the New Inn—is shiny as a new car. It comes complete with a swimming pool not far from the beach and an auditorium with movable panels for large and small conventions, and it is close to an airstrip for private planes, where the flying farmer and the Humboldt tycoon can swoop in to be with the wife and kids after a hot day on the combine or at the bank.

Past Dixon's Bay the *Queen* veers off on the chop of darkening waves. The public-address system rattles with anecdote and public reminiscence. Back there, the skipper tells his passengers, is the monument commemorating the Spirit Lake Massacre, the only genuine massacre in Iowa history, when some renegade Sioux did in more than fifty of the first settlers. The massacre has long since become a cliché, and the *Queen*'s passengers strain to catch some ineffable legend from the twilight itself.

Points and headlands vanish in this hour when cottagers are still reluctant to go inside and turn on their lights and television. Lake and prairie become one interminable waterway where the *Queen* trails after the *Ben Lennox,* the *Hiawatha,* and the *Favorite,* a long argosy steaming against the current of time in pursuit of happiness.

Somewhere along this eastern shore there is a reef of submerged boulders. Years ago a high-school class from some little Iowa town came up to the lake on its Senior Sneak Day. And somehow—no one knows how, for there were no survivors—some of them got into trouble out on the reef. Then the others must have formed a line, holding each other's hands because not all of them could swim, to go after those in trouble. According to the tale, they all drowned, holding hands faithfully.

No monument commemorates the tragedy, and the public-address system does not repeat the story as the *Queen* goes by the rocks. It's a brutal, paltry part of the legend of an inland people and can be interpreted as you please. Either the kids panicked like Iowa sheep or they weren't willing to come back without those they cared for. What there is in the story that says the most about Iowans, and perhaps about their celebrated loyalty to their lakes, is that they held hands with their own just as long as they could.

... R. Verlin Cassill, 1966

Abbie Gardner

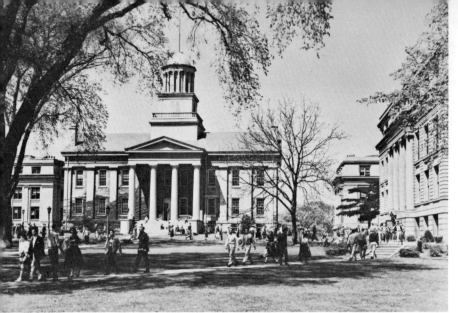

Old Capitol, Iowa City

Higher Education in Iowa

GEORGE C. DUFFIELD CAME INTO IOWA in 1837; nine years later, in 1846, his grandson Phil Stong pointed out, Iowa built its first college. The state has always valued higher education. Today, in Iowa, there are three state universities, twenty-five private colleges, and one private university, and a dozen-odd two-year colleges.

Some of these have caught the attention of Iowa's authors. Bess Streeter Aldrich's Miss Bishop *tells of a teacher whose whole career was spent at the University of Northern Iowa's predecessor; Ruth Suckow's* A Part of the Institution *is based on Grinnell College, as is, in part, her* The Bonney Family. *Both Tom Duncan's* We Pluck This Flower *and Phil Stong's* If School Keeps *have settings on the campus of Drake University.*

But, as Wallace Stegner said, it is the University of Iowa campus which has been a center for writers since 1915. Inevitably writers in this century write about subjects they've experienced, and inevitably, therefore, the University of Iowa has been written about.

One of the writers who went to school at Iowa was Calvin Kentfield of Keokuk; his 1963 Holiday *article on his alma mater follows. He was born in 1924, graduated from the Keokuk High School in 1942 and came to Iowa to prepare himself to be an artist. But a later year as a merchant seaman persuaded him to become a writer. He was the author of several novels before his untimely death.*

State University of Iowa

IN SOUTHEASTERN IOWA, on the banks of the Iowa River, lies Iowa City, a town of modest proportions and progressive intent. For many miles in every direction stretch pastures, fields of corn, grazing land, and irregular woods of oak, maple, and hickory. The farmhouses are large, the dogs friendly, and the hogs—some pink, some black-and-white, some brown—lying in the barnyards near bins of corn are numerous and fat. There are television aerials on the farmhouse roofs: mud-spattered pickup trucks by the barn doors; and conservative convictions in the minds of the natives, who, whether they know it or not, pay out taxes to foster research in audiology, quantum mechanics, and pedantics, as well as classes in mycology, life drawing optics, harp, epistemology, Hebrew, biostatics, poetry writing, golf, Russian, Wordsworth, and (for women only) relaxation.

These endeavors and many, many more are activated each autumn at the State University of Iowa. At that time the skies achieve a high, distant blue brushed with hazy cirrus, lending to the large, pleasantly rolling landscape an air of bemused preoccupation. The oaks turn red and the maples yellow, the river flows languidly, and the gray squirrels on the campus lay up acorns for the snowy winter to come. The song-birds prepare to depart from the campus, and the Thunderbirds and Jaguars return.

While the earth expires, Iowa City springs alive with boys and girls eager for fun, knowledge, and each other. They come from all over the state of Iowa and the Midwest—from Strawberry Point and Center-ville, Lone Tree and What Cheer; from Chicago, New York, San Francisco, and New Orleans; from Bombay and Karachi, Rio and Bogotá, Strasbourg, Kiel, Seoul, Monrovia, Alicante, Sarajevo, Addis Ababa, Calgary and Cairo; from Greece, Saudi Arabia, The Netherlands, Ireland, Vietnam, Nigeria, Mexico, Japan, Sweden, Australia, Kenya, and England. In those few square miles of river valley and the soft hills that flank it, they congregate for three seasons of each year, creating a bizarre oasis in this rich agricultural wasteland. Some years ago those persons whose job it is to think up such things began to tout Iowa City as the "Athens of America," referring, of course, to Athens, Greece, presumably in the Golden Age; but the name carried such a pompous air of self-congratulation that it quickly became a joke and has survived, healthily, as such.

Last fall I joined that throng, arriving a few days before Homecoming weekend. I realized as I drove into the town that twenty years had passed by since my parents had brought me there as a freshman and let me out on my own. That was a year after the beginning of the war, and I was one of a few more than 5,000 students. The enrollment has now passed 12,000. Still, one undergraduate, a girl from western Illinois, remarked to me, "I looked over Urbana (University of Illinois), but it's so *big*. Here at Iowa you don't get lost."

I knew exactly what she meant. Five thousand or 12,000, local or international, there was in 1942, and there is today, a feeling of a small town and a close community. Partly this is because the core of the University stands squarely in the center of town, directly opposite the business district—a scant few blocks of clothing stores, bookstores, drugstores, taverns, and hotels. Take away the University, and Iowa City would become any other Pleasantville, sitting on a hill above the shallow green valley of the meandering river.

I should mention that the town does contain eccentrics who are hardly typical of Midwestern towns in general—strange descendents of pioneers who like Victorian houses on quiet elm-lined streets, and a race of twisted women known in aggregate as the "Iowa City landlady." However, townspeople will probably take exception. The community is growing in all directions, and new tracts and industries and four-lane highways are being added all the time. The town is, as always, an ever-growing urban center for a rich agricultural hinterland, and it now has over 33,000 permanent residents.

Still, the town seems small and close, and no fresh student from Albia or Marathon or Grundy Center need fall victim to urban malaise or an oppressive feeling of lostness, as he might in Minneapolis (Univ. of Minnesota) or Columbus (Ohio State) or even Evanston (Northwestern) or Madison (Univ. of Wisconsin). Coming at age seventeen from the immurement of Keokuk, my hometown, this closeness worked to my advantage.

I didn't know, though, about another quality of life at SUI—the outrageous winter. As the leaves fall and the skies turn cold, as the wind comes howling down the river valley; as the winter sets in and drags on and on and on until you think spring will never come; as the weariness of work and tension of confinement mount through February and March—then that closeness and intimacy can work to the grave disadvantage of some, particularly the more high-strung members of the student body, or the foreigners or easterners unaccustomed to such long incarceration. Violent acts have become part of the folk history of Iowa City—acts bred in the icy entombment of winter that erupt in the spring, when the earth itself breaks out.

I stepped into this history in my freshman year when, in my dorm, the Law Commons, one of the boys—an exceptionally bright fellow—hanged himself on his closet door with the cord of his bathrobe. I remember returning to lunch with a group and seeing his body stretched out on the ice-crusted common, waiting for the coroner. We all stared in horror and amazement at one of our own fellows who had been alive at breakfast, and some cynical wag passing by said, "What's the matter with you guys, you never seen a stiff before?"

Over a period of a few years another boy shot himself because he thought he had failed his comprehensives, a sorority girl gave herself to fifteen eager fraternity boys during an early-spring rite on the riverbank, and an Independent girl was raped nine times by a carful of boys. (Afterward, she said to me, "You know, if I wanted to, I could let this ruin my life.") There was the student who accidentally murdered his girl during an intimate scene in his fraternity house; the Princess Café murder; the gratuitous shooting of Irene Kenney, the most popular barmistress in town. There have been any number of violent parties, almost invariably toward the bitter end of winter, after which the guests return the next morning to help the host wipe up the blood. During my most recent visit, I asked a professor I had not seen for years how things were going. He replied, "Oh, everything's about normal. Tonight I have one boy in jail and another in psycho."

He meant that half as a joke, of course, and rightly so, because "normal" student life at SUI is something else again. Its social center is the Iowa Memorial Union in general, and in particular the Gold Feather Room, which I visited on several occasions during the week leading up to Homecoming. There a student can get a sandwich, a cheap lunch, a soda or a coffee between classes. He can play the jukebox, study, talk, play bridge or chess. On the same floor are a bowling alley and a pool hall for his convenience and distraction.

The Gold Feather Room is the rendezvous of the "faceless ones"— as their detractors call them—the great mass who pay their tuition, cram for exams, cheer at the games, date on Saturday, fill up the dorms, the taverns and the center of the curve of grades. An articulate political-science major, a junior from Mason City, expressed this opinion.

"Most of the boys want to *get by*, that's all, as quickly as they can," he said, "so they can get out and start making *money*. And the girls want to sit up all night in curlers talking about boys, and have neat dates, and get out and get married to the boys who are out making *money*. There seems to be a celebration of the average."

We were having coffee in the Gold Feather Room. The place was full. The jukebox was playing *Moon River*. During the momentary lacunae in the music we could hear the crash of strikes and spares in the bowling alley. At a table directly adjacent to us four girls were playing bridge. All four were wearing sweaters and snapping nervously at cigarettes. Two of them were in curlers (covered with scarves); and one of them remarked in a voice designed for maximum shock effect, "Well, the only thing *I* can think of to do tonight is go out and get *drunk.*"

"As long as they look like everybody else and know everybody else looks like them," my companion pursued, "and *think* that way, then they're strictly neat. There," he said, pointing to a couple just leaving a table, "there go Miss Average and her stud." It was a crew-cut boy in cords, sneakers, and a windbreaker; and a girl in a sweater and plaid pleated skirt, her hairdo short and moderately *bouffant.* I had to admit that I *had* seen them around the campus many times over.

"You know what they'll do?" he said, leaning back. "And don't think I'm exaggerating, because I'm not. They'll go to a lecture, say Literature, and they'll sit there with a transistor radio plugged into their ears, listening to *Rhythm Rambles* and taking down the lecture on a portable tape. You think I'm kidding?" I shook my head. "And another thing, you can't be too dumb or too smart or you're something else, you understand?"

I obtained a different view on that last remark at the Phi Gamma Delta fraternity house. It sits on the west side of the river, on the hill above the valley, along with a cluster of other fraternity houses. Each of them is architecturally emulative of some international or domestic manorial style. The Delta Upsilon, for instance, is Mount Vernon Southern; Delta Chi is fairly French Provincial, and Phi Gam is English Country House, the most popular style of all.

I joined the brothers just after lunch in the cluttered room of the president, Wally Snyder. He introduced me proudly to the chapter's three prized possessions: The Brain, an engineering student with a grade average of 3.7; Lonnie Rogers, a first-string halfback for the Hawkeyes; and the boy who was pinned to Judy Ann Shimek, one of the finalists in the Miss SUI Homecoming Queen competition. Except for President Snyder, who wore a suit and tie, the invariable costume of the others was slacks and sweater. Inevitably, we got to talking about girls.

"Do you find it works to your disadvantage," I asked, "to have twice as many boys in school as girls?"

They all looked at each other and smiled—a little smugly, I thought. Then one of them shoved his hands in his pockets, rocked a little on the balls of his feet, and shrugged his cashmere shoulders. "It doesn't seem to bother *us,*" he said. He looked around at his brothers, who concurred by shaking their heads. "If you want a neat date," he went on, encouraged, "somebody you can take to the Homecoming party and introduce to your folks or go home with for the weekend, that's easy, or, I mean, it all depends on what you want. If you want the other kind. . . ."

"You mean," I said, "depending upon what mood you're in, all you have to do is pick up the phone and you can get pretty much whatever you want?"

"That's right," he said, nodding and smiling. "Maybe not the *first* time, but, *you* know, the *second* anyway."

"I wish somebody would give *me* some of those numbers," said President Snyder.

"There's definitely a difference, I'd say," the other boy went on, "between a girl who's a senior in high school and a freshman in college; I mean. I wouldn't say they get exactly *loose*, but. . . ."

"Do you have any restrictions on whom you can date? Do you have to date sorority girls?"

"Oh no," President Snyder said. "We can date anybody we want to."

"Independents are the best for my money," one of the others said, and the rest nodded. "Though it's strictly up to the individual."

"Do you have any restrictions on whom you can pledge into the fraternity? Can you pledge Jews if you want to, or Negroes?"

I addressed the question to Wally Snyder, who replied, "There's nothing written in our constitution any more that says we *can't*, only as far as I know there aren't any Negroes in fraternities at Iowa now. One was pledged a while back, then he was de-pledged."

"And it's not fair for us to rush the Jewish fellas. I mean, there aren't that many Jews come here, and they've got two fraternities of their own, and we get along with them just fine."

There was general concurrence on that point too.

Later in the afternoon I asked the same question of Miss Jane Hobart, a sociology senior from Lake City and president of the Iowa chapter of Alpha Phi sorority.

First she said, "I'd rather not answer that question." Then, after a little prodding, she went on, "I know that there's nothing written down in the national charter that says we can't, we've just never *had* any. Jewish girls, I mean. I know some of the chapters do."

"What about Negroes?" I asked.

She looked at the two other girls who were with us in the lounge. "There aren't any Negro girls being rushed this year, are there?" The others shook their heads.

The Alpha Phi chapter is new (1961) on the Iowa campus, and the house is a remodeled Victorian mansion, one of the most indigenously Midwestern structures in town. The three girls and I (and a chaperone, an alumni advisor) were sitting in the carpeted lounge that was once in the mansion's parlor. All three girls wore skirts and sweaters, with their sorority pins shining conspicuously on their breasts. They sat in their chairs with their feet together, their backs straight, their hands laid properly upon their laps. All of them were quite pretty. They were seriously made up and wore their hair in the careful, casual manner prescribed for the occasion. It was the official image that was being presented—something the boys generally had not bothered with. Out of the corner of my eye, however, I caught a glimpse of a more natural picture—a fourth girl, apparently unbriefed, slouching down the stairs in open-collared blouse and slacks. Miss Hobart said:

"I feel that the standard, accepted picture of sorority life is not true. Here at Iowa, anyway, the girls are not just interested in social life, they desire good academic accomplishment as well. We Greeks do a lot we don't always get credit for."

Another girl spoke up, "I have to go to class, but I'd just like to say something before I go. I love the sorority. It's done more for me than I can ever repay. It teaches you the social graces, and it teaches you to work together, I mean, we all pitch in to keep the house clean, and we get our own breakfast. I think that's just as much part of an education as going to classes. I'm going to miss it terribly when I graduate. I mean, the picture people have of so-called sororities is practically ridiculous. I just wanted to say that, that's all."

The Greeks, those students affiliated with the social fraternities, are a minority at Iowa. The majority of the undergraduates are Independents, who consider the Greeks, if they consider them at all, snobs and social pushers. The Greeks, on the other hand, maintain that if anybody's a snob it's an Independent, at least in his attitude toward Greeks. "We get along with everybody," a Greek boy told me. "I joined a fraternity because it helps you get ahead when you get out. You've got contacts. I think that's why most of the men are here, either that or because their dads or their big brothers came here and pledged."

Most of the Independent boys live in Hillcrest and Quadrangle, a complex of dormitories, which is constantly being enlarged, on the west side of the river, near the athletic facilities. Most of the girls live on the east side in two residences—the older Currier Hall and the new (1957) Burge Hall.

Burge houses nearly 1,300 girls; each girl pays $880 a year for board and room. The dormitory is an intricate brick-and-steel warren of modernistic-motel tendencies. There are three girls in nearly every room; four dining rooms; a vast kitchen complex that serves a chow line three times a day. With the exception of the telephones in every room and certain other amenities (such as little locked wire cages like rabbit hutches in the basement for the overnight drying of essential small clothes), it unavoidably brings to mind that renowned City of Women, that semi-prison that used to – and perhaps still does – crown the hilltop of Casablanca.

When I was an undergraduate, the dormitory girls were due in by 10:30 at night and were penalized for late minutes. The 10:25 scene at the gates of Currier was heartrending indeed, with the last-minute, desperate, passionate leave-taking destined to be cut off with the peremptory brutality of the bell. I can remember staggering off many a time into the snow, cheeks flushed, eyes blurred, wondering what had happened to me. This has not changed, but there is a difference now in the hour – midnight – and in the abolishment of penalties for those late minutes, too many of which could once cause a girl to lose her weekend. The mothers and fathers of Iowa still may sleep soundly after midnight (1 A.M. on weekends), knowing that their daughters are safe within the walls of Adelaide Burge and in the company of only their roommates. The boys of the Quadrangle and Hillcrest, of course, are not required to keep special hours, and this "double standard" has caused many a fight for reform lost by student governments throughout the years.

But given freedom and a little peace and quiet, "anybody who wants an *education* at Iowa can get it." I put that in quotes because it's the invariable response to criticism that defenders of the University make. And of course it's perfectly true, as any serious graduate student will tell you. The graduate students are the most devoted to acquisition of knowledge. There are close to four thousand of them, a quarter of the entire enrollment. They are in psychology, engineering, medicine, law, science, and the arts. Some of them are married and raising families, living in University housing or in town; the rest live wherever they please, in whatever atmosphere suits them best.

Many of them teach part-time. William Murray, for instance, who came originally from Ireland, has a wife and child, works for his Ph.D. in English (with a novel as thesis), teaches technical writing to engineers, and privately tutors football players in English. (The single academic requirement every undergraduate must satisfy goes by the high-sounding name of Rhetoric. It is, of course, reading and writing, and it presents some difficulty – particularly the writing part – to those students, some of them athletes, who came to college unprepared for such a trial.) Murray lives as do many graduate students – quietly, with his family and friendly dog in an apartment in town, separate from the University. His life is ordered, routine, constructive and moving toward a foreseeable goal; quite the opposite, in fact, of that of his friend David Wham, also a graduate student, who lives in a bizarre aggregation of dwellings known for a while as Dizzy Land, but now called "Black's Graduate Houses."

Murray and I went to see Wham on Friday evening, after the Homecoming parade, and I recognized Dizzy Land to be the direct descendant of The Flop House and the Cockroach Arms, dwellings famous in my day as harbors of free thought, free living, and free thinking—hotbeds of intellectual ferment and dissent. A party was in progress, or rather a series of parties more or less allied, in small dark chambers with stained-glass windows, quarts of beer, low couches, folk songs, and cool jazz. In Wham's compartment were two girls and a typewriter.

It was really more of a procession than a party, and by the time our contribution, a bottle of bourbon, was exhausted and Murray and I left, we had been visited by advanced student practitioners of nearly every science and art known to man. The conversation had run mostly to movies, and at one point someone had cried out in genuine distress, "Why doesn't anybody talk about *books* anymore?" Wham himself I recognized as an Iowa phenomenon that I was pleased to discover had not become extinct—very young, burning with undisciplined and uncheckable energy, talent, and ambition, always broke, likely to be seen in the worst weather without a coat, his hands in his pockets, stalking the streets of Iowa City alone, distracted, the desire for overnight fame raging in his head.

He is one of about a hundred members of the now famous Writers' Workshops developed and promoted by native Iowa poet and professor Paul Engle and currently headed by R. V. Cassill, Vance Bourjaily, Mark Strand, and others. An amazing percentage of America's literary talent has touched upon the Workshops in some way or other; Engle has overcome formidable barriers of the mind—first by convincing the University that creative writing is as deserving of college credit as the study or criticism of it, and second by convincing such unlikely organizations as the Maytag Company of Newton, Iowa, and the Merchants' National Bank of Cedar Rapids that they should support it by putting up money for scholarships.

Resistance, however, has not entirely ceased. Vance Bourjaily tells about a farmer who came into the Lighthouse, a restaurant and bar in North Liberty—a tiny town a few miles north of Iowa City—where Bourjaily lives and does his writing in a studio in back of his house. The farmer said to the bartender, "Did you know you've got a writer living here in this town, right here in this town?" The bartender nodded. "Well, *I* did," said the farmer. "And you know he *writes* them out in the barn. They're not fit to write in the house with his wife and family."

The Workshops—Poetry Workshop, Fiction Workshop, Undergraduate Workshop, Fiction Writing and some others—evolved back in the late Thirties and early Forties. The Iowa English Department was then a part of the Augustan-sounding *School of Letters*. It had achieved considerable national attention because of the New Humanism of Norman Foerster and was growing downright famous through the writings and lectures of the New Critics René Wellek and Austin Warren, a remarkable pair of sophisticated sensibilities who brought to Iowa some of the cultivation of Central Europe and New England (Wellek is Viennese, Warren a Bostonian).

During that Golden Age of Criticism the idea of a creative workshop developed, and Paul Engle became its chief champion. Unfortunately, the marvelous and dreamy concept of a centrum of literary culture, of creative writers dwelling side by side in vital harmony with the great critics of the day and with Elizabethan, Chaucerian, and Victorian scholars, did not come to pass. First went Norman Foerster, then the School of Letters, and finally Wellek left and Warren absconded to Ann Arbor. The English Department was created, including the Workshops, but it was split, physically as well as philosophically. The scholars stayed on their hill in University Hall, their ancestral home, and the Workshops moved down to the riverbank, into "temporary" war buildings. Down there Engle held his ground against "the hill." Largely through his monumental talents of promotion and persuasion, the Workshops grew in size and reputation.

But Engle was not alone responsible; there was also Baldwin Maxwell, then head of the department, now retired, who for all those tolerant years, despite protests in many forms—including, I suspect, a few arising from his own convictions—allowed the Workshops to thrive. An impeccable Elizabethan scholar with a precise, amused, Eastern manner that always comes as a gentle surprise in the interior of the continent, he told me over tall bourbons as we watched—or pretended to watch—the Homecoming parade, that he "never was much of an administrator. I always rather let things take their natural course."

We were above the Airliner Café, peering out of a second-story window. The Kalona High School Band went by, followed by an elaborate float illustrating *I Love You Truly*. "If you write about the University," Maxwell said to me, smiling, clutching his bourbon to his natty waistcoat, "try to find a few words to say about something *besides* that Writers' Workshop. That's all we ever hear about around here."

Dr. Maxwell was succeeded by John Gerber, an able man, and with Maxwell went his easy, personal way of nonadministration. C. C. Wylie is gone too, and with *him* went the one-hour course in astronomy that consisted chiefly of magic-lantern slides of old Pontiacs with holes ripped in their tops by falling meteorites and occasional ice-cold field trips to the top of the Physics Building to seek out and name the constellations. Now there is James Van Allen and his astrophysics, and the Physics Building is now a national center for space-science research, clamoring for room to expand.

In an article entitled "Education in the Space Age," published in *The Iowa Alumni Review,* Dewey B. Stuit, Dean of the College of Liberal Arts, wrote in his Thursday-luncheon style:

"'The greater size of our colleges and universities and the increased emphasis upon democratic procedures will produce changes in the techniques of administration. The day of the 'one-man show' whether it be a department head, dean, president, principal or superintendent is over. . . . The old-time administrator who tried to run everything from his own desk belongs to a bygone era. . . . Indeed, as I see it, the years ahead will witness increased reliance on the team approach to college and university administration."

In this team approach, in which the electronic computer is captain and calls the plays, Iowa is quite representative of the big Big-Ten, state-supported schools where, if one listens to Dean Stuit's talk of "socio-economic groups," "communication skills," and "percentiles," one unavoidably concludes the majority of students (who, incidentally, are in Liberal Arts) are being not so much educated as processed and packaged like some natural agricultural material. Illinois and Indiana and Purdue are the same; they run their admission exams by electronic testing machines—examinations in which an answer is either true or false or is one of a few preselected choices. Grades are assigned according to precalibrated curves in some cases; and I recall that as far back as 1949, when after a good deal of backing and filling I finally graduated, I stepped up to the platform to receive my degree from President Hancher and was handed instead a blank pasteboard tube which I turned in with my cap and gown after the ceremony. The diploma itself arrived later by first-class mail.

These shenanigans, of course, have nothing whatever to do with education, but in a way the young people of the Midwest *are* a kind of raw agricultural material; perhaps commercial processing techniques are the only possible way to deal with them. That incredibly large crop of war babies, full-grown and desirous of a recognizable and acceptable shape that will fit neatly and attractively on the market shelf with other shapes equally recognizable and acceptable, has stormed the gates of the University. And the University, being tax-supported, cannot turn away anyone.

The interstices between the old classrooms and laboratories have been filled in with new buildings and parking lots. Though the school is expanding into the farmland to the west, the green spaces of the lawns and the river banks at the University's center are being devoured. I heard so much criticism of the kind of building that was being erected that I asked President Virgil Hancher about it when I talked to him in his office in Old Capitol.

Old Capitol is a fine, simple, elegantly proportioned building on top of the hill overlooking the river—Iowa City was the state capital until 1857, and the capitol building, after the government removed to Des Moines, formed the nucleus of the State University.

"Each new building is a discrete example of a different architect's work," President Hancher said. "Ideally, we would have an architect who plans all the buildings and follows some kind of overall campus projection, but this simply is not the policy of the Board."

President Hancher explained that the practice of the State Board of Regents, which governs all of Iowa's state-supported schools, is to employ only architects from the state of Iowa, and seldom to employ the same architect twice in the same area. This means there can be little discrimination for or against quality, and little planning; and also that the architect receives his commission without competition. The results are nearly always unsatisfactory and frequently grotesque—as are, for instance, the new art-faculty studios, whose meager north light is partially obstructed by a maze of pipes and heating units. The new Law School addition is described by one lawyer as a labyrinth. Many of its windows do not open; the building was designed to be air-conditioned, but the air conditioning has not yet been installed, for lack of funds. Iowa City is a furnace in the summer. "All we can do," President Hancher said, "is to hope for money to install air conditioning some time in the future."

In general, he is proud of the expansion of the University and of the added facilities for research and adult education; the improvements in classes and personnel in surgery and speech pathology; the fine arts; fringe benefits, and the retirement plan for the faculty. All of this has taken place during his suzerainty, which began in 1940.

He is due to retire in 1964, and there is already a good deal of speculation and political maneuvering concerning his successor. I asked him if he had any idea who it might be, and he smiled, shaking his head. "It's generally accepted practice that an outgoing president makes no recommendations as to his successor, and I believe that's the way it should be. However, I think that the president should be someone of the cloth. I came here directly out of law practice, and I don't recommend it." After twenty-two years in the president's office he still has the air of a man who doesn't quite believe that he's there.

President Hancher had asked the state legislature for some ten million dollars for new buildings for the years 1963-65. In the next few years the enrollment will be unthinkable in relation to the facilities. All those kids will have to be housed, fed, and, in some way or other, taught. The most significant fact about SUI, it seems to me, is the immanent dichotomy between two factions. One is that ravenous horde that cannot be turned away, that must be processed, fed canned courses a hundred at a time, and sped on their way with just enough memory of sport and spectacle, good fellowship, first booze and first love, moonlight twist, and close shaves at finals, to last them till marriage. The other is the medics and lawyers, the painters and poets, the mathematicians and classical scholars who, by their devotion and their dedication, manage to keep the pride and prestige of the University healthy and alive.

Two such men, who would expire on a team of any kind, I visited after leaving President Hancher. One was James Van Allen, Head of the Department of Physics and Astronomy; the other was Frederick Bargebuhr, the Jewish representative in the School of Religion. These men, engrossed in such different work and so different in personality, are nevertheless very much alike in the love and intensity they bring to their milieu. Bargebuhr is an almost classic absent-minded German professor, a man of enormous warmth and humor, who is likely to walk out of a restaurant without his coat or arrive at lunch instead of dinner. He is probably the only authority in the world on the Hebrew vizier-poets who lived and flourished so lavishly during the Abbasid caliphate in Granada, and on the Jewish origins of the Alhambra. To a small group of students, devotedly solicitous, he teaches Hebrew, Arabic, and Old Testament studies.

Van Allen's field, as everybody knows who follows his government's nuclear and space experiments, is space science. Van Allen is a pleasant, relaxed, everyday sort of man, going about his labors with his pipe in his hand, his jacket off, his shirt sleeves rolled to the elbows. It was simply not true, he declared, that he was elusive, aloof, or difficult to see, or that, as one reporter said of him, the last thing in the world he wanted to come in contact with was a student. "This year," he said, "I'm teaching Freshman Physics." And I could see that he was tickled to death at the idea.

The international reputation of Iowa has been made and maintained by Van Allen and others, such as Alexandre Aspel in Romance languages, William Bean in internal medicine, Gustav Bergmann in philosophy, Mauricio Lasansky and Humbert Albrizio in art, Ignacio Vives Ponseti in orthopedic surgery, Hunter Rouse in hydraulic engineering. When I first came to the University, nearly all of the foreign students had been attracted by the Hydraulics Laboratory on the Iowa River, and most of them were young men from India or China or the Near East. When I returned some years later, the diversity of nationality had increased, as had the attractions. Through the years art, music, theater, and the writers' workshops, along with psychology and English, had drawn a large proportion of non-Midwesterners. I could be mistaken, but I believe that among the Big Ten schools, Iowa has been most successful in its seduction of students from abroad. Well, maybe it *is* the Athens of America after all—Athens, that is, in the Golden Age.

Van Allen, however, is a native Iowan graduated from Iowa Wesleyan College, a Methodist school there, and shows no indication of wanting to leave in spite of a freeway laid past his new house in Iowa City. His brother, Maurice Van Allen, is also a resident of Iowa City, a neurologist at the University Hospital.

"What do you think of their blasting a hole in your belt?" I asked him, referring to the high-altitude explosions over Johnson Island designed to disturb the rings of radiation named for him.

"I'm against it," he said, "not because I'm positive at this point that it's likely to do any damage to the human race or to a natural phenomenon—though, of course, we're not sure yet—but because testing on such a large scale constitutes an act of terrorism in the eyes of the world. I would not have objected to a smaller test purely as scientific experiment. That's what I'm working on right now."

He pointed with his pipe to a stack of diagrammed papers on the desk between us. "The data from those tests. It's very interesting."

In the course of our conversation I discovered that he believes that science and religion are not too disparate. "God made Nature, and science is simply finding out how God's universe is put together."

I asked him about federal subsidies for research by himself and his graduate assistants, who have brought such satisfying publicity to the University. "I spend half my time going back and forth to Washington," he said. "NASA or the Air Force, for instance, they don't come to us with projects. If we wish to launch a program of research—the magnetic field of Venus, for instance—we try to persuade them to support us. If we're turned down, then we have to find some other support for the project or else give it up."

As he spoke, I was reminded of the remark made by John Weaver, dean of the University's Graduate College, to the effect that a research-minded Federal government *uses* rather than *aids* higher education.

In the middle of the week before Homecoming, the fine warm weather worsened as a cold front moved in from the northwest. It brought low temperatures, heavy clouds, and, finally, the year's first snow, falling most of one night and changing to rain before morning. The cold weather brought a different look to the campus. The girls came out in fur-collared waterproofs and bright wool coats, the boys in hooded jackets. Some wore earmuffs. Their noses turned red, and they began to snuffle.

The fallen leaves whirled and sped along the gutters and across the green of Old Capitol. The windows of those student beer-and-argument resorts—Joe's, Kenney's, and the Airliner—steamed up, blanking out the smiling faces and modestly exposed limbs of young ladies whose posters solicited the University men on the street to vote for them for Miss SUI—*Judy's a Jewel; Sure and It's Sharon; Operation Holly; Like Love, Like Lana; Cinder-Elza*—including that of Miss Margie Walsh, the junior in Nursing who was elected.

The Dolphin Show was coming up, too, at the Fieldhouse pool, with a Far East theme: *Mood Oriental.* The superb Iowa String Quartet was scheduled to play, the art faculty were preparing to show their works in the new gallery, the University Theater was to open its winter season with *The Importance of Being Earnest.* Homecoming badges were being pressed upon passersby at the windy corners of Washington and Clinton Streets, Iowa and Dubuque. Stan Kenton was on his way for the Homecoming Dance (which would be eschewed by the Greeks in favor of their private parties) in the Iowa Memorial Union. The Union was also preparing for the reception of alumni. There was something, in fact, for everyone at the last fall festival before the hard winter set in.

Friday morning the Homecoming fever was beginning to rise. *The Daily Iowan,* the student newspaper, was delivered as usual before breakfast to University doors. Managing Editor Larry Hatfield, a senior from Bedford, Iowa, a harsh critic of practically everything, particularly football and the moral and political apathy of his fellow students, led off sarcastically in his column, *File 13:*

> Homecoming—the alumni are here (be respectful), the football team is preparing for the Spoilermakers (be hopeful), taverns are stocked up on beer (be careful), afternoon classes are called off (be thankful), Miss SUI is chosen (be worshipful) and Sunday will follow (be restful).

Before the machinery of higher education was switched off at twelve-twenty, and the bonfires of harvest pageantry piled high and set ablaze, there were some people and places I wanted to see. One was Forest Evashevski, known to stranger and friend as Evy. And from the moment I stepped into his office in the Fieldhouse and shook his gigantic hand, I was Cal.

Evy was a Michigan star, and head football coach for the Iowa Hawkeyes from 1952 through the Golden Age, 1956-60. Now he has moved up to Director of Intercollegiate Athletics, after picking as his successor his backfield coach, Jerry Burns. Iowa was nothing in football before Evy came, and during his years there the best gridiron talent in the country wanted to come to Iowa to play for him. Matt Szykowny, Hawkeye quarterback from Pittsburgh, told me, "I knew I wanted to be an engineer and play football, and Evy brought me and some of the fellas here, and he took us around and showed us everything, and, well, he sold me."

Evy's office is like nothing else in the University. The walls are hung with mementos, photographs of teams, bronze plaques. One of the plaques, presented by the Cedar Rapids Sales Executive Club, says, "Forest Evashevski—Iowa's Top Salesman." The furniture is modernistic—there is a coffee table offering one book, *Osborn on Leisure;* a peach-colored telephone; an enormous desk covered with athletic programs, checks, and commemorative fountain-pen sets. It was the office of a business executive whose product was sports. He explained that Iowa Athletics (nothing whatever to do with University Physical Education) was a separate, self-liquidating organization, under faculty and regent control but receiving no funds from the taxpayers. "All our salaries— coaches and trainers and such—and all teams' expenses are paid from the profits of Big Ten ball."

"What do you do with what's left over?" I asked, remembering President Hancher's comments upon the huge expenses of big-time football.

"We turn it back in," said Evy. "We've made improvements in the stadium, there's that press box—a half million, paid for in five years by the profits from TV. There's the new golf course, and then we help some research, like in the University Hospital, some research on knees, and . . ."

"What about athletic scholarships?"

"Oh, yes, there are some of those. We don't pay any faculty salaries, though, the academic faculty. You could see what that could lead to. Some of the teachers might get it into their heads that it was to their advantage to have a good football team."

"I understand that now there are some minimum scholastic requirements for athletes," I said.

"Oh yes." He fished through some papers at the side of his desk and then through a drawer; then he called to the woman in the outer office, then called her a second time, saying, "Never mind, I found it." It was a little blue book, which he opened to a double page of figures and averages.

"Here, he said, running a thick forefinger down the columns of numbers. "There, ah, there it is, it's all there." He clearly could not see them, but he was reluctant to slip on the bifocals that were lying on his desk. As with so many physical people, the petty failures of the body seemed almost intolerable annoyances.

"Do you like it now?" I asked. "I mean, being athletic director instead of coach." I smiled. "Being a desk man."

He leaned back in his leather chair, clasped his hands behind his head. "Well, to tell the truth, I miss contact with the boys, getting to know them. Now they're just names or numbers to me."

Leaving the Fieldhouse, I walked over to the stadium. It has been greatly enlarged since I was in school. The weather was sharp and damp, and University workmen were rolling the wet tarpaulins off the playing field in preparation for the grueling contest the next day. The Hawkeyes were in a severe slump, and it was predicted that the powerful Purdue Boilermakers would rivet them mercilessly to their native earth. The game had been sold out (at five dollars a seat, except for the students, who go free) since Lord-knows-when, but I had managed a seat through the President's office. I hadn't seen an Iowa football game in a long time, and I was looking forward to it.

I spent the morning looking at other things I had not seen for a long time. I stopped in the Art Building, where the gallery was being hung with work by members of the faculty. There were engravings by Mauricio Lasansky, who has made the Iowa print department the most vigorous and influential in the country; there were paintings by Stuart Edie, by Eugene Ludins, and by Byron Burford, who had just received a purchase prize of $2,000 from the Ford Foundation; there was sculpture by Humbert Albrizio.

Up the hill from the Art Building, at the top of a flight of broad, stone steps, I made an effort to reacquaint myself with what used to be the Law Commons, the dormitory in which I was originally housed as a freshman in those grimly uncertain days at the beginning of World War II. The old dorm had been converted to offices and seminar rooms, and the new Law building had been tacked on. It was now past one o'clock, and the students had gone off, free until Monday.

I wandered around, vainly trying to get my bearings in a nearly deserted complex of halls and stairways. A few boys were in the new library, and two young men were sitting on a table in the lounge with a chess board between them; but the mood of the place, in fact of the entire University, on that suspended Friday afternoon, was expressed cryptically by the inscription on the blackboard next to the judge's bench in the empty trial courtroom: NO SMOKING, NO DRINKING, NO EATING, NO STUDYING BY ORDER OF THE DEAN.

During the afternoon the Greeks and the Independents completed their competing floats illustrating the titles of songs. The bloodthirsty alumni poured into town, displacing the traveling salesmen at the Hotel Jefferson. Corsages arrived by the dozen at the desk at Burge Hall, in whose lounge was a milling, restless throng of boys waiting for their afternoon dates to step out of the elevators. The taverns jammed up at lunchtime and stayed that way. At the Airliner I saw one boy's head droop hopelessly toward the bar at not quite three in the afternoon.

The streets were cleared at dark, and the parade, headed by the President of the Student Senate, the President of the Iowa City Chamber of Commerce, the Mayor of Iowa City, and President Hancher, passed by with many bands, drum corps, and girls. The queen was crowned, the parties began. I have mentioned the one I attended at Dizzy Land, and there were many others in private homes and fraternities and roadhouses on the outskirts. Though it was the dark of the harvest moon, and overcast, several groups engaged enthusiastically in hayrides, and one fraternity abandoned themselves to a Peppermint Lounge Party.

There were a good many hangovers on Saturday morning, but not nearly as many as there would be on Sunday.

The sky had cleared during the night, and the weather, after the unseasonable snowfall, had pulled another prodigious switch, offering a Saturday as dry as summer and nearly as hot. There were over 60,000 people at the game. The gigantic steel-and-concrete conning tower of a press box was alive with announcers, reporters, experts, analysts, and cameramen. Planes and helicopters hovered overhead.

The marching band marched, and the famous Scottish Highlanders (all women) played their bagpipes, did their Highland Fling and their one and only original Drum Dance. The Hawkeyes tried, failed, and trailed off the field in near-tears and abject defeat. I sat through the whole spectacle in a very choice section of the visitors' stands, practically surrounded by the governor, his retinue and most of the state legislature.

When the whole thing was over, and the crowd was dispersing in a mood of perfect petulance, one woman said to her representative husband, "Well, I surely did enjoy the band." One senator said to another, grinning as he tossed away his four-color, fifty-four-page, fifty-cent program, "Well, that was a waste of a good afternoon."

I was reminded of the remark made to me by President Hancher, who was making a multimillion-dollar request for next season. "I have never known a single instance," he said, "when winning or losing a game affected the way a legislature votes." And in that, I felt as I left the packed and noisy stands, he was doubtless right.

. . . Calvin Kentfield, 1963

RAGBRAI riders reach the Mississippi

Getting Around Iowa

THE INDIANS TRAVELED over their beloved Iowa prairies and on its lakes and rivers on foot, on horseback, or in dugouts and canoes. The first white settlers, as Herbert Quick told us a few pages back, came on foot, horseback or by any sort of conveyance that could be drawn by horse, mule, or ox. Then came the trains, next the automobiles, finally the airplane.

Most recently, a nineteenth-century development, the bicycle, has come into vogue—a vogue emphasized once a year for the past few years by the Des Moines Register-sponsored Register's Annual Great Bicycle Ride Across Iowa—RAGBRAI, for short.

Gary Gildner, who with his wife Judith, was a native Michigander and who now teaches at Drake (his wife is an editor at Ames) is one of those who forsakes the automobile for the bicycle. (The whole family cycles.) When he tours around his adopted state, as he does when he meets with public school students and others to discuss his favorite subject, poetry, he rents an automobile.

The Gildners are the compilers of a collection of poems about Iowa, Out of This World *(1975) from which "Touring the Hawkeye State" is taken.*

Touring the Hawkeye State

I saw the best parts of Iowa covered with New Jersey tea,
    partridge pea, rattlesnake master, and Culver's root,
    I saw Chief Keokuk's "X" in the county courthouse in Keokuk,
    home of John L. Lewis and Elsa Maxwell

I saw sweet William, wild rye, I saw the Iowa Watershed Divide
    running through the business district of Orient,
    I saw the outskirts of Adair and the locomotive wheel
    marking the spot where Jesse James derailed the Chicago,
    Rock Island and Pacific and knocked off engineer Rafferty
    and ran with the loot to Missouri

I saw gayfeather, blazing star, and butterfly weed,
    I saw where Henry Lott murdered Two Fingers on the banks
    of Bloody Run, where Dr. William S. Pitts, a dentist,
    wrote hymns, taught singing and practiced
    in Nashua in Chicasaw County,
    home of The Little Brown Church in the Vale,
    I saw Osage, home of Hamlin Garland

I saw the home of Iowa's only one-eyed governor, Bill Larrabee,
    and Clarinda, home of Glenn Miller,
    and Humboldt, home of Frank Gotch, who hammerlocked
    the Russian Lion Hackenschmidt for the world
    wrestling championship, and Grundy Center,
    home of Herbert Quick, author of *The Hawkeye,*
    The Invisible Woman, and others

I saw the braided rugs that Grant Wood's mother made
    from Grant's old jeans, where the *Bertrand* went down
    on her maiden voyage, taking boxes of Dr. Hostetter's
    Celebrated Stomach Bitters, and the Fairview Cemetery
    where Amelia Jenks Bloomer, of *The Lily,* lies buried,
    I saw her Turkish pantaloons,

I saw the only Holstein museum in America
    and Mama Ormsby Burke's neck chain and milk stool
    and the west branch of the Wapsinonoc and the modest
    two-room cottage that sheltered young Herbert Hoover
    and Peru, where the first Delicious apple tree grew,
    and Newton, home of Emerson Hough, author of *Mississippi*
    Bubble

I saw the summit of Floyd's Bluff and the lightning-
    struck obelisk south of Sioux City
    near Interstate 29, the final resting place
    of the bones of Sergeant Charles Floyd
    who died of a busted gut under Lewis and Clark,
    their only loss on the whole trip,
    I saw Oskaloosa where Frederic K. Logan
    composed "Over the Hills" and "Missouri Waltz"

I saw the Walnut, Turkey, Pony, Plum, and Honey creeks,
    the Polecat River, Spirit Lake, the park where John Brown
    drilled for Harper's Ferry, Eisenhower's Mamie's
    home in Boone, the home of John "Duke" Wayne, née Marion M.
    Morrison, in Winterset, Billy Sunday's mother's grave
    a peg from Story County's Sewage Plant,
    where Billy saw the light, where he came back
    to gather souls, in Garner, after shagging flies in center
    for the Chicago White Stockings

I saw ½ mile west of Orient where Henry Agard Wallace,
    experimentalist and Republican, Democrat and Progressive,
    breeder of chickens, strawberries, and hybrid corn
    and Iowa's only U.S. Vice President was born,
    on a nine-acre tract of virgin prairie
    in West of Orient I saw pink and white beardtongue

I saw where Jenny Lind and Tom Thumb appeared
    in Stone City, where Cyphert Talley, a Baptist preacher,
    was killed in the Talley or Skunk River War
    in Sigourney, where the Sac-Fox council
    started the Black Hawk War in Toolesboro,
    where Chief Wapello and his friend General Street
    are buried in the same plot along the C. B. & G.
    right-of-way in Agency

I saw the trails worn in the sod by trekking Mormons,
    the Corning farm of Howard Townsend, historic communist,
    blue-eyed grass and Jerusalem artichoke,
    war clubs, knives, scrapers, grinders, and threshers,
    hickory, basswood, hackberry, wahoo, and burr,
    a Victorian parlor, a low-growing yew,
    a rare folding bathtub, a belfry stocked with birds

. . . Gary Gildner

Ragbrai--Polly Kemp (1979)

· BIRTHPLACE PHIL STONG ← PITTSBURG·

Iowa

IT IS MOST APPROPRIATE that Paul Engle's 1956 Holiday *article on his native state should close this book. It wraps up in Engle's fine poetic-prose style all that has been said about Iowa in this book, and some more. And for most of Engle's three-score-and-ten years, he has been our own "Mr. Iowa Literature," excelling in that respect even his predecessor, John Towner Frederick. Engle's reputation as poet, novelist, writer, and teacher is international, and that last adjective is not a mere figure of speech. Since he founded the International Writers' Workshop on the University of Iowa campus a few years back, Engle's associates have included not only his wife, Nieh Hua-Ling, a native of China, but also writers from all the continents and several lesser domains.*

Still, for all that, he has remained an Iowan, in person, at heart, and in spirit. Of all of the famed group of Iowa authors, he and his Cedar Falls peer, James Hearst, have alone remained in Iowa, to write about their state and to teach its students.

Iowa

IOWA IS THE HEARTLAND OF THE HEARTLAND.

Its greatest single force is dirt – fat dirt; out of its soil each year more wealth is produced than in all the gold mines of the world. Gently the land rises and falls, not flat, not broken into steep hills, but always tilting its fertile face to the sun.

When a military highway was needed from Dubuque to the Missouri border in the early days of the mounted dragoons, a farmer was hired. He yoked up ten oxen to a long sod-breaking plow and headed south. Day after day they moved, ahead of them the untouched grass and grove, behind them a lengthening furrow of black dirt. No sound but the man's yell to his animals, and the silken, tearing rip of the plow splitting that sod for the first time ever. It was natural for Iowa to use for its military road only the peaceful oxen and the plow. For this is an abundant land.

And when last year the Soviet Union sent agricultural experts to America to find out what free men working on their own land could raise, it was natural that the Russians should come first to Iowa. And when the Red farmers arrived they were given, in once "isolationist" Iowa, a wealthy welcome, told everything they wanted to know, shown all the methods and secrets of production. They went to the First Presbyterian Church in Jefferson and held hymnbooks, probably for the first time in their lives, watched 4-H boys demonstrate how to kill corn borers, and 4-H girls bake sweet rolls. They lifted their arms at the right time in the Iowa song for the line "That's where the tall corn grows," and they saw their first real drugstore with a soda fountain and ate "Tummy Busters. Eat Two and Get a Free One – 49 cents plus one cent tax." For this is an abundant land.

Iowa is the middlest of the Middle West. Its life and people are balanced and solid. It is a country of the small town, the average comfortable life. There are no great fortunes and there is no poverty. But it has the highest standard of living for its area in the world and it has a quarter of all the best land in America.

Look at the map of Iowa, the Missouri wavering down the west side and the Mississippi down the east. Jutting eastward is a fine round pot belly, the broad Mississippi bending around it like a belt. For this is an abundant land.

Iowa carries nothing to excess save its virtues and its weather. It has been the place of the sensible medium, and of the peace that goes with it. The only Quaker President, Herbert Hoover, came from a little Iowa town. There has never been a war on Iowa soil, or a battle of any consequence. One massacre by the Sioux of a few white settlers. John Brown trained his men at a Quaker settlement, where they did strange calisthenics and drilled with wooden swords. One of his men was censured for hugging girls, which was as violent an act as any of the group committed in Iowa. When the time for fighting came, Brown left his peaceful settlement, where the Quakers had assisted him without knowing his wicked purpose, and went off to bloody Harpers Ferry. Iowa men marched off to Vicksburg, but the Civil War never came to their state.

When my grandfather rode with the Fifth Iowa Cavalry in the '60s, he chased the Sioux in Dakota Territory but never caught up with him. Inkpadutah, the leader of the Sioux who massacred thirty-two men, women, and children at Spirit Lake, realized that Iowa was too peaceful for such wild goings-on, and fled west.

Kentucky was the Dark and Bloody Ground, but Iowa has always been the Bright and Bloodless Ground.

Of the Missouri River the old saying is: too thick to drink, too thin to plow. But Iowa is just right to plow, no waste land, no swamps, no mountains, no large forests. Glaciers scoured off the soil from other states and dumped it on this lucky land, giving Iowa its long reaches of loam. After grass had grown and died for centuries, sinking its roots so deep that prairie fires couldn't burn them out, the soil became as rich as the side of a fat hog.

Then the settlers came, and the sod-breaking plows, with their great oak beams to hold the point of the plow down against the tough buck of the roots, and the great crops began to spring up. France had its Field of the Cloth of Gold, but Iowa still has its Fields of the Cloth of Green.

The common shape of Iowa landscape is the little valley, with tiny streams everywhere like veins meshing a marvelous body. And along all of the streams, wooded slopes with willow, elm, maple, hickory, black walnut. The streams are everywhere, the dark rivers with the silt of fields: Raccoon, Coon, Wolf, Catfish, Mosquito, Polecat, Opossum, Pike, Turkey, Skunk, Cedar, Crabapple, Squaw, and Five Barrel Creek, so called because dragoons found five barrels of whisky buried near it. And most lyrical of all, in the high hills of northeastern Iowa, the Tête de Mort (call it Teddymore), proof that the French once were here, and that a band of Dakotahs was killed by Sac Indians and scalped and thrown over a cliff.

There is no soft nonsense about the seasons in Iowa. Winter is a savage season; blizzards out of the west rattle the teeth in your skull. Frost goes deep in the fallow ground; snow piles up and when the ice comes, impenetrable, squirrels scamper over it hungrily. But then will come the incredible May morning when the sun drips a gold life on the land, seeds jump in delight under the plowed fields, the sprouted corn turns the countryside into tufted quilts, and the pigs squirm out into the light of day ("Sows opened weak on the Chicago market" says the radio report) and calves jump stiff-legged around the barn. The air itself has the quality of food and breathing is nourishment. The pastures glitter with green.

Then summer overwhelms us. We can hear the crops growing, the corn up an inch a day, the pigs grunting their growth as they crunch their food—more elaborately planned and mixed than that of any child (buttermilk, yeast, fish, soybeans, sugar, corn, limestone, cobalt, acetate, zinc carbonate, linseed oil, rolled oats, fish liver, manganese sulphate, vitamins, antibiotics, riboflavin, and many others). The porkers have had their "one-shot wormer" and are busy hanging bacon on their slick sides. The whole state turns into a skillet, frying human, animal, and plant life. Midnight differs a few degrees from intense noon. Corn grows tall and men grow limp. People droop by night and drop by day. But everything flourishes.

Autumn is the Iowa season. All of the winter's frozen rest, the spring plowing, the summer cultivating, move toward the final act of harvest. The land browns, oats ripen, corn begins to dent, hay is cut, the alfalfa for the third time. As the long corn leaves turn brittle the air itself turns crisp and tree leaves burn the branches for a while before falling. It is a season truly called "the fall." Things come to earth, the crops to barn, the kids to school. The delirious activity of summer slows down, as the urgency of jobs to get done before it's too late falls away.

Between summer and autumn come the county fairs, with their rows of Jerseys, Guernseys (with the highest butter-fat content in their milk), of Holsteins (the largest producers of milk in bulk), the mouse-colored Brown Swiss with their calves looking like heavy-boned fawns, the glistening flanks of Black Angus beef steers, polished and combed, or the ruddy Herefords with their white faces. And there is usually a single hog litter totaling a ton. The wildly carved running horses on the merry-go-round carry children to the same sweet and brassy tunes. The exhibits of farm machinery are fantastic, the prize squash, pumpkin, corn, startle the eye with their size. And of course there are the formidable yet delicate and fluffy cakes with blue and red prize ribbons on them, the prize pickels, canned beans, enough to shatter the stablest stomach. Along the race track where the horses are jogging with their light sulkies and the old-time horsemen with their legs straddling the shafts, families are engaged in that most typical, most delightful Iowa activity—consuming food.

What people come? Farmers with their families, faces tanned but a sharp white line around the neck where the shirt collar kept off the sun, with the deliberate walk of men accustomed to plowed fields and bumpy pastures. They watch the fat-steer judging and the heavy draft-horse judging, look at the machinery, take a suspicious glance at the Kewpie doll stands and the jaded girlie shows, but mostly they talk, talk to other farmers they haven't seen in a coon's age. (What is the age of a coon?) Everywhere clusters of men arguing weather, crops, prices (today's prices are mentioned in the tone of voice one uses coming home from a funeral), politics, the Government (in the tone one uses for a difficult uncle you don't really want around but whose wealth might be needed later on).

The women are here, too, and the kids; it's a family affair, something for everybody, the home-convenience exhibits for the ladies and the Ferris wheel for the screaming kids. But town people are here too, especially the ones who grew up on farms and moved away. They've changed some, they walk a little faster and gesture more abruptly, but they still like the smells of the barns and the bawl of the calves and the leathery tang of harness being soaped for the afternoon's first trotting heat. You can take the boy out of the farm but you can't take the farm out of the boy.

Across the top of the Great Seal of Iowa is the motto: Our Liberties We Prize and Our Rights We Will Maintain. And to prove that those rights will be maintained, a soldier with rifle stands in the foreground, a plow and a great swirling flag behind him. To a surprising extent, they are maintained, although now and then there is a little uncertainty as to just whose rights are meant. A few years ago the body of a GI was refused burial at a Sioux City cemetery, although he had died protecting his country's liberties, because he was too much a 100 per cent American, a real Indian. But this is rare. It is a matter of pride that the first case to come before the Supreme Court of Iowa territory gave freedom to a Negro slave. And this same regard for human liberty came up a century later when a Negro Army officer stationed at a radar base near Waverly could not find housing for his family, although an apartment was available. When the other tenants heard about it, they petitioned to have him as a neighbor and welcomed his family with a celebration.

There has always been a sense of the just in Iowa. More than a hundred years ago when the defiant Sac Chief Black Hawk was presented to Andy Jackson in Washington he looked him in the eye and said simply, "I am a man and you are another."

Even obscenity gets a fair hearing. A few years ago the ladies of Dubuque were frightened by the appearance of comics, reprints, pocket books near schools. Hearings were held and the naughty evidence was introduced, such fiction as that of Erskine Caldwell, Richard Bissell (Dubuque's own, author of *A Stretch on the River* and *The Pajama Game*), and the usual popular novels, along with some gruesome comics and a history of art which charmingly proved that the female nude had interested more artists than had bowls of fruit or happy children. But in the end, the decision taken was the moderate, middle one to be expected of Iowa people: the chance of censorship was worse than the chance of indiscriminate novels being read. One argument of real power in a state essentially rural-minded was that the corset sections of mail-order catalogs contained more photographs of undressed models than any of the books being questioned.

When the Russians came to Iowa they expected to find the fields full of people. As they were driven along the roads between the luxuriant corn and oats and alfalfa, with the yards and pastures full of hogs and cattle, they kept asking, "But where are the workers?" Usually they were told that a man and his wife and children, with an occasional hired man, farmed the place. One of them exclaimed, "By you one man – by us a hundred." What he did not realize was that this staggering production of food by a few people was done by the same class of farmers the Soviet had murdered in the early '30s. They had never seen a husking hook fastened to a glove. They kept asking at the agricultural college at Ames who was their *boss* in Washington, and could not believe that the college operated independently of the Federal Government. When they asked Guy Stover, Jr., a farmer near Reinbeck, who told him what to plant, he replied: "Nobody tells me what to plant. Nobody. I can let the whole farm grow up in weeds if I want to and nobody can say a thing."

They ate meals of roast beef, vegetables, ice cream, angel-food cake, salad, milk, all of which came from the same farm. They discovered that small-town newspapers in Iowa were thicker than Russia's national dailies. They had their first experience of motels, a dime store, golf, a country club. They discovered, as the Charles City *Press* put it, every reason under the sun why the Iowa farmer produced twenty times as much food as the Russian farmer, except the main one, the freedom under which the Iowa farmer operates.

The Russians came in the hope of learning how to feed their people. That was natural, for men and women have always come to Iowa with hope. In the 1850s came a group of Germans calling itself The Community of True Inspiration, who believed that God still spoke directly to man. They settled between Iowa City and Grinnell and built seven little Amana villages in the medieval manner, the families living close together in the communities and going out to work in the fields. They had the wisdom to realize that the Lord could best be served with good land rather than poor, and took up 26,000 acres of rich bottom soil and wooded hills along the Iowa River. They ate in communal houses (five times a day, in leisure and abundance, with excellent grape and dandelion wine brought out to those working in the fields at noon). All property save clothing and furniture was held in common. Each adult received a tiny sum known as "year-money" for odd expenses, the least-skilled worker in the hog house receiving the same housing and maintenance as the most responsible farm head. God was worshiped not in churches but in houses without cross or decoration, and no music save the unaccompanied human voice grandly ringing out the hymns written by their own brilliant prophet Christian Metz.

They flourished in their isolated, abundant, and devout life until the wicked world came to them by newspaper, paved road, car, radio, and the young people began to yearn for the things they saw others having, like bicycles and Sunday baseball. They voted to dissolve the old communal-property idea and to form a corporation in which everyone worked for a salary. Each adult was given one share of Class A voting stock; when issued in 1932 a share was worth fifty-four dollars—today it is worth $3400. Houses are painted, cars are everywhere, television aerials rise as high as the native hickory and oak trees.

Again Iowa released the energies of people who came to her. Working with odd items from local shops, George Foerstner and others created a little freezer. And now in the cornfields at Middle Amana, where oxen loafed not long ago and daily prayers out of the early 18th Century were uttered in praise of God and in disparagement of weak man, there is a bright new factory from which more home freezers are sold than from any other plant in the world. And where the name *Amana* used to mean a shy young girl under a black sunbonnet, now it means movie star Laraine Day opening an Amana freezer wide, as she widely smiles, on television.

Iowa has always believed in bringing together the holy and the useful. Dutch who would not conform to the established church in Holland came in 1847 to found the town of Pella, where every May the old Dutch clothes and the wooden shoes come out, and there is dancing in the street. Why shouldn't they dance? They're in Iowa raising tulips, and raising the hem of their long dresses, oh so slightly.

And the French came to start their own idealistic community at Icaria on the Nodaway. Property was held in common, but alas, not the zeal for work. A dance hall was built, however, with plenty of zeal and native wood, but soon there were only individual men and women working their own lives.

The Hungarians came after the failure of the 1848 revolt against

Austria. But they were aristocrats full of zeal to build a New Buda in Northwestern Iowa, and what the land needed was a sharp plow, not an edged sword.

The Norwegians came to northeastern Iowa, in the handsome hill country, to settle the town of Decorah and found Luther College. Some crossed the frozen Mississippi in the depth of winter, proving the stern devotion of a faith that could build log cabins in a wilderness and a hundred years later produce blond, unbeaten football teams with Viking names.

Naturally, the Mennonites came here to build their fine farms, with that same combination of hard work and solid faith. Around Kalona they wrestled with some hard questions: Was it right to drive an automobile? (Most drive buggies; a few, cars with the chrome painted out.) Was it proper to use a tractor with metal tires but not with rubber tires? Would pickles tied to the feet cure a child of convulsions? Should the preachers forbid turkey roasts, ice-cream suppers, imposing weddings, laces, corsets, Christmas trees? The men in their beards, the women and children in their black bonnets and high shoes, come into Iowa City to shop, and to peer quietly at the naughty world. And then go home to work their rich farms with their old simplicity.

The Czechs came to Spillville in the northeastern country, where Antonin Dvořák came to write his music in the peaceful valley where his native language was still spoken. And signs across part of Cedar Rapids today are in Czech, and the Sokols do their fine gymnastics and the kolaches are made with prunes or poppy seeds. Once a Czech girl named Jaroslava Holobulova graduated from Coe College at the top of her class.

But most amusing of all the peoples who came to Iowa were the English younger sons who settled in Le Mars in the northwest to learn farming in the 1880s. They brought to Iowa their own sporting ways; cricket practice was held on Broken Kettle Creek, and the Le Mars cricket team beat St. Paul. Polo was played against Cherokee and Council Bluffs. But the polo ball proved more attractive than the humble pumpkin, and the younger sons left the plow in the furrow and rode into town to "paint the place a rip, staring red."

But the purpose of these gay British boys, since the place was Iowa, was to learn how to raise food. A visiting newspaperman wrote about them: "The young men who make up this community are . . . graduates of Oxford or Cambridge. On one farm I met two tall and handsome young farmers whose uncle had been a distinguished member of Parliament. The last time I had seen them was in a London drawing room. This time they tramped me through the mud and manure of the barnyard to show me some newly bought stock. They were boarding with a Dutch farmer at three dollars a week in order to learn practical farming. . . . Another young farmer had been an admiral in the Royal Navy, another had been connected with a Shanghai bank. There was a brother to Lord Ducie, not to speak of future baronets, viscounts, and honorables. . . ."

But real liberty had its price. One of the Englishmen wrote that he could no longer stand the Iowa attitude: "The other evening on the closing of the House of Lords (as they had named a saloon), I was standing with four or five friends talking when the deputy marshal comes up and requests me in his usually suave manner to 'cheese this racket.' Liberty is constantly jammed down your throat here, but it seems to me an exploded theory, when an officer can do what he likes with your right of speech." Discouraged by equal parts of being told to cheese it and of hard work, the younger sons gave up their western ghosts and left.

The English were the gayest of all the Iowa settlers. More solid were the "Hook-and-Eye Dutch" who refused to put up the tops of their buggies because the sun was no harder on them than on the horse.

But no matter what their origins, Iowa people believed in education. With the lowest rate of illiteracy in the United States, it is natural that one of the country's largest manufcturers of fountain pens should be the W. A. Sheaffer Pen plant, at Fort Madison, and that one of the finest state-wide newspapers should be the Des Moines *Register,* unique today in having an editorial page with generous convictions and the courage to express them. It opposed Senator McCarthy long before more timid papers did so; it began the protest which resulted in Ladejinsky being cleared; it invited the Russians to visit Iowa; it approved Dr. Robert J. Oppenheimer being invited to speak at Iowa State College when many colleges refused to have him. In all this, it remains stanchly Republican, believing, with the mixture of idealism and practicality which has always distinguished the people of Iowa, that personal freedom is nothing but old-fashioned right, and every man's due.

The Cowles family is a solid example of what human character can mean to a state, through its many gifts to colleges, the foundation it has endowed, and through dramatizing in the pages of the *Register* the fact that a nation's security lies as much in its ideals as in its bombs, and that liberties must be prized, even at the risk of offending subscribers.

Even in liquor, Iowa has chosen the medium way. Knowing the strong temperance feeling among the people, and yet suspecting that, since it was mentioned in the Old Testament, drinking might be here to stay, the state compromised. Under the fancy that a man would remain soberer if he took a bottle home, where there was no one to observe but the kiddies, all bars (save for beer) were outlawed. State liquor stores were set up without advertising or decoration. Some dramatic things have happened as a result.

Because of a fear that liquor purchases might be criticized by their neighbors, many people in the first year drove to the next town to buy where they might be unrecognized. On the way, they would pass the cars of those from the next town hurrying over to *their* liquor store to buy in secret. One enterprising newspaper, the Eagle Grove *Eagle*, discovered that, on the basis of gross liquor sales, Eagle Grove and nearby Clarion had exchanged populations. Any action connected with the naughty word "liquor" is news. The Iowa attorney general, willing to have his name honorably connected with the role of a white knight crusading against the dark dragon booze, obtained a plane and went off in what the *Anamosa Journal* lyrically described as an "aerial sashay," raiding thirty places across the state. Liquor was found in only three. But the attorney general is going to make Iowa "cracker-dry," he says. He'll need a big box of crackers.

The demon rum even lurks behind innocent beef cattle, causing Governor Hoegh (a firm "dry") embarrassment. At last year's Iowa State Fair, the governor accepted the grand-champion baby beef, only to discover that it was owned by the Storz Brewing Company of Omaha. He gave it away for charity. And at the Waterloo Cattle Congress he agreed to pose with the grand-champion bull, a colossal animal, and then found that it belonged to a Milwaukee brewer named Pabst. It's a delicate thing when the governor of the state producing the finest fat cattle can't be photographed with a baby beef or giant bull without first sniffing them for fumes of alcohol.

But in the long run, Iowa's system works out for the average best. It returns an annual profit to the state of several million dollars, so that drinking might be called patriotic. At the same time that those who loathe the spectacle of public bars are spared that hideous sight, their neighbors who like a nip are allowed to buy all they wish.

Realizing that the surest way to produce a balanced people was to educate them, the first General Assembly to meet in Iowa founded a university. Later came the first law school west of the Mississippi. And since the state believes that fertility in the arts should try to equal fertility in the soil, it was only natural that the University of Iowa should have been the first in America to bring all the creative arts to the campus, boldly and with honor to the artist. Students were encouraged to write plays, novels, poetry, short stories, compose a string quartet or a symphony, to paint in oil or gouache or water colors, to carve in wood or stone or metal, or to act in plays.

At Iowa, the creative artist is equal to the scholar: Philip Bezanson of the University Music Department composed a piano concerto which was conducted by Dimitri Mitropoulos with the New York Philharmonic Orchestra, and the soloist was John Sims of the music department; and in the same field house where the Iowa basketball team won the Big Ten championship in 1955 and 1956, Mitropoulos conducted the Berlioz *Requiem*. University of Iowa painters and sculptors exhibit in the finest shows in the country; more poets from the University of Iowa were represented in the 1955 *New Campus Writing* than from any other institution. Tennessee Williams wrote some of his first plays at the superb University theater. Some thirty novels have been published out of the Fiction Workshop.

This congenial attitude toward the arts has had some remarkable effects on the personality of the state. In Des Moines the state capitol is so extreme an example of ornate decoration that it has the complex beauty of the grotesque (the people, however, seem to love it). Across town, out Grand Avenue, with its 19th Century big houses covered with gingerbread, is the new municipal Art Center, designed by Eliel Saarinen, the 20th Century architect from Finland. On the walls may be an exhibit of modern art; its variety and abundance will amaze you.

Go to one of the most congenial cities for art in America, Cedar Rapids. In the home of Owen Elliott, president of the board of trustees of Coe College (Presbyterian), you will find Renoir, Braque, Bonnard, Matisse. At Coe College itself there has been a long-term exhibit of the most advanced art from the Solomon R. Guggenheim Museum in New York. For fifty years Cedar Rapids has had its own art association and for many years its own symphony orchestra. It was not chance that Grant Wood painted his first oils here; dozens were bought locally long before he became famous. (I remember the time he painted on a canvas—for a startled eighth-grade art class I belonged to—the sound of a piece of music, following the sound over the curves and whirls with his brush.) It was in the country around Cedar Rapids that he found the neat and formal landscape for his paintings. Here were the artificial-looking trees, which he had seen first on his mother's china, trees rounded by the steady wind before Wood rounded them on his own imagined hills. Here he saw the patterned corn, the young sprouts lined across the fields like knots tied on a guilt. Wood painted the birthplace of Herbert Hoover at nearby West Branch (settled by the same Quakers who had befriended John Brown in the bloody days). With his instinct for order, which he found in the cultivated and controlled Iowa landscape, he cleaned up the field beyond the little white house. When a resident of West Branch saw the painting, he remarked gratefully, "Well, Grant, that's the house all right, and we sure thank you for mowing them weeds."

So it is natural that in Cedar Rapids there should live Marvin Cone, the country's leading painter of all the shapes and richness and variety of wooden barns, and all the intricate, many-doored interiors of haunted houses. For he, too, has found in the Iowa scene a pattern and a pride.

Every summer at the county fairs one sees the letters "4-H" everywhere. They stand for Head, Heart, Hands, Health, and are an effort not only to make better farmers out of the young people but to give them better lives, to improve the style of clothes worn by the girls and the style of public speaking used by the boys. Some of the finest baby-beef steers in the world are owned by 4-H boys and girls, who feed them, brush them, keep records of costs and diet, tend them like pets, and then compete at the fairs, selling them for the fanciest prices, often over a thousand dollars for one animal. Girls compete in the same ring with boys and sometimes beat them. It's a fine sight to see a young girl leading a Black Angus curried to glossy brilliance or a Hereford to a glowing ruddiness; and at times a tearful sight when a creature which has been pampered and worked over for a year is sold for slaughter.

When the 4-H members take part in a contest, there is no public posturing in bathing suits. The *healthiest* boy and girl from each county are chosen, and compete in a state-wide and then a national contest. For the girls, there is no mere beauty contest, but one for the best groomed—in clothes each has made—but many of these girls would brighten a bathing suit too.

The Iowa farmer has come a long way since the frontier grace at meals: *Mush is rough, Mush is tough, Thank Thee Lord, We've got enough.* His problem is no longer getting enough mush, but producing too much beef, pork, corn, wheat. When nearly everybody else in America has been increasing his income, the farmer's has dropped by 30 per cent. He was urged to raise as much food as possible, and the wars exaggerated this. But suddenly, just when the farmer had bought more machines to produce more food, there is too much food. Corn is sealed in round metal bins outside every town in Iowa. Too many hogs go to market (you can't let a hog wait, and you can't tell it to stop eating; when it's ready for market it's got to go), and the price is down to half what it was not long ago.

Now the farmer is traditionally "agin the Guvment," but of late years he has turned, kicking and screaming most of the time, to that same Government which he has cussed out with such pleasure. He doesn't want controls. The old phrase "independent as a hog on ice" is a wonderfully and miserably accurate description of the farmer's position. A fat hog sliding across the ice is the least independent thing in the world. The farmer wants to be his own boss, he doesn't want anyone telling *him* what to do, but he finds the market a mighty slippery place. He looks at his corn-fattened beef cattle, or his hogs, and knows he will get barely his cost back, and maybe not that. So he looks toward that suspicious and remote city called Washington. He wants to remain individualistic, but he doesn't want to go bankrupt. When the same situation rose in the early thirties, the farmers overturned milk trucks, brought guns to auctions and forced the sale of foreclosed farms for a dollar. These people were called "sons of wild jackasses."

The result is a mild schizophrenia on the farms. Leave me alone but help me. The younger farmers accept the curious combination of the individual going his own way (my father, born on a farm, used to say that a real country was one where a man could go to hell the way he wanted to) and the Government stretching out a long, helping arm from Washington. In maybe ten years our population will have increased so fast all farm produce will be eaten. But can the farmer wait? To a man with a rope around his neck, hanging from a tree, it doesn't matter if his feet are sixteen feet off the ground or one sixteenth of an inch. Will that old wild jackass blood come out at this autumn's election?

The state grows with the times, too, for in 1956 industrial production surpassed agricultural. New factories are coming in, many small and specialized ones to the smaller towns. The big cereal plants, the agricultural machinery factories, the Quaker Oats in Cedar Rapids where entire boxcars of grain are picked up and rolled over on their sides, an aluminum factory on the Mississippi, all expand the state's income and alter its rural character.

Even in fighting, Iowa men have struck a balance. In 1870 two men fought until they were, as the old account says, a mangled mass. Both were arrested, whereupon each said that it had all been for fun, just to see whether a man from Kentucky could beat a man from Maine. The loser even argued that the winner should not be fined because, after all, he had won.

The famous Iowa 34th Division of World War II fought from North Africa to Sicily to Italy to Germany, still looking after those plain rights. Yet Buffalo Bill, born down at Le Claire on the Mississippi, had to leave Iowa for a more violent life.

Iowa balances a furious physical climate with a congenial human climate, for the hearts of the people are as abundant as the land around them. Graced from the beginning with a fullness of food, they have made abundance and creativeness an integral part of their rights and liberties. If there is hope anywhere in this wicked world or in these many states, it is certainly here, exploding like popcorn in a pan. (Of course Iowa raises more popcorn than any other state.) When a farmer falls sick at harvest time, neighbors move in with fifteen corn pickers and gather his crop in a day. When the young writers, musicians, painters, sculptors of the United States want a sympathetic community as an alternative to New York, here is a university welcoming them not merely as students but as artists. When Marvin Cone needed a year away from teaching so that he could paint without distraction, businessmen (those same maligned businessmen of whose stony hearts we read) put together a purse of money and told him to spend it anywhere he wished. And he painted more in one year than in any other five.

Suddenly, those outrageous seasons no longer matter in the face of the life, the people, the hope. They become rather a source of pride that one survives them, a source of that very abundant fertility which hard work meets halfway, between heaven and earth, between the two great rivers.

. . . Paul Engle, 1956

· HOME OF ABBIE GARDNER — OKOBOJI LAKE. IOWA ·

Walla
Lak

German Town
Hancock Co

Ruth Suckow—
Hawarden

☆ *Cherokee*

Joan Liffring-Zug
Remsen ★

MacKinlay Kante
Webster City

B. Paul Chic ine—
"Ding" Dar ing—
Josephine Herbst—
Sioux C ty

Iowa Great Lakes

Gary Gildner—
William J. Wagner—
Michael Walker—
Des Moines

John Towner Frederick—
Corning ☆

IO